OCEANS VENTURED

OCEANS VENTURED

WINNING THE COLD WAR AT SEA

JOHN LEHMAN

W. W. Norton & Company

Independent Publishers Since 1923

New York | London

For information about permission to reproduce selections from this book, write to
Permissions, W. W. Norton & Company, Inc., 500 Fifth Avenue, New York, NY 10110

For information about special discounts for bulk purchases, please contact
W. W. Norton Special Sales at specialsales@wwnorton.com or 800-233-4830

Manufacturing by LSC Communications, Harrisonburg
Book design by Marysarah Quinn
Production manager: Anna Oler

ISBN: 978-0-393-25425-9

W. W. Norton & Company, Inc., 500 Fifth Avenue, New York, N.Y. 10110
www.wwnorton.com

W. W. Norton & Company Ltd., 15 Carlisle Street, London W1D 3BS

1 2 3 4 5 6 7 8 9 0

FOR MY SEA-DADDIES
─────

Lt. Cmdr. John Lehman, Sr., USNR

Adm. Arleigh Burke, USN

Navy Secretary John Warner

Adm. Bud Zumwalt, USN

Adm. Jim Holloway III, USN

MCPO John Tower, USNR

CONTENTS

AUTHOR'S NOTE

My INTEREST IN geopolitics began when I was listening to my father, John Lehman, Sr., at the dinner table. He was what Annapolis grads called a "ninety-day wonder," having left his career as an industrial engineer in the middle of World War II to be commissioned at Navy Officer Candidate School. He had been skipper of LCS-18, the most heavily armed class of ship per ton in the U.S. fleet. He saw almost constant action with the Fifth and Third Fleets during the final twelve months of the Pacific War. While he loved the navy and was offered a career commission after the war, he went back to the business world instead but read widely in history and current affairs. While he rarely talked about his own experiences of the war, he commented freely on the progress of the Cold War and American policy. Those family seminars sparked my intense interest in military naval and foreign policy in college and graduate school.

In addition to the then-required core curricula of Aristotle and Plato, Thucydides and Cicero, Macaulay and Gibbon, Spykman and Mahan, I loved reading contemporaries like Samuel Huntington, Henry Kissinger, and Robert Strausz-Hupé. As an undergraduate at St. Joseph's University, I studied under James Dougherty, a protégé and colleague of Strausz-Hupé. At that time I met Richard Allen, a co-founder of the Georgetown University Center for Strategic Studies (now the independent Center for Strategic and International Studies) who later became President Ronald Reagan's first national security adviser. I worked for a number of years as a summer assistant to Allen.

At Cambridge University, I studied under Sir Elihu Lauterpacht, my director of studies, who was to become my dear and late lamented friend; E. H. Carr, the noted socialist-realist; and F. H. Hinsley—all very much in the realist school. Back at the University of Pennsylvania's Foreign Policy Research Institute to complete my doctorate in American foreign policy, I worked directly under Strausz-Hupé, William Kintner, and my dissertation supervisor Ambassador Covey Oliver, and through them I met Henry Kissinger.

The intellectual foundations of national security strategy were the focus of my academic studies, but I was equally fascinated by the actual operational realities of national power. Strausz-Hupé and Kissinger, both army veterans of World War II, often pointed out that diplomatic power was the shadow cast by military and naval power. Operational practice interested me even more than theory, and as an undergraduate I joined the Ready Reserve, and after graduation from Cambridge, I was commissioned as a naval intelligence officer. I then earned my navy wings, first as a bombardier-navigator and later as a pilot.

As a Squadron Augment reservist, I served short, temporary active-duty tours several times in Vietnam and more often in the Mediterranean with squadrons aboard the aircraft carriers *Saratoga, Independence, Forrestal,* and *America*. Periodic active duty in operational squadrons, which I continued for twenty-five years, kept me immersed in the realities of tactics and strategy, and the shortcomings and opportunities involving hardware, technology, and blue-water operations.

I could not have pursued this nonstandard career in the Naval Reserve without the help of what in the navy are known as "sea-daddies." The first was, of course, my father. The next was the retired admiral and former chief of naval operations (CNO) Arleigh Burke. He was the mentor who sponsored my navy commissioning. Another was the retired admiral and former CNO James Holloway, a naval aviator and strategist with distinguished service in combat in World War II, Korea, Vietnam, and the mortal combat of Washington, D.C. I first met him aboard *Saratoga* off Vietnam, and we became fast friends. He was an invaluable mentor.

It was because of the combination of national security education and some real-world experience that Dick Allen recruited me to the National Security Council staff when he was appointed deputy national security advisor in 1969. When Allen left for the private sector, I worked directly for Henry Kissinger. In that capacity I worked with George H. W. Bush during his progress through Congress, the CIA, and China.

When George H. W. Bush made his first run for the presidency in 1980, he asked me to join him as a defense adviser. After Bush dropped out of the running, Dick Allen, national security policy adviser to Ronald Reagan, asked me to join his team. I became, in effect, the naval expert on the Reagan team. Since I was simultaneously participating in the Sea Plan 2000 planning effort, which was then under way at the Naval War College at Newport, and in the bipartisan effort of Senators Henry "Scoop" Jackson (D-WA) and John Tower (R-TX) to forge a strong alternative to the policies of President Jimmy Carter, I became a two-way conduit between these groups and candidate Reagan and his team. Thus when Senator Tower, a World War II navy combat veteran and a master chief petty officer in the Naval Reserve, was appointed chairman of the Republican Platform Committee in 1980, he appointed me to oversee the drafting of the platform's national security planks. So it was that the senatorial policy study group, the Sea Plan 2000 study, and the Reagan Maritime Strategy became as one.

In 1981, when Dick Allen was appointed national security adviser to the president, he recruited me to the National Security Council staff because of my combination of national security education and some real-world experience. That same year Senator Tower became chairman of the Senate Armed Services Committee. He, along with Senator Jackson, was decisive in convincing Reagan to accept Allen's urging that I be chosen as navy secretary. Senator John Warner (R-VA), a veteran of both the navy and the marines and a former navy secretary himself, urged me to seek that job and helped shepherd my nomination through the Senate. Adm. Bud Zumwalt, while CNO, helped me to complete my navy flight training and to understand the racial problems in the navy. They also became my "sea-daddies."

PREFACE

"OUTLAW ONE, JOKER; your target is angels twenty-eight, bearing 040 at ninety-one miles closing."

"Roger that, Joker, got him." Joker was the call sign for the E-2C Hawkeye radar surveillance aircraft from the navy's newest aircraft carrier, USS *Dwight D. Eisenhower*. Outlaw One was the call sign of the lead of two F-14 Tomcat fighter interceptors from the *Ike*. The target was a Soviet Tu-95 Bear bomber. Joker's system could see everything from the sea surface to the edge of space for a radius of three hundred miles. Joker had tactical control of all NATO aircraft assigned to his sector.

But in this case, there was a very high level of command attention, and the Hawkeye controller merely acted as a relay to Vice Adm. James "Ace" Lyons, the commander of the NATO Striking Fleet Atlantic, aboard his command ship, *Mount Whitney*. The F-14 pilot moved his throttles to full military power, without afterburner to conserve fuel, closing on the target at 590 knots. In less than six minutes, the F-14 crew had visual contact with the Bear flying at 28,000 feet between cloud layers. The Tomcat immediately broke right to come around and rendezvous with the bomber from behind.

Using well-established procedures agreed to in the landmark

agreement between the United States and the Soviet Union called the Incidents at Sea Agreement, Outlaw One joined up in formation with the Bear coming up level with the pilot and saluting. He then dropped back just a few feet off and slightly behind the port wing-tip of the Russian bomber. The Bear was a unique weapon, without counterpart in NATO forces. A modern, very large swept-wing turboprop-powered airplane, it could carry a wide array of anti-surface and antiship weapons. This Bear was carrying two Raduga antiship missiles and 23mm cannon for self-defense in the nose, tail, and side blisters. Completing the rendezvous, Outlaw One reported to Joker and was surprised to hear in response the gruff voice of Admiral Lyons.

The admiral made it very clear that this was a very delicate moment, warning the two aviators to watch the Russian crew very carefully for any flight path changes or unusual behavior. During the Cold War, intercepts like this one between American fighters and Bears were routine over European and even western Atlantic and Caribbean waters, but no one could remember ever running such an intercept off the North Cape of Norway, almost within sight of the Soviet Union. This was unprecedented, and tensions were high. The F-14 was the outrider for a huge armada of eighty-three NATO naval ships surging north in late summer 1981 in the Norwegian Sea. It was the first such exercise this far north by NATO for more than twenty years, and this was the very first contact between the two potential adversaries.

While the Soviet Northern Fleet Command knew that something big was up and had launched a special radar satellite specifically to track the NATO fleet, they had been caught flat-footed. The U.S. Navy had developed and practiced very sophisticated cover and deception tactics, and Lyons had become a master in their use in large operations. Using classified electronic gear that simulated through emissions a large carrier force, he sent a small group of combatants heading southeast from Norfolk, while the main fleet proceeded north in total electronic silence and under the dense cloud cover normal in that season in those high latitudes. It wasn't until they were well into the Norwegian Sea that the Soviets realized they had been completely snookered. They had failed to detect an armada of eighty-three ships until it was within striking range of the Soviet Union itself.

The alarmed Soviet command mobilized all available ships and aircraft to find the carrier strike groups. Lyons had decided to wake them up with a surprise. One of his battle group commanders, Rear Adm. Jerry Tuttle, launched a flight of Tomcats, Intruder strike aircraft, Prowler electronic attack jets, and KA-6 tankers to give the Soviets a flyby nearly a thousand miles away from the carriers. Based on intelligence, they homed in on a group of Bears being refueled in the air just outside the twelve-mile limit near Murmansk. Without warning, they roared close by in formation as the refueling Russians stared in disbelief.

It had become orthodoxy in NATO headquarters that in an era of détente, operating so close to the Soviet Union on NATO's northern flank was too provocative. All such large naval exercises had been essentially prohibited for more than twenty years by the Supreme Allied Commander Europe, who up to that point had almost always been a U.S. Army general.

But in fact, this exercise originated not in NATO but in the White House of newly elected President Reagan. It had not even gone through the process of bureaucratic review in Brussels. Its full extent became known outside naval circles only after the exercise was successfully completed in the autumn of 1981, when the Soviet Union burst into the media with protests and alarms. Those alarms were soon echoed by those in Washington and in Europe who had viewed Reagan as a naïve cowboy who might provoke a dangerous crisis or worse. Even some in the U.S. Navy, remembering that the Soviets, Chinese, and North Koreans had shot down many allied aircraft during the Cold War with much less provocation than this exercise, had for years strongly opposed taking the fleet into far northern waters and now joined the alarmists. They had been convinced that the Soviets would react violently and would not hesitate to fire on NATO aircraft or ships operating so close to their nuclear bases in the Kola Peninsula and the White Sea. The more extreme alarmists feared that it could provide the spark to set off the powder keg of war. Reagan and his navy leaders, however, knew better. They knew from closely held intelligence just what the reaction would be.

Thus it was that the three-star commander of the NATO Striking Fleet was in conversation with the two lieutenants flying within a few feet of the Russian Bear. The bomber crew kept on a steady course, heading for where they hoped the large fleet was. But Outlaw One reported considerable activity in the gun blister thirty feet off their starboard wing that could mean the unlimbering of the 23mm cannon. The Tomcat pilot was spring-loaded to execute a violent split S if a gun appeared. The silence mounted until, in the flat emotionless tone of naval aviators, Admiral Lyons heard, "The Russian airmen have just taped a *Playboy* centerfold over the gun-port Plexiglas."

INTRODUCTION

Since World War II, major changes of direction in American national security policy have been rare. Presidential elections have always included strong differences on some issues: Ike promised to end the Korean War; Jack Kennedy campaigned against Ike's "missile gap"; and Nixon campaigned against Johnson's conduct of the Vietnam War. But Ronald Reagan's 1980 campaign against the Carter administration represented something wholly different: a fundamental rejection of the administration's policy of détente and convergence with the Soviet Union. Reagan promised a robust increase in defense spending to build significantly the size and capability of American military and naval forces. He rejected the Soviet-declared Brezhnev Doctrine and made clear his intention to pursue a "forward strategy." When asked back in January 1977 about his policy toward the Cold War, he had famously replied, "We win and they lose, what do you think of that?" In addition to pursuing the declared policies, he also intended to launch a highly classified program to exploit Soviet economic, political, military, and psychological vulnerabilities.

This posture was not merely campaign rhetoric—Reagan was quite serious. While specifically calling for increases in all the services, including new missiles and aircraft, the most prominent part of the changes he advocated was a new forward Maritime Strategy based on a six-hundred-ship navy. He believed that a strategic framework had evolved in which East and West had rough parity in nuclear weapons; that the Warsaw Pact, with its 280 divisions, had a de facto superiority in land forces; but that geography and history had given the Western alliance an inherent naval superiority that should be exploited.

Reagan's worldview had deep roots. From his entry into national politics in the mid-1960s, it was clear he did not share the received orthodoxy of the Republican and Democratic establishments on matters of national security policy. He was convinced that the country was embarked on the wrong path: a losing path in the Cold War. Unschooled on these matters, in preparation for his first run for president in 1975; he began to read widely in the academic and journalistic literature. He simply could not follow the logic of establishment experts like Arthur Schlesinger, Jr., James Reston, and others in journals like *Foreign Affairs*, the *New York Times*, the *Washington Post*, and the *Los Angeles Times*, praising the growth of the Soviet economy, the superiority of their education and medical systems and calling for accommodation, convergence and détente.

Reagan found far more persuasive logic in a loose archipelago of policy experts like Richard Allen (formerly at Georgetown and the Hoover Institution), Robert Strausz-Hupé and William Kintner at the Foreign Policy Research Institute at the University of Pennsylvania, Samuel Huntington at Harvard, William Van Cleave at USC, Robert Conquest in the UK, and a group of innovative thinkers at the Rand Corporation led by Fred Iklé, Jim Schlesinger and Henry Rowen. These scholarly voices were distinctly at odds with establishment views. A former leading member of these "realists" was Henry Kissinger. His role as national security adviser to Richard Nixon and then as secretary of state had taken him out of play in that period. After Reagan became president however, he consulted with Kissinger frequently.

At Reagan's invitation Allen began to spend time with him including travel abroad, which began in 1978. Allen became in effect Reagan's director of studies in national security. He introduced Reagan to those mentioned above. This group along with Reagan's friends, George Shultz and William Casey, became his trusted advisers on defense and foreign policy.

While each of these experts had unique perspectives and insights on the balance of power and international affairs, they shared a policy view that questioned the long-established defensive national strategy of containment and deterrence as being an insufficient framework to bring about a successful end to the Cold War. In Allen's landmark book *Peace or Peaceful Co-existence*, and Strausz-Hupé and Kintner's *Protracted Conflict*, and *A Forward Strategy for America*, Reagan found a view that resonated. These books and others advocated not simply accepting the status quo of the division of a Communist and non-Communist world but adding to containment and deterrence a third leg of proactive rollback of Soviet ideology, political influence, and military power. Thus, by the time Ronald Reagan ran for president for the second time in 1980, he had been participating in a five-year seminar on a personal basis with the best minds in the "realist school" of national security.

With that preparation, Reagan went into the 1980 campaign with a fully thought-through national security plan. Allen recruited and organized teams of like-minded experts to add depth and breadth, facts and numbers, to Reagan's plan to change national policy.

In contrast to Reagan's hawkish views, President Gerald Ford's fervent belief in détente was appreciated by the Soviets. A former Ford staffer recalls that "[Vladimir] Putin's covert support for Donald Trump [in 2016] has not been the first time Russia aspired to influence an American presidential election." At the 1975 Helsinki Summit, "forty-two years ago, a Russian leader privately pledged his government's support for a president's reelection: 'We for our part will do everything we can to make that happen,' Leonid Brezhnev said to Gerald Ford. I know, because I'm the last surviving participant in those events."

With the help of Senator John Tower, a strong Reagan ally and chairman of the Republican Platform Committee, Reagan's policies were incorporated almost word for word into the Republican platform in July 1980. It was not surprising then that during this period Reagan began publicly calling for maritime superiority, including in his principal national security campaign speech in Chicago in March 1980. By the time Reagan secured the Republican nomination, the six-hundred-ship navy had become a central plank in the Republican platform.

In the navy, Reagan and Allen had found just what they needed to symbolize the change Reagan intended in American strategy. The maritime strategy behind Reagan's plank was based on principles of offense that had long been fundamental to the navy, ably articulated by Alfred Thayer Mahan, who wrote and taught at the Naval War College in the late nineteenth century. Beginning with his classic book *The Influence of Sea Power upon History*, Mahan declared that the United States must acquire and maintain "command of the seas." That principle required that the navy always have the power to defeat the naval forces of any power or combination of powers that could be potential adversaries. Assistant Secretary of the Navy Theodore Roosevelt was one of his first converts. From Roosevelt's time through the early Cold War, ensuring "command of the seas" was the principle around which navy thinking, shipbuilding, and training were organized as well as the unquestioned basis of national policy.

The culture of the U.S. Navy, especially since the days of Mahan and Roosevelt, has been based on forward operations and offense, not on defense. In Mahan's words, "The general principle of the decisive superiority of offensive power over defensive is applicable throughout, to the operations of a war, to the design of a battleship, to the scheme of building a whole navy."

The long ordeal of the Vietnam War, however, for a decade shifted naval operations away from ensuring "command of the seas" to providing tactical support to land forces ashore and a strategic bombing campaign against North Vietnam. As the war dragged on, the huge funding requirement resulted in a steady decline in numbers of ships and a disastrous decline in the readiness and maintenance of much of the fleet. As numbers declined, remaining ships stayed deployed much longer, ten and eleven months instead of six. Morale and retention of experienced sailors and airmen sank as the quality of life became less tolerable.

The Soviet Union had seized this opportunity to challenge American naval supremacy with a massive shipbuilding program and an offensive blue-water strategy led by another disciple of Mahan's, Admiral of the Fleet of the Soviet Union Sergei Gorshkov. By the end of the Vietnam War, he had built, deployed, and exercised a combatant fleet of over 550 warships—not counting some 850 armed coastal defense craft and over 750 auxiliaries.

In 1974, contrasting the declining American fleet with the expanding Soviet fleet, Adm. Elmo Zumwalt, recently retired as chief of naval operations, testified that "the odds are that the U.S. would now lose a naval war to the Soviet Union."

Helped in no small measure by national fatigue after the long war, and the debilitating effects of the Watergate scandal, Jimmy Carter was elected in 1976 with the intention of cutting defense and deemphasizing the navy.

Although Carter was a 1947 graduate of the Naval Academy, he did not have a head for strategy. He did not grasp that diplomatic power is the shadow cast by military and naval power. He believed instead that soft power and diplomacy could be substituted for military power. The result was White House–led Policy Review Memorandum no. 10, intended to establish the national policy that embodied this unusual worldview. Under that Carter directive, all the forces were to be cut. Pay for all the services was frozen; the army was to be reduced by several divisions, and the air force was to have its MX missile and B-1 bomber canceled. But the navy was to bear the brunt of the cuts, fundamentally reducing the fleet to a defensive posture with a principal role in NATO of convoying supplies flowing across the Atlantic. Under this plan, all future nuclear carriers were to be canceled in favor of building smaller nonnuclear flattops, and some older conventionally powered carriers were to be retired early. The White House favored a global strategy they called the "swing strategy," which justified a smaller navy. It entailed moving the U.S. Pacific Fleet from the Pacific to reinforce the Atlantic Fleet in the event of war, based on the unrealistic belief that all-out war with the Soviet Union could be contained in Europe and not involve the Pacific theater.

By 1978, the U.S. Navy had been reduced to 464 active warships and thirteen carriers. The USSR was not slow in taking advantage of this fading of deterrence, fomenting revolution in Central America and establishing a forward naval presence in the South China Sea at former U.S. bases in Vietnam. In late 1979, it invaded Afghanistan and in 1980 began to suppress the Solidarity movement in Poland. In none of these cases was there a meaningful American response. (The United States did boycott the Moscow Olympics.)

In April 1980 the Pentagon answered President Carter's request for a military option to rescue the American hostages in Tehran with a plan called Operation Eagle Claw, an ill-conceived multiservice formula for catastrophe that duly took place a few weeks later, with Carter unfairly given the blame.

In November, Ronald Reagan won the presidency in a landslide.

Ronald Reagan formally adopted his naval strategy (which ran in parallel with an internal navy study called Sea Plan 2000) in July 1980. The next step for his team was to add to it the actions that could enable him to launch implementation immediately upon taking office. In 1980 Richard Allen organized his teams of experts, including congressional and Pentagon budget experts working on their own time, to prepare a detailed new defense budget and a budget supplemental for additional funding, to be submitted to Congress immediately after the inauguration. These supplemental and new budgets included funds for expanding and modernizing the

National Security Advisor Richard Allen with President Reagan. *(National Archives)*

army, commencing the MX strategic missile and B-1 bomber, and building a six-hundred-ship navy, including fifteen carrier battle groups. These budgetary initiatives would certainly get the attention of friend and foe alike in signaling a national change of direction. But something more tangible and globally visible was needed, and the navy provided it.

Shortly after the election, the president-elect had named Dick Allen to be his national security adviser. Allen and Bill Casey led a small group to organize the new administration's national security agenda and to assist Reagan in choosing his national security team. Two of the earliest appointments were Caspar Weinberger as secretary of defense and myself as secretary of the navy.

One of my first actions was to recall Rear Adm. James A. "Ace" Lyons back from his command in the Pacific to head up my transition team. I had served under Lyons years before, in June and July 1976, on the carrier *America*, where his aggressive leadership and his grasp of strategy had impressed me. Over the next four years, we had often crossed paths in the navy and in the Washington policy world, particularly when we both were participating in the Sea Plan 2000 effort. He was very much a part of the thinking that became Ronald Reagan's strategy.

Led by Lyons, the transition team began immediately to work with the chief of naval operations, Adm. Thomas Hayward, on the priorities to enable the rebuilding and reassertion of U.S. naval power that supported Ronald Reagan's policies. Chief among these was the establishment and implementation of a strategy to achieve unquestioned naval supremacy, and to make sure that the world, and especially the Soviet Union, understood that policy change.

Allen wanted the new strategy to be publicly proclaimed and explained soon after the inauguration, in presidential speeches and congressional testimony starting with the confirmation hearings for the secretaries of defense and navy. But actions speak a lot louder than words. Lyons had persuaded me that the rather routine annual NATO naval exercises planned for the fall could rapidly be reorganized to conform to the new Reagan military and naval strategy and could dramatically demonstrate to friend and foe that there was indeed a new game in town. I provided Allen with the plan to take the fleet north in force within months of the inauguration as the navy's contribution to Reagan's overall forward strategy. Allen and Casey, with the support of Weinberger and Hayward, got approval from Reagan to begin planning for that bold action at sea almost immediately. Thus began Ocean Venture '81.

The importance of naval exercises and operations at sea is little understood outside the navy. They train sailors at all levels to operate complex systems and technology in the unforgiving world of the great sea, to operate large fleets of submarine, surface, aircraft, and space platforms, and to integrate with American land and air forces and the forces of our allies. They also innovate, develop, and test new tactics. Far more important than strategic documents, books, and war plans, the actual operations in exercises at sea demonstrate to allies and potential enemies how the United States actually intends to act when and if conflict breaks out. Ever since Theodore Roosevelt sent the Great White Fleet around the world, adversaries have been riveted on how the U.S. Navy performed at sea.

During the Cold War, including the Korean and Vietnam Wars, navy air, submarine, surface, and riverine forces conducted offensive operations of many dimensions. The United States and its naval allies maintained large fleets and exercised them regularly in the Mediterranean, Atlantic, Pacific, and Arctic, including sensitive areas close in to the Soviet Union. During the Cold War, huge annual exercises of the United States and NATO and other friendly navies were commonplace in all the troubled waters of the globe.

Beginning in the mid-1960s, the rapidly growing Soviet fleet began its own open-ocean exercises, demonstrating that the USSR intended to challenge American command of the seas. Thereupon U.S. operations began to pull back. The immediate cause was, of course, the increasing requirements for carrier operations off Vietnam, but the balance was shifting. Emphasis gradually changed from offensive to defensive thinking; from naval power projection to convoy escort and to creating imaginary barriers from Greenland to Iceland and Iceland to the UK and across the various Mediterranean narrows and in the Pacific, across the straits between Japanese islands, in an effort to keep the growing Soviet fleet hemmed in and away from Atlantic and Pacific sea-lanes. Such a naïve naval Maginot Line would, of course, likely leave millions of Norwegian, Icelandic, Danish, Italian, Greek, Turkish, Japanese, and Korean allies stranded behind enemy lines. Little consideration was paid to the ability of U.S. and allied naval forces to prevent Soviet forces from deploying south toward the allied sea-lanes in the first place

At-sea exercises were particularly important in the heavily operational culture of the U.S. Navy in inculcating the principles of the Maritime Strategy into the navy. Most navy officers are not scribes or theorists or war gamers; they are operators. It is the exercises and operations at sea—not the documents or war games—that matter to them, and that has been the secret of their historic successes.

But by 1981, U.S. Navy exercises had often become routinized and focused solely on fleet training. The other functions of exercises at sea—especially signaling to adversaries—had been neglected or prohibited. That had sent a signal to them and indeed to our allies. Worse, the exercises had become predictable—in their geography, force dispositions, tactics, and demonstrated role in U.S. policy. The Soviets became comfortable in their knowledge of U.S. Navy capabilities and intentions and increasingly confident in their own ability to counter them.

This all would end with Ocean Venture '81, a massive naval operation into the northern seas that the Soviets viewed as their maritime sphere of influence. It was approved by Reagan before his inauguration and launched just seven months after he entered the White House. Updated and refined, these exercises under different names were repeated every year thereafter, until the Soviet Union and its navy collapsed at the end of the decade. Through the decade these operations grew in numbers, effectiveness, global reach, and innovation in offensive warfare. The jolt to Soviet perceptions and to the growth in confidence of American allies was magnified as the fleet was augmented with all the new technology, defenses, and striking capability made possible by the Reagan budget increases.

Simultaneously, of course, the air force's new B-1 and MX programs, as well as the modernization and expansion of the army and marine corps, left no doubt that Reagan was not bluffing. This, along with the dysfunctional Soviet economy as the price of oil collapsed through the decade, was the reality that destroyed the Soviets' belief that history was on their side. They came to understand that all the enormous economic sacrifices to build the massive Soviet Armed Forces had in fact left them worse off. It was the shadow of this American naval and military power that gave Reagan the leverage to begin the process of negotiation with Mikhail Gorbachev that led, soon after his retirement, to a peaceful end to the Cold War.

This book tells the story of how a new president's determination to change the nation's course came together with a powerful strategy that could be implemented immediately through highly visible and dramatic operations. While in itself the naval buildup and forward strategy did not end the Cold War, it did fundamentally change what the Soviets liked to call "the correlation of forces." The realization by a new Soviet leadership that the global balance of military power was rapidly shifting against them and that their failing economy prevented them from keeping up gave Reagan the leverage to negotiate the web of treaties and agreements that brought about the end of the Soviet Union and the Cold War, so skillfully handled in the end by George Bush, Margaret Thatcher, Helmut Kohl, and Mikhail Gorbachev.

Despite all that has been written on the Maritime Strategy, this story has not yet been told. The scribes and planners and war gamers and historians and analysts and journalists have all written their books. The operators—being operators—haven't. This is also their story: how they won command of the seas and helped to bring about a peaceful end to the Cold War.

OCEANS VENTURED

The Philadelphia-based privateer *Fair American* captured twenty-nine British merchant ships. The ship's physician, Dr. George Lehman, was my fourth great-grandfather. *(Courtesy of the Naval History and Heritage Command. Model in the U.S. Naval Academy Museum Collection.)*

CHAPTER 1

American Naval Strategy and Operations in the Cold War

PART I: *The Iron Curtain Descends*

Think tanks try to make strategic planning seem complex, but it is in fact quite simple: the first duty of the U.S. government is to provide for the country's common defense. The art and science of planning and directing military, diplomatic, economic, and all other means to maintain the long-term security of the nation is what constitutes national security strategy.

Naval strategy is derived from and dependent on national security strategy, as determined by the president and Congress. The fundamental task of U.S. naval strategy is to prevent the seas from being a medium of attack against us; to ensure the free commercial use of the seas; and to enable the seas to be a reliable avenue of attack against our enemies. How we achieve those objectives is dependent on the nature of our vulnerabilities, the strengths of our maritime forces, and the nature of the threat from our enemies. All these change over time.

In the American War of Independence, our vulnerabilities were great as we were so heavily dependent on seaborne commerce. Our naval forces, consisting of converted merchantmen, privateers, and small combatants but no ships of the line, were no match for the Royal Navy. American strengths were ships of superior design and quality (captured American-built ships were often taken directly into the Royal Navy), abundant skilled seafarers, and a thriving capital market that enabled a rapid building, outfitting, and manning of fast, well-armed privateers. The British enemy possessed the largest fleet in the world, powerfully armed and skilled in naval combat from decades of war with the French and other continental powers. For the Americans, the balance dictated a *guerre de course*, that is, a strategy of attacking the enemy's seaborne commerce, and they waged it with great success. According to records at Lloyd's of London, American privateers captured 2,600 British merchant ships, 12 percent of their entire merchant fleet, causing enormous financial loss to British elites and eventually contributing materially to pressure in London to negotiate an end to the war. Daring and aggressive American sea captains like John Paul Jones, working out of forward French and Dutch ports, successfully carried the war to British waters, even raiding the United Kingdom itself.

In the two Barbary Wars against Muslim state-sponsored terror, which consisted of seizing and holding for ransom American seaborne commerce across the Atlantic and in the Mediterranean, naval strategy was a straightforward counterattack against the corsairs and their ports, which enabled successful negotiated settlements.

Once again in the War of 1812, naval strategy reverted to a forward global *guerre de course*, and once again privateers played a significant role, capturing some seven hundred British merchantmen. While still far from a match for the Royal Navy, the U.S. Navy had grown into a serious and effective force since the War of Independence, often ranging aggressively throughout the globe. The six superfrigates that had been built at the beginning of the century for the newly reestablished U.S. Navy were generally judged to be the finest warships in the age of sail. They were very successful against the Royal Navy in individual combats.

During the Civil War, Union naval strategy was a combination of *guerre de course* and offensive amphibious warfare. The former, which targets enemy commerce rather than enemy navy, took the form of

The USS *Constitution* defeating the HMS *Java*.
(Courtesy of the Naval History and Heritage Command.)

aggressive blockading of the entire South and relentless global pursuit of its commerce raiders, while waging offensive amphibious riverine warfare and providing gunfire support to the Union Army throughout the South.

Confederate naval strategy was also a global *guerre de course*, targeted on Union commerce, and it was quite successful. British-built commerce raiders like the *Alabama*, and privateers like *Rattlesnake*, roamed all over the world preying on Yankee commerce. In the Pacific, they virtually eliminated the American whaling industry, dealing it a blow from which it never fully recovered.

In 1884, after the Civil War, one of the most visionary of naval leaders, Rear Adm. Stephen B. Luce, established the U.S. Naval War College in Newport, Rhode Island, in an effort to establish grand strategy as the core of U.S. Navy thinking.

Two years later Capt. Alfred Thayer Mahan succeeded Luce as president of the War College. Mahan's focus was on what today

For the river war in the South, the Union Navy converted dozens of double-ended New York Harbor ferries into gunboats and amphibious assault craft, which proved to be among the most useful craft in the war. *(From "Pictures of U.S. Navy Ships 1775–1941," a leaflet produced by the National Archives Trust Fund Board, 1974.)*

would be called geopolitics, although the term was not invented until the 1930s. In 1890, Mahan published *The Influence of Sea Power upon History, 1660–1783*, a history of naval warfare that brought together ideas that had developed primarily in the U.S. Navy and the Royal Navy into a coherent strategy of naval warfare. Mahan was also influenced by then-current academic theories holding that the rapidly growing U.S. economy, to avoid stagnation, must find markets across the seas.

Mahan believed that a large merchant marine and, most importantly, a strong global navy were essential for America's future. He believed that the United States must build and maintain sufficient naval forces to ensure "command of the seas." The concept required a navy fleet clearly superior in numbers and firepower to be able to defeat not just any potential adversary but any likely coalition of

LEFT: Adm. Stephen B. Luce, USN. *(U.S. Naval Institute.)*
RIGHT: Alfred Thayer Mahan. *(U.S. Naval Institute.)*

naval powers. Successful naval strategy, he argued, must be based on the principle of offense, the ability and the will to seek out and bring an enemy fleet to battle and destroy it. Mahan's strategic theories rapidly became established orthodoxy in the U.S. Navy, and they heavily influence, if not dominate, U.S. naval strategy and operations to the present day.

By the time of the Spanish-American War, the U.S. Navy, formed on the Mahanian model, was still only the sixth largest in the world, but Spain's obsolescent navy suffered from decades of neglect and essentially was without strategy. Thus when war broke out over the sinking of the USS *Maine* (which modern technical analysis has shown was almost certainly an accident in which Spain played no part), U.S. Navy strategy was to "go right at 'em," resulting in

The cruiser USS *Olympia*, Dewey's flagship at Manila Bay. *(U.S. Naval Institute.)*

the one-sided victories at Santiago, Cuba, and Manila Bay that led directly to Spain suing for peace and an end to the ten-week war. Had Spain not surrendered when it did, the next step in the American plan would have been to aggressively deploy the U.S. fleet forward across the Atlantic against Spain itself.

By 1906, thanks to TR's building program, the U.S. fleet had risen to third largest in the world. By the onset of World War I, Kaiser Wilhelm had built a large modern German fleet explicitly on the Mahanian model. (He had ordered every German naval officer to read Mahan.) Britain, for its part, had built an equally modern and even larger Mahanian Royal Navy fleet, commanded by leaders who were true believers in the church of Mahan and his friend Adm. Lord Jackie Fisher.

The war's only major confrontation between the main German and British battle fleets was fought in 1916 at Jutland, in the eastern part of the North Sea (known to NATO naval commanders of a later generation as the Baltic Approaches). At Jutland, the British Royal Navy's immense Grand Fleet and the Imperial German Navy's smaller High Seas Fleet fought in lines of massive steel battleships and battle cruisers armed with huge and deadly long-range guns. The battle, the last major battle ever fought mainly by battleships, lasted for two straight days.

The British and German gunnery equipment and procedures differed significantly: The British favored using centralized gun-firing directors, while the Germans used directors that could not fire all guns at once. In firing salvos, British gunners used a "bracket system" while the Germans used a "ladder system." (American battleship captains of the 1980s would routinely study both systems, plus others.)

After the battle the two fleets retired back to their home bases, savagely bloodied but still intact, both sides claiming victory. The British had lost more ships—the Royal Navy lost nearly double the tonnage and twice as many sailors as the Germans. But they succeeded in containing the German fleet, preventing it from breaking out of the North Sea into the North Atlantic. On the other hand, the German fleet continued to pose a threat, requiring the British to keep their battleships concentrated in the North Sea.

The following year, frustrated by the stalemate, the Germans would turn to unrestricted submarine warfare to break the Royal Navy blockade, an act that would pull the United States into the war on the side of Britain and her allies. But the kaiser's timidity in risking his fleet after Jutland resulted in the successful seaborne resupply of the Allies by North America and allowed the combined British, American, and Allied navies to blockade the Central Powers. The successful blockade was decisive in ending the war.

The close relationship between the Royal Navy and the U.S. Navy resulted in the controversial decision effectively to integrate American capital ships into the British fleet. U.S. Navy battleships worked out of forward bases in the British Isles. An American anti-submarine destroyer force, however, was kept together and operated

The Battle of Jutland. *(Courtesy of the Naval History and Heritage Command.)*

out of Queenstown, Ireland, and made a significant contribution against the German U-boats.

While naval strategy derives from national strategy, the interwar period illustrates that when a national strategy changes direction, a change in naval strategy does not automatically follow.

After World War I, the Wilson administration's national security strategy, largely driven by the powerful navy secretary, Josephus Daniels, fully supported Mahanian precepts. It submitted navy budgets to build the navy in size and quality second to none. As with Wilson's League of Nations, however, Congress would not support it. The naval buildup became an issue in the 1920 presidential campaign, and when Republican Warren Harding was elected, he supported naval disarmament.

None of the other victorious but exhausted allies except Japan were willing or able to support large naval expenditures, and so when

Harding called for a naval disarmament conference, it was fully supported. The conference convened at Washington in November 1921. The resulting treaty put strict limits on capital ships on all signatories, with a proportionate ratio of 5:5:3 for United States, the UK, and Japan and proportionately less for others. It also required a ten-year moratorium on building any capital ships (surprisingly overlooking aircraft carriers in the definition) and an immediate stop to construction under way. In addition, the Japanese demanded and got a complete ban on Britain, United States, and themselves constructing or fortifying any naval bases in the Pacific, which sealed the fate of Guam, Hong Kong, and the Philippines two decades later.

The treaty was subsequently modified in 1930 and again in 1936, but by then Japan had ignored and then formally withdrawn from its limitations. Because of the severe effects of the depression in Britain and the United States, those governments continued to adhere to the treaty limits until 1936. That delay in rebuilding their navies cost them dearly in the early years of World War II.

The U.S. Navy, however, did not abandon Mahan when the Republican administrations indulged in naval disarmament and wishful thinking. Maritime supremacy remained navy orthodoxy as it awaited a more enlightened national strategy. Massive annual "fleet problems" at sea tested aggressive new procedures, tactics, operations, and equipment, especially carrier aviation and amphibious assaults. Strategic planning and war-gaming continued at the Naval War College through the 1930s. *War Plan Orange*, the strategy document for a war against Japan, was first drafted in 1911, and it was war-gamed and updated regularly through the 1930s. Adm. Chester Nimitz wrote, after World War II, that he had not faced a single situation in the Pacific, except for kamikazes, that had not been war-gamed at Newport in the 1930s.

President Franklin Roosevelt had served for eight years as assistant navy secretary in the Wilson administration and was a thoroughgoing navalist. The severe depression in his first term removed any possibility that the navy would escape the strictures of the naval

The war game room at the Naval War College. *(U.S. Naval Institute.)*

disarmament treaties. But with Roosevelt working with Carl Vinson and other navy supporters in Congress, major navy rearmament and shipbuilding acts were passed in 1936, 1938, and 1940, without which victory in the Pacific War would have been impossible.

The maritime strategy in the Pacific after Pearl Harbor was pure Mahan and pure offense: seek out the enemy fleet and destroy it; use the resulting command of the seas to deliver and support American land forces to conquer and occupy the island chains defending the Japanese homeland; seek out enemy commerce and logistics and destroy them; impose a commercial and military blockade and destroy the enemy economy. But the end game was a subject of much disagreement between national and naval strategy. The national strategy in 1945 was to invade Japan; the navy opposed any invasion of Japan until the blockade and strategic bombing had eliminated Japan's ability to fight. The navy had also opposed unsuccessfully

Gen. Douglas MacArthur's determination to invade the Philippines, which naval strategists viewed as a costly and irrelevant backwater that would delay the collapse of the enemy, which it probably did.

In the 1945 battle for Okinawa, the navy fought Japanese kamikazes for one hundred straight days. It lost more sailors than in all previous wars combined as well as more than thirty destroyers. Four carriers were put out of action. Because of this outcome, the navy stood solidly behind President Truman's decision to use the atomic bomb against Japan.

The naval war in Europe was also conducted along Mahanist principles. Hitler and the German General Staff were antinaval-

The carrier *Enterprise* under kamikaze attack at Okinawa. One kamikaze hit blew the forward elevator some 120 meters into the air. *(Cmdr. William H. Balden's World War II scrapbook, National Naval Aviation Museum Photograph Collection.)*

A German U-boat. *(Courtesy of the Naval History and Heritage Command.)*

ist and had little interest in naval power, believing that they could neutralize a repeat of the Allied blockade of the continent, as had happened in World War I, by seizing control of all Europe from the Atlantic to the Urals, removing any need for seaborne commerce. While ceding command of the seas to the Allies, Nazi naval strategy was *guerre de course*, building submarines and surface commerce raiders and a few large surface combatants that were doomed to operate without sufficient air support. Only reluctantly did Hitler realize, in 1942, what success the submarine force could have in destroying the Atlantic Bridge, and he belatedly ramped up submarine construction. But by the time the new subs joined the force in numbers, Allied tactics, intelligence, and air superiority over the seas had decisively gained the upper hand. It became a slaughter, with nearly seven hundred enemy subs sunk by the war's end.

The Allies' naval strategy in Europe used command of the seas with great effectiveness, not only in neutralizing the Nazi submarines and commerce raiders but in providing the invaluable flexibility of delivering amphibious land forces wherever national strategy chose from North Africa, Italy, the Normandy invasion, and the landings in the South of France. Once the Allied forces were established ashore, Allied navies supported the land campaign with

The fleet off Normandy during the D-Day invasion. *(U.S. Coast Guard photograph.)*

massive naval gunfire, air support and intelligence, and an endless resupply of soldiers, beans, and bullets.

THE COLD WAR BEGINS

The U.S. Navy ended World War II with more than seven thousand ships, including ninety-nine aircraft carriers. Washington plunged immediately into an understandable political rush to bring the boys home. Many politicians demanded that the navy mothball, scrap, or otherwise dispose of this massive and expensive fleet. The expected rush to reap the peace dividend soon morphed into an existential political battle over whether to maintain a blue-water fleet at all.

World War II had barely ended when the Soviet Union, having secured rule over its western neighbors in Eastern Europe, contin-

The only known photograph of the four *Iowa*-class battleships sailing together: USS *Iowa*, *Wisconsin*, *Missouri*, and *New
Jersey*. *(Official U.S. Navy photograph, National Archives.)*

ued its momentum. To press its advantage, it made a bold attempt
to bring Turkey and Iran into its orbit and thus advance two of its
historic geopolitical vital interests; to secure a major oil supply and
to control the Dardanelles.

Historians generally place the beginning of the Cold War on
March 4, 1946. On that day, the Soviet Union invaded Azerbaijan,
the northwestern province of Iran, massed troops on the Turkish border, and launched an offensive by Communist rebels inside
Greece, effectively starting the Greek Civil War.

President Harry Truman's reaction was immediate. On March
22, he dispatched the battleship *Missouri* to Turkey and Greece,
arriving on April 5. His administration was deeply divided between
those who hoped for cordial postwar relations with the Soviet Union

and those who were convinced that the USSR must be confronted and contained. In that context, the White House put out the cover story that it was taking the remains of the deceased Turkish ambassador to the United States back to Istanbul, but Truman made it quite clear that the purpose was to demonstrate his commitment to block the Soviet moves with real power if necessary. No one in Europe had ever seen such a powerful warship deployed there, let alone one flying an American flag. And the *Missouri* was fraught with high-recognition symbolism, having just appeared in movie theaters around the globe as the site of the signing of Japan's surrender to

TOP: The USS *Missouri* off Istanbul.
(U.S. Navy photograph, National Archives.)
BOTTOM: Turkish stamp commemorating the enormous impact of the USS *Missouri* arriving in Istanbul to signal U.S. determination to block the Soviet threat to Turkey.

American naval and military might, and bearing the name of the home state of the president himself.

Soviet troops were removed from Iran within the year, but East-West relations continued to deteriorate rapidly as the new global balance of power became the Cold War. The deep divide on policy within the administration continued between those committed to the rapid demobilization of the U.S. military and détente with the Soviet Union and those committed to maintaining a large naval and military deterrent to contain Soviet and Chinese expansion. The divide continued right up until North Korea invaded South Korea in June 1950.

While the political battles raged in Washington, the navy was rapidly refocusing on the emerging need for containment of Soviet expansion.

The wartime creation of carrier striking forces, amphibious assault forces, forward submarine patrols, and the ability to refuel and resupply the fleet under way at sea had enabled a revolutionary new fleet deployment model to emerge in the late 1940s: combat-credible forward naval presence. As the Soviet Union emerged as a global threat to U.S. interests, the development of a global U.S. alliance system required the clear ability to defend those allies exposed on the northern flank, Norway and Denmark; those in the eastern Mediterranean, Turkey and Greece; and those in the western Pacific, Korea, and Japan. Thus came about the practice of keeping large powerful naval forces always deployed and operating in the western Pacific, the eastern Mediterranean, and the North Atlantic, and of making regular forays into the Arctic, Norwegian, Baltic, and Black Seas. Precedents were set of carrying out large, multinational sea exercises close to Soviet shores, developing and testing tactics, strengthening allied interoperability, and probing Soviet defenses and vulnerabilities. A strong political motivation was, of course, to demonstrate allied and U.S. resolve to the Soviets, especially in the Norwegian Sea and the eastern Mediterranean.

With Scandinavia an obvious area vulnerable to Soviet threat, the navy began to relearn the hard lessons of Arctic operations with Operation Frostbite, a two-week exercise in March 1946 with the large new carrier *Midway* and other warships operating in the Labrador Sea/Davis Strait. In June and July, a U.S. Navy task force visited ports in Scandinavia and the Low Countries. Annual Atlantic Fleet cold weather exercises continued through 1949, when the Truman administration began its massive but short-lived naval disarmament.

In September 1947, the new carrier *Franklin D. Roosevelt* and its escorts visited Athens, followed later in the fall by the carrier *Randolph*, beginning the long Cold War pattern of regular deployments of carriers to the eastern Mediterranean. This became formalized gradually as the need to contain Soviet expansion came to dominate navy thinking. In April 1948, the Sixth Fleet was established as the navy began keeping forces in the Mediterranean for six months, then replacing them with fresh units, thereby establishing a powerful permanent forward carrier and amphibious presence there.

Everything changed after President Truman's reelection and his appointment of Louis A. Johnson as secretary of defense. Johnson had a mandate to drastically cut the defense budget and slash the navy fleet, which he did immediately. An unintended consequence was to signal to the Soviets and Chinese that the United States would not interfere with their plans for expansion in Asia.

The Truman administration was divided over the nation's future relationship with the Soviet Union. Many entertained the hope and belief that close cooperation with the Soviets, including sharing nuclear secrets, would eliminate the need for maintaining large armed forces, while others felt that the Soviets were bent on making further incursions in Europe and Asia and viewed capitalist America as an implacable enemy. The result was a schizophrenic administration. On the one hand, Truman confronted Soviet incursions by deploying the battleship *Missouri* to Istanbul in 1946 and by announcing the Truman Doctrine to help Greece and Turkey against Soviet pressures in 1947. Administration skeptics arranged to have the prestigious Council on Foreign Relations publish an article by George Kennan, a State Department foreign service officer, that called for the containment of Soviet expansion by diplomatic, economic, and if necessary military confrontation. The article, heavily edited by Forrestal and Dean Acheson, became the basis of NATO, the Marshall Plan, and more than forty years of a national strategy of containment of an aggressive Soviet Union.

But on the other hand, the administration pushed seriously in 1946 and '47 for the "Baruch Plan" to turn over all nuclear weapons to United Nations control, then began a massive disarmament program in 1949. Flush with victory and having developed powerful new fleet and multinational operational carrier task force capabilities, the navy felt its Mahanian maritime strategy was vindicated and undertook to continue developing the strategy for the postwar world, a world that in its view involved a new and powerful adversary, the Soviet Union.

President Franklin Roosevelt, with his love of sailing and the sea and his eight years in the Navy Department, had been a naval person to the point that in White House meetings, he had often forgotten himself and referred to the navy as "us" and the army as "them." President Truman, however, was an army veteran who occasionally vented his resentment of the navy. He was known to agree with the comment of his first chairman of the Joint Chiefs of Staff, Army Gen. Omar Bradley, who referred to the navy leadership as "a bunch of fancy Dans."

The stage was set for one of the bitterest political battles in Washington history when the "détentists" in the administration and their allies in Congress set about to massively reduce and reorder the defense establishment. This campaign included efforts not only to reduce the fleet well below the normal postwar shrinkage planned, but to transfer navy and marine aviation to a newly created Department of the Air Force and to put the marine corps under the

LEFT: James Forrestal. *(U.S. Naval Institute.)*
RIGHT: Carl Vinson. *(U.S. Naval Institute.)*

army. This titanic struggle raged for three years, including headline events such as the release of the Collins Report and the "Revolt of the Admirals."

But the navy had very strong supporters in Congress like Carl Vinson, chairman of the House Naval Affairs Committee, and an exceptional leader in its secretary, James Forrestal. The culminating legislation, the National Security Act Amendments of 1949, preserved the Navy Department, with its aviation and its marine corps largely intact, but placed it within a new Defense Department that included the Department of the Army, the Department of the Navy, and the new Department of the Air Force. To reach this compromise, Carl Vinson and other powerful navy supporters insisted that Secretary Forrestal be installed as the first secretary of defense. (The latter, a particularly bitter pill for the White House, was necessary to gain passage of the legislation. Truman had originally chosen War Secretary Robert Patterson to be secretary of defense, but Patterson turned him down for personal reasons.)

The navy's victory was to be temporary, however. Soon after Truman was reelected in 1948, he fired Forrestal, who had been in office only eighteen months. Exhausted by four years of war and four years of bitter vicious political infighting, Forrestal was admitted to Bethesda Naval Hospital shortly after he was fired. He died on May 22, 1949, under puzzling circumstances, an apparent suicide.

Closely advised by White House special assistant Clark Clifford, a passionate advocate of détente and reconciliation with the Soviet Union, Truman, greatly strengthened by his reelection, was determined to install his loyalists in the Pentagon, drastically reduce defense spending, and cut the navy down to size politically as well as physically. On March 29, 1949, he named his campaign finance chairman from the recent campaign, Louis A. Johnson, to be the second secretary of defense. Truman had essentially adopted the air force position during the acrimonious unification legislative battle: the country's defense did not need a large navy, and the air force's new strategic nuclear bomber, the B-36, was all that would be needed for strategic deterrence. Johnson was told to get it done.

Less than a month after his appointment, Johnson ordered the cancellation and dismantling of the navy's first new supercarrier, the *United States*, then about 5 percent completed. Navy Secretary John L. Sullivan had not been consulted and, after finding that Truman backed Johnson, promptly resigned. The senior admirals, including the chief of naval operations, Louis Denfeld, lined the steps of the Mall entrance at the Pentagon and gave him three cheers as he departed. Although none of them followed Sullivan's example by resigning, Denfeld and many other admirals and captains were nevertheless soon purged by Johnson for not falling into line as he proceeded to dismantle the navy and marine force structure.

Johnson made no bones about his intention: "There's no reason for having a Navy and Marine Corps. General [Omar] Bradley tells me

The B-36 strategic nuclear bomber.
(U.S. Air Force photograph.)

that amphibious operations are a thing of the past. We'll never have any more amphibious operations. That does away with the Marine Corps. And the Air Force can do anything the Navy can do nowadays, so that does away with the Navy." To carry out such a revolutionary change of defense strategy, Truman and Johnson selected Francis P. Matthews, a Truman loyalist and fundraiser. Matthews famously noted that the only naval expertise he had was rowing a boat on a lake.

While Johnson lost a few battles to navalists in Congress, he was able largely to carry out his naval disarmament, transferring the funding to the air force to build a thousand B-36s. In little more than a year, the fleet was reduced from 700 to 634 ships, with only five aircraft carriers deployable. All battleships were decommissioned except *Missouri*, and that only because President Truman personally intervened. The marine corps was gutted, from six divisions and five air wings to just two each, with fewer than 75,000 leathernecks on active duty.

The navy, committed as it was in a bitter struggle for survival between 1946 and 1950, did not resume maneuvers on the scale and model of the interwar years. Not only was it impossible to plan with fleet numbers in free fall, but the shift in funding away from the navy left little money for steaming and flying.

Despite the Berlin Blockade, the tightening Soviet grip on Eastern Europe, and growing doubts in the administration, the nation was fully embarked on a strategy of hope for conciliation with the Soviets through the United Nations, backstopped by faith that nuclear bombers alone could deter any future conflict. The NATO alliance was consummated in 1949, but it had no combined command structure besides a series of planning groups, and no exercise program. A day of reckoning could not be far off. As in the 1930s, the rapid shift in national policy away from maritime superiority did not change the need for naval strategy. It was put on the shelf awaiting a better day, which, in this case, was not long in coming.

The real world intruded with stunning swiftness. The Soviet Union and Mao Zedong's China had watched in disbelief as the United States disarmed its navy, marine corps, and army and made it clear that it would not fight another land war in Asia. Opportunity beckoned irresistibly.

On June 25, 1950, the North Korean Army, supported by the Soviet Union and China, swept across the demilitarized zone separating North and South, driving United States and South Korean forces into a tiny pocket on the southern tip of the peninsula.

THE KOREAN WAR, 1950–1953

President Truman immediately realized that a nuclear response was not a real option and called for the imposition of a full naval blockade. He was appalled to find that the navy no longer had sufficient deployable ships to enforce such a blockade.

All air bases in South Korea had been overrun, and the air force had to fly such missions as it could from Japan, well beyond the combat range of its fighters. The B-36 could not be used without fighter escort because, contrary to the case made to Congress, the Soviet Union did indeed have a fighter, the MiG-15 (powered by British designed Rolls-Royce engines) that could shoot it down at altitude. North Korean forces had the MiGs in large numbers, although flown mostly by Russian pilots.

Luckily, the disarmament had not yet taken full effect, and both the U.S. Navy and the Royal Navy presciently had on scene small but combat-capable forward fleets. They rapidly began to reconstitute their forces to surge to Korean waters. The U.S. Navy immediately employed its still-overwhelming command of the seas to provide air superiority over the battlefield, naval gunfire and close air support to the land forces, minesweeping, logistics support, and delivery ashore of marine and army ground forces in MacArthur's brilliant amphibious assault at Inchon.

Luckily, of the five deployable navy carriers, one, the *Valley Forge*, was operating in the theater. For the first months of the war, it was the only source of fighter and close air support for U.S. forces. It soon became clear that the rapid postwar disarmament by the United States had left all the services unable to provide an immediate effective response.

Truman instantly realized that in turning away from his more hawkish cabinet members (Forrestal, Marshall, and Acheson) and adopting instead the policies of his most optimistic and naïve advisers (Clifford, Johnson, Baruch et al.), he had blundered. He changed course immediately and directed the preparation of a new defense budget triple the size of his previous one. He directed an initial emergency reactivation of 381 warships by April 1951 and the immediate restart of the canceled supercarrier program. In a significant gesture, Congress directed that the first supercarrier, launched in 1954, be named *Forrestal*. Within three months of the invasion, Defense Secretary Johnson was forced to resign in disgrace. While certainly deserving some blame, he became the scapegoat for carrying out the presidential decision to slash the defense budget. He was replaced by Gen. George C. Marshall as the third secretary of defense.

Fortunately, the majority of fleet ships had not yet been retired, mothballed, and scrapped, and the navy was able rapidly to reconstitute a powerful fleet, fully manned by Pacific War veterans recalled and activated from the Ready Reserves. In a bold *coup de main* just three months after the invasion, the Seventh Fleet carried out MacArthur's brilliant surprise amphibious landing of marine and army forces at Inchon, almost cutting off the North Korean Army and forcing them into headlong retreat out of South Korea.

Truman, however, knew that he could not leave Europe, the Mediterranean, and the Middle East without sufficient forces to deter

Carrier aircraft over Korea. *(U.S. Naval Institute.)*

further Soviet incursions. Even as he prosecuted the Korean War, he continued to reactivate sufficient ships and aircraft to strengthen the Atlantic and Mediterranean Fleets and the modest naval presence in the Persian Gulf.

When NATO was established in April 1949, the navy had begun carrying out annual joint and combined exercises with Canadian, Dutch, Norwegian, British, and French naval forces on in the eastern Atlantic and Mediterranean, and those continued throughout the Korean War.

In 1952, the navy lost command autonomy in the Mediterranean when U.S. naval forces in Europe were subsumed under the U.S. Army–dominated European Command, for European contingencies including general war. While this made sense for unity of command, it had the unintended consequence of almost eliminating the naval perspective in NATO defense strategy, since allied army staff colleges viewed the principal role of naval power was to secure supplies to armies. That view soon settled into orthodoxy at NATO military headquarters.

With the Communist attack in Korea, the replacement of Louis Johnson by George Marshall, and the trebling of the defense budget, the U.S. Navy began once again to hold routine large-scale exercises. These were usually conducted with allied navies, in close proximity to both the Soviet Union and American allies as part of the U.S. policy of containment, using surge forces as well as powerful fleet units that were routinely forward-deployed.

Operation Mainbrace, in September 1952, was the first major NATO naval exercise in the North Atlantic. Planned and sponsored by Adm. Sir Patrick Brind RN, it included operations in the Norwegian, Barents, North, and Baltic Seas, including carrier operations off Vestfjord and amphibious assaults in Denmark. This massive exercise was for basic training in combined and joint naval operations and intended to send a strong message to the Soviets that the distraction of Korea did not make the West vulnerable. More than one hundred major warships from nine NATO navies participated, including six U.S., three British, and one Canadian aircraft carrier and one U.S. and one British battleship. In the exercise they practiced and demonstrated offensive strike, amphibious, and antisubmarine operations. The overall scenario was to demonstrate massive capability to support any land battle in NATO's northern region (Norway and Denmark).

Other major NATO exercises took place in the fall of 1952 in NATO's central and southern regions. In November, an even larger combined exercise, Operation Long Step, involving 170 warships, was carried out in the eastern Mediterranean to demonstrate to the Soviets NATO's intention and capability to defeat an invasion of NATO's Mediterranean members. The exercise concluded with a large-scale amphibious landing in Turkey involving three thousand French, Italian, and Greek troops and a U.S. Marine battalion.

PART II: *Containment and Détente*

Following the first use of atomic bombs against Japan and the development of the much more powerful hydrogen bomb, a doctrine for the possible use of these weapons began to develop in the nuclear laboratories at Los Alamos, New Mexico, and Livermore, California. When the Soviet Union acquired a nuclear capability, strategic thinkers emerged in the armed services and academia. Edward Teller, Henry Kissinger, Bernard Schriever, Herman Kahn, Thomas Schelling, Fred Iklé, and others, while never achieving consensus, evolved a strategy in which ballistic missiles and long-range bombers would deliver thousands of intercontinental nuclear weapons, which came to be called strategic weapons. Matched by the Soviets, it came to be called deterrence by Mutual Assured Destruction or MAD.

For the military balance in Europe, the Warsaw Pact was able to field far more army divisions than NATO. To even the balance, the United States deployed hundreds of smaller nuclear weapons to be delivered by short- and medium-range missiles and by land and carrier-based fighter-bombers, which came to be called tactical weapons. This doctrine of flexible response came to be the foundation of NATO defense policy in the Cold War.

When the navy deployed the first Polaris nuclear missile submarine, the *George Washington*, in 1960, with strategic nuclear ballistic

LEFT TO RIGHT:
A-1 Skyraider aircraft.
A-3 Skywarrior strategic bomber.
A-4 Skyhawk attack aircraft.
(*U.S. Naval Institute.*)

missiles, the navy began efforts to have the carriers relieved of the strategic nuclear strike role but not the tactical nuclear role. (The Soviets might be forgiven for failing to appreciate the distinction.)

NUCLEAR STRATEGY

While the navy had lost the major battle in 1949 to the air force over a role for aircraft carriers in strategic nuclear deterrence, the battle was renewed in 1954. That was the year NATO formally adopted the policy of using tactical nuclear weapons to back up its conventional forces confronting the Warsaw Pact. By then, the Warsaw Pact had deployed 180 armored, motorized, and infantry divisions along the West German border, with another hundred divisions in reserve. NATO divisions faced far superior Warsaw Pact conventional forces across the border. Following the new flexible response doctrine, NATO adopted the use of nuclear weapons for tactical purposes to counter Soviet superiority in conventional forces, including infantry and tank divisions. It was thought that use of nuclear weapons on the battlefield against Soviet forces would not necessarily escalate to all-out strategic nuclear war.

As part of this policy change, navy carriers were given a nuclear strike role against Soviet targets from launch points from the Norwegian Sea to the eastern Mediterranean. With the deployment of the *Forrestal*-class carriers and the A-3 Skywarrior, A-4 Skyhawk, and A-1 Skyraider aircraft in 1957, the navy finally achieved a realistic,

highly reliable, and very credible nuclear weapons delivery capability. As a result, the Second and Sixth Fleets and the NATO Striking Fleets focused more on training for "tactical" nuclear strikes on Soviet and Warsaw Pact forces invading Central Europe and less on interdiction and battlefield support for NATO flanks.

As American and Soviet nuclear strategy evolved into the standoff known as MAD, the navy's role changed significantly. On July 1, 1961, the U.S. government formally adopted the first Single Integrated Operational Plan (SIOP), which assigned specific targets for the air force and navy carrier aircraft to hit with nuclear weapons, in the event of Soviet strategic nuclear attack on the United States. The SIOP and its successors had the effect of constraining navy carrier operations, requiring carriers to be within range of a fixed launch point in order to attack their preplanned targets. Thus in March 1962, a carrier group led by *Wasp* operated in the Baltic Sea to send a clear signal to the Soviets that Russian forces and cities were now vulnerable to nuclear attack from the sea. While *Wasp* was a sub-hunting carrier, others of its class were nuclear attack carriers.

But those nuclear weapons assignments brought serious problems for navy planners. The targeting constraints bit into the fleets' basic needs for movement, cover, and deception. Moreover, the secure storage and maintenance of nuclear weapons required much additional manpower and shipboard space, and the costs soon became apparent. Many in the navy planning world began to have doubts about the nuclear role for carriers, and those doubts would soon grow into a broad desire to get rid of these cumbersome weapons. It was a clear case of national strategy conflicting with naval strategy. The navy finally succeeded in offloading nuclear weapons from the carriers during the Reagan and Bush administrations, when naval strategy and national strategy emphasizing nuclear reductions and conventional deterrence were once again one and the same.

The Great Sea, as has often been said, is an environment utterly unforgiving of any carelessness, incapacity, or neglect. Deeply embedded in navy culture is a strong suspicion of theorists and planners unless they have earned their reputations in operations at sea. Following World War II, with the rapid growth of new technologies, weapons, and tactics, this skepticism resulted in the creation of a team of civilian scientists and operations analysts. It was the job of these specialized civilians to go to sea and act as unbiased fact-based analysts and judges of the effectiveness of weapons, electronics, equipment, tactics, and overall operations.

These teams grew into the Operations Evaluation Group (OEG), and they still today go to sea with the sailors in actual exercises and operations to gather hard data on performance of guns, missiles, radars, sonars, communications, ships, and aircraft. Their data provide fleet commanders with a reality feedback loop that acts constantly to refine and update systems, tactics, and strategy. As the Cold War progressed, the OEG was folded into a broader studies and analysis organization with an expanded mandate to support navy and marine corps strategy and tactical development. This combined group was the Center for Naval Analyses (CNA), and it became a central player in developing strategy and tactics throughout the Cold War. (In the 1980s, the CNA's tactical exercise analyst embedded in the Third Fleet, Christine Fox, was the role model for Kelly McGillis's character Charlie in the movie *Top Gun*. Fox would years later become acting deputy secretary of defense.)

THE CUBAN MISSILE CRISIS

After U-2 spy planes established the presence of Russian nuclear ballistic missiles in Cuba, President John F. Kennedy, on October 14, 1962, declared the immediate blockade (styled a "quarantine") of Cuba, to be enforced by the U.S. Second Fleet and other Atlantic Fleet units. The navy went on global alert. By November 20, the crisis was over, and the withdrawal of the missiles begun. The world had once again learned to appreciate the meaning of Mahan's "command of the seas" concept.

Among other lessons, the Soviets took this one to heart. Adm.

Soviets withdraw the missiles from Cuba. *(U.S. Navy, National Naval Aviation Museum Photograph Collection.)*

Sergei Gorshkov, appointed commander in chief of the Soviet Navy in 1956, finally had the leverage he needed to persuade the Politburo to support his building a true blue-water navy to acquire naval supremacy over the United States. His program commenced at once. Within two years, he established a permanent naval presence in the Mediterranean, soon institutionalized into the Fifth Operational Squadron, or Fifth Eskadra.

THE VIETNAM WAR

In 1964, President Lyndon Johnson's administration chose to use the Tonkin Gulf incident as a *casus belli* despite the skepticism of navy leaders. The navy once again found itself devoting its attention to providing logistics, naval gunfire support, close air support, and riverine and special forces combat support to army and marine forces ashore.

But as had not been the case in Korea, command of the seas was used increasingly for employing the navy's carriers in the strategic bombing of North Vietnam. While the navy disagreed intensely with the rules of engagement and tactical restrictions imposed by national strategy, there was no disagreement about the necessity to maintain global maritime supremacy. So while the increasing war effort meant less money available for maintenance of the fleet and increased strain on morale and retention, the navy continued large-scale naval exercises with NATO in the Norwegian Sea and the eastern Mediterranean.

In addition to carrying out its logistical responsibilities, providing naval gunfire support and tactical air support for the marines and army ashore, the navy created a new "brown-water navy" for a kind of riverine warfare not seen since the American Civil War. Also, as had not been the case in Korea, carrier aircraft were increasingly assigned to a strategic bombing campaign against industrial and infrastructure targets in North Vietnam.

The Soviet Navy meanwhile continued its aggressive building and deployment campaign, deploying its first Yankee-class nuclear ballistic missile submarines, establishing permanent fleet presence in the Indian Ocean as well as the Mediterranean, and holding unprecedented large-scale Soviet and Warsaw Pact joint exercises, including naval exercises in the North Atlantic and in the Norwegian, Barents, and Baltic Seas.

With growing Soviet global fleet operations and their considerable focus on countering U.S. carriers, the navy expanded its research and development program to accelerate deployment of acoustic and electronic cover and deception systems. These proved to be highly effective in countering the ability of submarines and surface ships to find the carriers.

OPERATION AZORIAN
In March 1968, about fifteen hundred miles northwest of Hawaii in water several miles deep, the Soviet missile submarine K-129

A *Yankee*-class nuclear ballistic missile submarine. *(Official U.S. Navy photograph.)*

sank with all hands. The U.S. Navy was, of course, intensely interested. K-129 was a conventionally powered Golf II-class submarine designed to carry three nuclear ballistic missiles on cruises within range of the U.S. West Coast. The Soviet Navy tried for months to locate the sub but failed. After a suitable interval, the U.S. Navy was able to locate and extensively photograph the sub using a specially outfitted submarine, *Halibut*. The navy immediately drew up plans to use *Halibut* to retrieve everything of intelligence value: codebooks, crypto and communications gear, nuclear warheads, and as many missiles and torpedoes as possible. The navy was confident that while it would take time and extensive cover and deception, it would be able to recover most of the invaluable equipment using only submersible equipment and without tipping off the Russians.

Unfortunately the Navy at that time had not salvaged a submarine deeper than 200 feet (the *Squalus*), and did not have the capability to lift such heavy objects from such depths. The White House

The Glomar Explorer. *(U.S. Naval Institute.)*

decided however that obtaining a Soviet nuclear warhead was worth taking greater risks.

National Security Adviser Henry Kissinger and CIA Director Richard Helms advised the president that the CIA should undertake a daring mission to salvage the Russian submarine, and President Nixon gave the go-ahead. In 1971, the CIA drew up a far more ambitious plan to recover the entire forward two-thirds of the sub, which had broken in two when it sank. A ship was designed to lower a grapple big enough to raise the entire section up into a huge chamber in the hull, then sail away with her. The navy objected strongly that it was far too risky and would not accomplish any more than the navy's own more time-consuming but far less risky plan. Navy objections were overruled. The ship was built and launched, in Operation Azorian, as the Hughes Glomar Explorer, owned by Global Marine Inc., with a cover story that Howard Hughes was supporting the deep-sea mining of manganese nodules.

The clandestine ship began operation in June 1974. Unfortunately, the sub section broke apart as it was being drawn into the ship, and two-thirds of it fell back to the sea bottom. But the forward third was successfully brought aboard, and a great deal of useful material was recovered—including, in some reports, two nuclear torpedoes. The bodies of six Russian sailors were also recovered and given formal military honors and buried at sea. Despite the navy's disappointment, the operation was in fact a major naval intelligence coup.

THE NIXON YEARS

Richard Nixon was elected president in 1968 on a pledge to end the war. American involvement ultimately ended in January 1973 with the signing of the Paris Peace Accords. Both Richard Nixon and his national security adviser, Henry Kissinger, were navalists committed to maintaining naval supremacy. There were unfortunately two obstacles to doing so in the face of the Soviet naval buildup. First, Congress was determined to get a major "peace dividend" by making deep cuts in the defense budget; second, Nixon and Kissinger were also committed to the conflicting strategy of pursuing détente and major arms control agreements with the Soviets. The result was an inconsistent national strategy. The president and his national security adviser never questioned the need to maintain naval supremacy and never doubted that they had it, but they also knew it was rapidly slipping away. They supported the modernization and repair of the Vietnam-worn fleet but did not have the votes in Congress to fund it. They also agreed with the Joint Chiefs of Staff to support the navy's new Trident submarine and nuclear-ballistic-missile system. On the other hand, in the spirit of détente, they did not challenge the growing political restrictions on naval exercises. as a result of congressional cuts, the fleet steadily shrank during the period.

SOVIET NAVAL STRATEGY

In April and May 1970, Admiral Gorshkov launched a massive Soviet naval exercise called Okean '70, creating global shock waves by ending all doubt that he was determined to seize the opportunity of American entrapment in Vietnam to wrest naval supremacy from the United States. It was the largest peacetime naval exercise held by any navy since World War II. Two hundred surface ships and submarines, plus land-based naval aviation, conducted simultaneous operations in the Barents, Norwegian, Baltic, Mediterranean, and Philippine Seas and in the Sea of Japan. They included intense anti-submarine, anticarrier, and amphibious operations.

Despite what was going on in the Pacific, NATO military staffs became focused solely on the balance of NATO/Warsaw Pact land, missile, and air forces in Central Europe, the Fulda Gap, and North German Plain, to the exclusion of all else. Naval power and its enormous potential deterrent influence was dropped from consideration. As a result, the size, importance, and publicity attending NATO multinational naval exercises steadily shrank.

THE MIDDLE EAST

From the beginning of the Cold War, periodic crises in the Middle East required naval operations. In 1958, in Operation Blue Bat, President Dwight Eisenhower ordered the navy to land a force of marines in Lebanon to stabilize a dangerous political deterioration and support the Lebanese government.

In September 1970, a new crisis erupted as the Palestine Liberation Organization sought to topple King Hussein of Jordan. With the fighting in Vietnam undiminished, President Nixon nevertheless deployed an additional carrier and amphibious assault ship to beef up the Sixth Fleet in the eastern Mediterranean, ready to intervene if necessary to save the king. The assigned U.S. carrier air wings off-loaded support aircraft and added more F-4 Phantoms to enable the establishment of complete around-the-clock air superiority and a no-fly zone over Jordan. A third carrier got under way from the East Coast. Two additional U.S. nuclear attack subs entered the Mediterranean, and the Royal Navy deployed two carriers there as well. The

Soviet Navy's Fifth Escadra increased to twenty surface combatants and six submarines.

During the crisis, Sixth Fleet experimented with operating carriers in the radar shadow of the coastal mountains of Cyprus to mask their presence. It worked so well that the tactic was refined in subsequent exercises and was incorporated into the far more mountainous coast and fjords of Norway in the Reagan administration's Maritime Strategy, as we shall see.

In September 1970, the new chief of naval operations, Adm. Elmo R. Zumwalt, launched a detailed, comprehensive, and coherent blueprint for initiatives the navy needed to take to regain momentum and prevent the Russians from gaining naval supremacy. The project was called Project SIXTY. It included many new programs that were essential to prevail against the new cruise missile, submarine, torpedo, Backfire bomber, and missile threats that the Soviets were beginning to deploy in large numbers in their growing blue-water fleet. It included new ship and aircraft systems needed to operate in Arctic waters as well as shallow tropical seas. It provided for planning and training to operate in those unfamiliar and difficult environments. Zumwalt's successor, Adm. James A. Holloway, revised and adjusted some of the priorities, and because of his skills in dealing with Congress, he was able to get funding for the development of most (but not all) of the initiatives, which were then eventually successfully funded and deployed by the navy during the Reagan administration.

NATO headquarters was increasingly fixated on the growing numerical superiority of Warsaw Pact army divisions along the East German, Polish, and Czech borders (known as the Central Front), with the result that NATO naval forces were seen as of less importance beyond convoying supplies across the Atlantic. The navy tried to get attention: in 1971, as Rear Adm. William Houser was returning his carrier task force to the United States from a Mediterranean deployment, he got navy orders to detour into the Bay of Biscay and North Sea and fly his fighters and bombers. The purpose was to demonstrate and remind the generals at NATO headquarters that naval vessels and strike aircraft could provide invaluable support to European commanders. Nevertheless attention to the naval balance steadily diminished.

NATO multinational naval exercises steadily shrank. In the early 1970s, as the perceived land balance continued to shift against NATO, an era of seeking arms control agreements and "détente" with the Soviets began. This led in turn to an ascendant view in NATO political circles that the annual naval exercises should be scaled back even more and made less provocative to the Soviets, by requiring them to stay south of the Greenland-UK line. By the end of the decade, the strategy shift from offense to defense of the Greenland-Iceland-UK (GIUK) Gap had become NATO orthodoxy.

Getting direct guidance from CNO Admiral Zumwalt, Vice Adm. Gerald Miller took command of the Sixth Fleet in October 1971:

> During this tour, I attempted to demonstrate the capabilities of the carrier task forces to support activities in Central Europe. I requested permission from my U.S. superior at the top of the command structure, a U.S. Air Force general, to launch four A-7 aircraft from the Aegean Sea in the Mediterranean and recover them on board a carrier operating off Bodø, Norway, in the Norwegian Sea. At the same time, four A-7s from the carrier in the Norwegian Sea would launch for the carrier in the Mediterranean. The next day all eight aircraft would return to their respective home bases. It was a relatively simple exercise in that Europe is not that large, and the aircraft had plenty of range and payload capabilities for the mission. After some time, I was granted permission to conduct the exercise, which went off very smoothly. It showed once again that carriers could support combat operations in the European landmass and contribute to either the combined or joint operations being conducted.

Navy Secretary and later Senator John Warner. *(U.S. Naval Institute.)*

As the Soviet fleet steadily increased in size and global operations, the interaction between them and U.S. and NATO operations became an issue. Soviet spy ships and combatants began to participate in allied naval exercises as uninvited guests, and U.S. and NATO combatants did the same in Soviet exercises. Close calls and actual collisions at sea soon took place. In the air, similar monitoring and surveillance of each other became routine, and there were many close calls. While political tensions remained high throughout the Cold War, the very close physical interaction of the two naval forces soon bred a grudging respect, then even admiration of the professionalism of the sailors of both fleets of these potential enemies. Nevertheless as incidents multiplied, it became imperative that something be done.

On May 25, 1972 a bilateral U.S.-Soviet Incidents at Sea Agreement (INCSEA) was signed during the Moscow Summit by U.S. navy secretary John Warner and Soviet Adm. Sergei Gorshkov. One of the negotiators was the director of Warner's uniformed navy staff, Rear Adm. Thomas B. Hayward, later Pacific Fleet commander, then chief of naval operations and a major player in the development of a forward naval strategy. The INCSEA agreement established annual U.S.-Soviet review conferences, which have taken place ever since. It is one of the most successful agreements in the history of arms control.

The following day, May 26, the United States and the Soviet Union signed a much more controversial arms control agreement. The Strategic Arms Limitation Talks (SALT) agreement limited land-based and submarine-launched nuclear ballistic missiles, strategic bombers, and antiballistic missile (ABM) systems, including a ban on sea-based ABM systems. Since the agreement gave the Soviets a three-to-two advantage in offensive weapons and gave up a large U.S. advantage in ABM systems, there was a storm in Congress. The State Department argued that that was the best deal they could get since the United States was not building missiles and the Soviets had already achieved a three-to-two advantage and were still building. They believed that the only leverage they had was to give up the U.S. advantage in ballistic missile defense. (The United States had an operational ABM system, while the Soviets did not.) To get Senate approval, the administration had to commit to develop and procure the new Trident missile and submarine system, the Tomahawk cruise missile, and the B-1 bomber, among other things.

OPERATION IVY BELLS

In October 1972, in one of the most consequential intelligence developments of the Cold War, the navy's Operation Ivy Bells began. The nuclear attack submarine *Halibut* began tapping Soviet military underwater communications lines in the Sea of Okhotsk. These operations would continue for about a decade, including similar operations in other areas, until National Security Agency (NSA) employee Ronald Pelton compromised them. It has been speculated that without the intelligence provided by this source, President Reagan would not have been able to conduct his forward naval strategy and his strategic diplomacy with confidence or in the way he did.

In November 1980, after Reagan's election as president, the navy reorganized how it distributed, limited, and protected its most sensitive intelligence. The director of naval intelligence (DNI), Rear

The USS *Halibut. (Official U.S. Navy photograph by P. Bubble.)*

Adm. Sumner Shapiro, established Soviet Doctrine Division OP-009J under Richard L. Haver, reporting directly to the DNI, to ensure the full exploitation of dramatic and sensitive Naval Intelligence breakthroughs made in the late 1970s. These intelligence sources were very closely held, and very few of the most senior decision makers in the government were given access to the intelligence derived from them. They provided a steady stream of insights into Soviet naval doctrine and strategy, the Soviets' means of fighting a war, their strengths and vulnerabilities, their perceptions of and prejudices against the United States, and their reactions to the increasingly aggressive American navy.

Some believe that because of that intelligence, the president and his navy leaders knew exactly how the Soviets would react to the new forward exercises beginning with Ocean Venture '81. As important, some believe that this intelligence made clear that as the exercises intensified over the next six years, the Soviets could not deal with the NATO naval onslaught, and that their own operations analysis in each exercise concluded that within a week of a NATO counterattack to a Warsaw Pact attack on the Central Front, they would in fact effectively lose their ability to defend the Northern Sea Frontier.

In October 1976, the navy launched its first operational space-borne ocean surveillance electronic intelligence (ELINT) spy satellite system, targeting Soviet ships at sea. Following Classic Wizard, as it was known, more ELINT satellites and their successors—White Cloud and Parcae—would follow throughout the 1970s and '80s.

In the early 1970s, NATO's successful containment of the Soviets led to an era of seeking arms control agreements and "détente" with them. This led in turn to an ascendant view in NATO political circles that the annual naval exercises could be scaled back and made less provocative to the Soviets, a view that much pleased NATO defense ministry budget cutters on both sides of the Atlantic. Naval focus was shifted to a kind of Maginot Line for the northern flank.

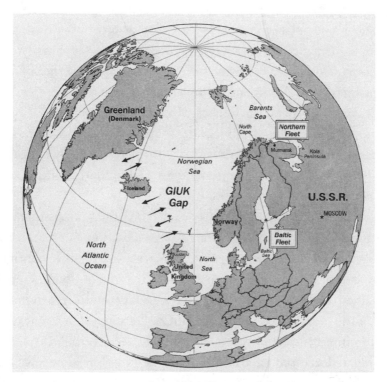

The Greenland–Iceland–United Kingdom (GIUK) Gap.
(Center for the Study of Intelligence, Central Intelligence Agency.)

Above the GIUK Gap, an imaginary line drawn from Greenland to Iceland to the UK, offensive naval exercises were not to be undertaken so as not to provoke the Soviet Union.

The Soviet Politburo, advised by Admiral Gorshkov, had a more accurate view of the threat that NATO naval superiority posed to Soviet objectives. In 1971, Soviet leader Leonid Brezhnev called for comprehensive mutual U.S.-Soviet limitations on naval deployments throughout the globe—a proposal regularly reaffirmed by Soviet spokesmen over the next several years.

The End of U.S. involvement in Vietnam

Ninety percent of the military assistance from the Soviet Union and China to North Vietnam reached the country through Haiphong Harbor. Since 1967, the navy had been advocating mining the harbor, but it had not been approved for fear of provoking both those powers to become more actively involved in the war. Finally, after the North launched its "Easter Offensive" invasion of the South in the spring of 1972, President Nixon approved the mining.

On May 8, Operation Pocket Money was launched. Navy and Marine aircraft flying from *Saratoga* and *Kitty Hawk* mined the approaches to Haiphong Harbor. The mining completely eliminated traffic in and out and was maintained for eight months, until the end of U.S. involvement in the war.

A day later the Operation Linebacker I, bombing campaign began. The purpose of this joint navy/air force operation was to interdict supply routes and military targets in North Vietnam. It continued until October 23. By then the army and air force of South Vietnam had rallied and counterattacked and were successfully driving the army of the North back across the DMZ. Despite these setbacks, the North refused to make any concessions in the peace talks.

Joint air force and navy bombing in the North resumed as Operation Linebacker II from December 18 to 29. This time it attacked more strategic targets around Hanoi and Haiphong and involved heavy use of B-52s in an effort to force the North to agree to a cease-fire and a settlement. Finally the North began to negotiate.

The Paris Peace Accords were signed by the United States and North Vietnam in Paris on January 29, 1973. The war was over for the United States, but not, unfortunately, for South Vietnam.

EAST-WEST MANEUVERING CONTINUES

After President Nixon was reelected in 1972, he intended to continue to seek arms control agreements with the Soviets. But he also wanted to keep pressure on them by building on the historic opening to China with steady warming of relations, and by supporting the navy's modernization efforts with new nuclear carriers, submarines, and missiles. The president's national security adviser, Henry Kissinger, privately encouraged naval leaders to continue to exercise closer to the Soviet Union and to demonstrate the ability to project power from the seas. Nixon and Kissinger never doubted the importance of maintaining maritime supremacy, nor did Gerald Ford, after he suc-ceeded Nixon. But that strategy was not fully understood elsewhere in the administration or in Congress, and many officials supported the NATO shift to using naval forces only defensively and keeping them away from provocative deployments close to the Soviets.

But neither the Washington bureaucracy nor that of NATO in Brussels really understood what went on in naval exercises, so the navy was left pretty much to itself as long as it did not cause any incidents or get into the press.

The Soviet arms buildup; the looming imbalance in nuclear, conventional, and now, for the first time, naval forces; and increasingly aggressive Soviet foreign policy pronouncements, all seemed to spur the Ford administration to focus even more on achieving arms control agreements. In the period leading up to the 1976 election, a bipartisan group led primarily by hawkish Democrats Paul

Nitze, retired Adm. Bud Zumwalt, Eugene Rostow, Max Kampelman, and Jeane Kirkpatrick, along with Republicans Ronald Reagan, George Shultz, Richard Allen, myself, and numerous others, found our concerns bordering on alarm. In November 1976, we formed an advocacy group under the resurrected name the Committee on the Present Danger (CPD). For the next four years, we published papers, gave speeches, organized conferences, and lobbied for rebuilding American nuclear, land, and naval forces to reestablish a balance. (Thirty-three Republican and Democratic members of the CPD later served in the administration of Ronald Reagan.)

At the beginning of 1976, at the instigation of Secretary of Defense Donald Rumsfeld, a former naval aviator, and Henry Kissinger, now secretary of state, the Ford administration launched a major new look at the navy's shipbuilding program. I was at the time deputy director of the Arms Control and Disarmament Agency, having followed Kissinger from the White House to the State Department, and I was Kissinger's representative on the study group. The yearlong study produced National Security Decision Memorandum (NSDM) 344, "Navy Shipbuilding Program," on January 18, 1977. Coming two days before the inauguration of President Carter, the study may have made the navy's heart beat faster, but it had no chance of enactment. It was, however, a good contrast to the coming Carter reductions. It called for attaining and maintaining an active force of six hundred ships.

As an offshoot of the study, the navy got closer to its wish to rid its surface ships of nuclear weapons. Carrier aircraft were withdrawn from the strategic part of the nuclear strike plan, but they remained in NATO's "tactical" strike planning. This freed the carriers from some launch-point restrictions on their mobility, although the carriers still carried, trained, and prepared for tactical nuclear missions.

Part III: *Defense Becomes Offense*

The Carter Years

When Naval Academy graduate Jimmy Carter was inaugurated president in 1977, the navy had high hopes. Those hopes were soon dashed as Carter surrounded himself with advisers who did not support increased naval power and who thought the navy budget was ripe for cutting. For secretary of defense, Carter selected Harold Brown, a former air force secretary highly respected by both Republicans and Democrats. Brown and his senior deputies and assistants were Eurocentric and viewed the navy's role as primarily to keep the Atlantic logistics bridge open by escorting convoys.

The navy was blessed, however, with the appointment of two strong leaders who were completely out of harmony with the new administration's arms reduction orthodoxy. Graham Claytor, a railroad CEO and decorated destroyer escort skipper in World War II, became secretary of the navy, and James Woolsey, counsel for the Senate Armed Services Committee and later CIA director, became navy undersecretary. Led by the chief of naval operations, Adm. James Holloway, a combat veteran of the Pacific War, Korea, and Vietnam, the navy had a unique and powerful triumvirate.

The common wisdom in the office of the secretary of defense, however, soon became that carriers and the surface navy could no longer survive in the age of technology, and that "naval supremacy" was dangerous fantasy. Holloway was ordered to remove the term from all his testimony before Congress.

The president supported this radical shift in postwar strategy so strongly that he vetoed the Fiscal Year 1978 Defense Bill because Congress had added a new nuclear carrier. Navy supporters in Congress fought back and almost had the votes to override the veto. The following year they succeeded, and the carrier was authorized and funded. (When I became navy secretary the following February, I named it *Theodore Roosevelt*. It was the first contract I negotiated as secretary. My wife Barbara was named the ship's sponsor and christened it when it was launched. Two decades later our son John III spent two combat tours in Iraq and Afghanistan flying Prowlers from its deck.)

During the Carter years, the navy once again had to salute the president and await a better day. A number of aggressive navy strategic thinkers kept the flame alive during the Carter years. Admiral Holloway was, of course, first among them. While he was forbidden to use the term *naval supremacy* in any testimony or prepared speeches, when asked his personal opinion during hearings, he did not hesitate to say that in his view American security required maritime supremacy.

Adm. Isaac C. (Ike) Kidd, Jr., commander in chief Atlantic from 1975 to 1978, was a firm believer in the principles of Mahan and forward offensive NATO operations through the Norwegian Sea to the Kola Peninsula. He made his personal views known at every opportunity, which made him quite unpopular in the administration. One of his disciples and his executive assistant, Capt. Frank Kelso, was later to become chief of naval operations.

Another aggressive strategist was Vice Adm. Thomas B. Hayward, who took over as commander of the Seventh Fleet in 1976. He was concerned that while the Seventh Fleet was exhausted from a decade of intensive Vietnam operations in Southeast Asia, the Soviets had built and deployed a capable new Pacific Fleet in northeastern Asia. Hayward began to reorient the Seventh Fleet toward prompt offensive war fighting against the Soviet Navy and Soviet conventional forces in the northwestern Pacific.

After a year of reorienting the Seventh Fleet, Hayward took command of the entire Pacific Fleet. He expanded the aggressive blueprint he had used in the Seventh Fleet to the entire Pacific. In the event that the Soviets started a war in Europe, far from "swinging" his fleet out of the Pacific, Hayward intended to use it immediately—forward, offensively, and to the north, against the Soviet Far East. In his view, this would put the Soviets on the defensive and either deter them from aggression or, if deterrence failed, defeat them by pinning them down and preventing their transfer to Europe. Hayward worked closely with his army and air force counterparts in integrating their role in operations.

One of the navy's more controversial strategists was Capt. James A. Lyons, Jr. "Ace" Lyons had alternated sea tours as an aggressive destroyerman with shore tours as a strategic planner on the joint staff and at navy headquarters. In July 1975, he became chief of staff of the carrier strike group in the Mediterranean, aboard first *Nimitz*, then *America*. One of his staff recalled that Lyons "reoriented the staff from an administrative bureaucracy to a war-fighting battle group team, operationally astute." Lyons was well known in the navy for developing and using dispersed formations, deception tactics, unpredictability, and bold electronic warfare.

I met Lyons the following summer in the eastern Mediterranean. I was deputy director of the Arms Control and Disarmament Agency and a reserve naval aviator, serving my annual active duty assigned to Attack Squadron 176 aboard *America*. (This was just after Operation Fluid Drive, the evacuation from Lebanon of U.S. citizens following the assassination of the U.S. ambassador in Beirut.) As both of us were deeply interested in strategy, we soon hit it off, and when off duty, we could often be found at a table in the wardroom talking strategy, operations and tactics. Our association would later have an impact on navy strategy, policy, operations, tactics, and exercises.

When autumn came, Lyons returned from the Mediterranean and reported as senior navy planner on the navy staff. He had a reputation as an aggressive and successful operator not only at sea but in the corridors of the Pentagon. He pulled strings and gathered around himself some of the brightest young naval officers, with skills and experience in national security policy, strategy, and political military affairs, such as Cmdr. Hank Mauz and Lt. Cmdr. Phil Dur. Their work greatly magnified Lyons's impact within the Pentagon, and his mentoring in turn accelerated their careers. All would later rise to positions of power and influence in their own right.

In October 1976, Lyons completed his strategy team with the addition of Lt. Cmdr. Peter Swartz, who had built a reputation as a navy strategy specialist with a distinguished academic record in international relations from the Johns Hopkins School of Advanced International Studies as well as in-country Vietnam War experience as a political warfare adviser to the Vietnamese Navy. Swartz was to become one of Lyons's top interagency gladiators in the coming battles. His meticulous research and fact-based logic enabled him to dominate debates with the fine points of navy strategy and policy.

Lyons and I met often for lunch at the Metropolitan Club (coincidentally, the same club where Assistant Navy Secretary Theodore Roosevelt had lunched frequently with Capt. Alfred Thayer Mahan.)

The change in direction of national strategy began on February 18, 1977, when President Carter signed out Presidential Review Memorandum 10 (PRM-10), directing a "Comprehensive Net Assessment and Military Force Posture Review." This review occasioned bitter discussions between the navy and other elements of the defense establishment, as the others sought to downplay navy contributions in a global war with the Soviets and shy away from aggressive forward naval operations. The review saw the navy's primary role in a global war with the Soviets as safeguarding the North Atlantic sea-lanes for the movement of U.S. military forces to central Europe. It would recommend cutting the navy's carrier force from thirteen ships to ten and result in publication of Presidential Decision 18 (PD-18), "U.S. National Strategy," six months later.

On May 5, President Carter put forward a budget with significant cuts in defense and began a series of arms control initiatives. That same day he called for the "complete demilitarization of the Indian Ocean," and later in the month he announced his decision to reduce U.S. force levels in Korea.

He also directed the State Department to renew its efforts to negotiate a Strategic Arms Limitation Treaty, SALT II, which had been stalled since the Ford administration. Republicans and conservative Democrats who viewed the draft subsequently negotiated saw it as hopelessly one-sided. Despite strong opposition from the Joint Chiefs of Staff, Carter signed the treaty in Vienna on June 17, 1979. This of course would deed our deterrent advantage to the Soviets. Predictably, the draft treaty failed to get Senate ratification.

On June 22, 1977, U.S.-Soviet Indian Ocean Arms Limitation Talks, initiated by President Carter, got under way. Admiral Hayward, Pacific Fleet commander, was the military representative on the U.S. delegation. The talks made no progress and were suspended in February 1978.

In June 1977, President Carter canceled development of the air force's B-1 bomber.

On June 30, he announced that the South East Asia Treaty Organization (SEATO) was dissolved after twenty-three years. The Central Treaty Organization (CENTO) was dissolved two years later.

On September 7, he signed the Torrijos-Carter Treaty, turning over control of the Panama Canal to Panama.

AN ALTERNATIVE STRATEGY EMERGES

When the review created by PRM-10 began, a month after the Carter inauguration, the navy sent in its first team. Ace Lyons coordinated and provided guidance on navy participation and arguments for his action officers, who included Peter Swartz, to use in the review. They faced off against Carter administration White house staffers. It soon became apparent that navy arguments, however compelling, were being ignored.

Every June the navy secretary hosts the Current Strategy Forum at the Naval War College in Newport, Rhode Island. That year the director of strategic research, Francis "Bing" West, ran the forum, and with navy secretary Graham Claytor's approval, he invited me.

The Black Pearl Restaurant,
Newport, R.I., birthplace of
the "napkin plan."
(Courtesy of Keith Cullen.)

(A former marine and later best-selling author, West was to become a major player in the Reagan national security arena.) I was out of government but was advising Admiral Holloway and Senators Tower and Jackson. After the formal sessions, Claytor, Woolsey, West, and I repaired to the Black Pearl restaurant after hours. Assisted by lobsters and refreshing beverages, a very lively discussion ensued. West took notes and from them sketched out a forward Norwegian Sea campaign on a napkin. The napkin became one of the roots of Sea Plan 2000, the study that Secretary Brown would soon authorize.

As expected, on August 24, 1977, President Carter signed PD-18, based on the PRM-10 review, downplaying navy contributions to national and global alliance defense. PD-18 was marked by essential agreement between the army, the air force, and the civilian Defense Department bureaucracy on the resources and force levels needed to address a range of representative scenarios. The major exception was in the area of naval forces, where navy estimates of force levels were so out of sync with those recommended by the army and air force that it undermined the credibility of the directive, especially in Congress.

Coincidentally one week later, on August 31, the prestigious International Institute for Strategic Studies (IISS) in London reported that NATO had become weaker in sea power and would no longer be able to control all sea areas of importance to the alliance at the start of a conflict.

Defense Secretary Brown was open-minded and analytical, but along with his under secretary for policy, Robert Komer (known as "Blowtorch Bob"), he believed carriers were obsolete and that naval power had little relevance to the Soviet threat to NATO. Brown, inordinately fearful of losing carriers in wartime, believed they had to be kept at least "1,500 nautical miles from Soviet land bases," if they were to survive long enough to win in a sea war. Otherwise, his chief naval concern was that resupply of forward allies by convoy must be able to take place thirty days after a conflict started. To Komer, "Offensive naval operations simply could not prevent the projection of Soviet power outward in Eurasia by land and sea. . . . It would be like sticking pins in the hide of an elephant."

Of course, not all Pentagon leaders agreed with such a radical change in defense policy. Navy secretary Claytor, his deputy Woolsey, and CNO Holloway argued that a "swing" strategy would abandon our Pacific allies to the Soviets, effectively neutralizing Japan; it would give China cause to throw in its lot with the Soviets, and it would free up substantial Soviet forces for reinforcement of their campaign in Europe. But their strong logic was ignored. They gritted their teeth and saluted, but they made clear in their congressional testimony that they had no enthusiasm for the new policy. Fleet commanders were not told to change their offensive planning and exercising against the potential Soviet adversary, and some very innovative strategy, forward operational concepts, and tactics continued to be developed.

Sea Plan 2000

When Admiral Holloway learned from Lyons and Woolsey that the conclusions of the PRM-10 study had been set in stone and that

navy views were being ignored, he recommended to Secretary Claytor that the navy develop its own fully researched and supported
study to set against PRM-10. On July 14, Claytor formally requested
Defense Secretary Brown to permit the Department of the Navy to
conduct its own force planning study, because the conclusions and
recommendations of PRM-10 did not include navy positions. Claytor, Woolsey, and West briefed Secretary Brown on the proposal,
including Claytor's intention to include me and a few other Republican advisers on the study team. To Claytor's surprise, Brown told
them that he believed they were wrong but to "go to it." Komer, who
participated in the meeting, in typically colorful fashion expressed
the view that the navy was "nuts" to dream of an offensive strategy,
but he did not throw up any roadblocks.

Holloway and Claytor organized a major naval policy and strategy study, to be conducted at the Naval War College and in Washington under the leadership of Bing West. The study, to be called
Sea Plan 2000, would have momentous effect. The War College
directed me and a few other defense thinkers to whom Reagan was
listening to participate. Both classical and innovative approaches to
strategy were involved in thinking through the latest technology as
it applied to naval operations. The study integrated the results of war
gaming and actual operations in recent years, all within a broad geopolitical framework that was grounded in the state of the NATO/
Warsaw Pact confrontation.

The deductive strategy began with the security requirements of
the United States, then surveyed threats to those interests in all areas
of the world. The analysis tallied army, air force, and coast guard
forces available to support naval operations, as well as allied naval
and air forces that could be counted on, and finally calculated navy
and marine corps force levels required to deter those threats. It went
on to recommend a structure for the U.S. fleet by ship and aircraft
type, with numbers and configurations. In its final form, the study
recommended a more aggressive approach to the use of naval forces

in the Cold War and included a force structure considerably larger than what was then in the administration plan.

Sea Plan 2000 benefited from the acquiescence of the office of the secretary of defense and the other military departments. Ironically, this comprehensive plan, undertaken and paid for by the Carter Pentagon, became one of the main sources for fleshing out Ronald Reagan's naval policy initiative and a critical part of his campaign platform. It was based on the latest thinking of operators and thinkers inside and outside the navy.

After the study was delivered, Bing West and the Naval War College began a series of annual "global war games" to explore the naval ramifications of a global war with the Soviets. The first one kicked off in the summer of 1979 (with Fred Iklé playing the role of the president), and for the first time the "napkin plan" was exercised. As West recalls:

> As dean of research at the Naval War College, I convened 200 officers and officials to conduct a full-scale NATO war game. The Warsaw Pact had attacked along the inner German border; what would happen next? Under the game rules, the clock advanced one game day per hour of real time. Per standard planning, in the game, our attack submarines were deployed along the GIUK [Greenland-Iceland-UK] Gap to prevent Soviet subs from sinking our convoys in the Atlantic. After the first day (D-Day plus 7 days), Blue [NATO] was losing badly. Under Secretary of the Navy Jim Woolsey was playing the role of NSC adviser, and John Lehman, not then in government, was the secretary of defense. A year earlier the three of us were eating lobsters at the Black Pearl Restaurant while sketching a major offensive move on a napkin. Now playing our roles in the war game, we sent our subs north to sink all Soviet vessels and subs, including ballistic missile submarines.

The next "day" John Lehman ordered the attack. At
the end of the game day (D-Day plus 8), Red [the Soviet
Union] had lost 30 percent of their submarines. John
then unleashed a strong carrier task force to attack the
bases in the Kola Peninsula, including harassing strikes
on a Russian missile field. The Red team had no credible
counter to a Blue offensive that was crippling their navy
and degrading their nuclear force by conventional means.
By the fourth day of the game (D-Day plus 32), the war
was raging on several fronts. Taking the offense at sea had
knocked Red off-stride.

When John Lehman became SecNav, . . . he insisted
on a maritime strategy that was offensive rather than
defensive. That significantly rattled the Soviet military
hierarchy, especially the Russian chief of naval operations,
who had no means of protecting his most valuable assets.

Meanwhile the Pacific Fleet commander, Admiral Hayward, and
his staff were refining and applying their Sea Strike concept. It represented a drastic transformation of the Pacific Fleet into a forward
offensive war-fighting force, capable of attacking vital Soviet interests
in the northwestern Pacific, to put the Soviets on the defensive. That
strategy would tie down Soviet assets in the Far East, preventing their
redeployment to Europe. It would keep Japan in the war as an active
ally and protect U.S. territory in the Aleutians. Sea Strike—always
classified—was widely briefed and discussed in the navy and elsewhere in 1977–78 and became one of the conceptual roots of Sea Plan
2000 and ultimately of the Maritime Strategy of the 1980s.

The Soviet naval buildup picked up speed. On August 17, 1977,
a Soviet nuclear-powered icebreaker reached the North Pole, the
first surface ship in history to do so. In 1978, the Soviet Navy commissioned the first of twenty-five Victor III-class much-improved
nuclear attack submarines they were to commission between 1978
and 1991. They had significantly lower radiated noise levels than any

A Soviet Victor III–class nuclear attack submarine. *(Official U.S. Navy photograph.)*

previous class of Soviet submarine—approaching U.S. Navy submarines in capabilities, especially quieting. The Victor III would be used to "delouse" Soviet strategic nuclear-missile-launching submarines (SSBNs) by attempting to detect U.S. nuclear and other attack submarines that might be trying to trail them.

That same year the Soviets also completed the first *Ivan Rogov*-class amphibious helicopter/dock landing ship. These ships could deliver ashore and support a fully equipped combat force. The Soviets would commission two more by 1990. In this period they also commissioned the first *Berezina*-class multiproduct fleet replenishment ship, the first Delta II-class SSBN, the *Kiev* and *Minsk* aircraft carriers, the *Kirov* nuclear battle cruiser, the first of fourteen *Sovremenny*-class antiship guided-missile destroyers, the first of twelve *Udaloy*-class antisubmarine destroyers, and the first of four *Balzam*-class large armed spy ships that could intercept radar, communications, and intelligence signals.

The Soviet Navy introduced an impressive new supersonic swing-wing bomber, the Tu-22 Backfire, equipped with supersonic antiship missiles. The Backfire was part of an effort to prevent U.S. naval forces from coming close to targets in the Soviet Union.

The rapid expansion of the Soviet Navy was, of course, not without its setbacks. In November 1975, a mutiny on a Soviet Navy's Baltic Fleet *Krivak* frigate caused sudden Soviet naval and air movements in the Baltic. The mutiny was quickly quashed, and the ringleaders were shot. The story would inspire Tom Clancy's plot in *The Hunt for Red October.*

At the same time, the American submariners' confidence in the total superiority of their technology began to tremble. Forward-deployed navy submarines began to experience serious difficulties in detecting and trailing Soviet SSBNs. This—retrospectively—was in large part a result of John Walker and his spy family passing navy submarine intelligence to the Soviets. Increasingly emboldened, the Soviets, with much fanfare, also visited Cuba with its first modern submarines.

As the Soviet naval challenge grew, the U.S. Navy took a new interest in Arctic waters. In the 1975 Icex exercise, Cmdr. Frank Kelso, later chief of naval operations, took the nuclear attack submarine *Bluefish* under the Greenland Sea and reached the North Pole. The navy wanted to make sure that its submariners became proficient in operating in the extremely dangerous environment under the polar ice cap. This was to ensure that the Soviet Union could not hide its nuclear missile submarines there and to make sure that American missile subs could not only hide under the ice but attack Russian SSBNs from anywhere in the polar seas.

The navy expanded its discussions with the air force to draw it further into naval strategy and operations. On September 2, 1975, the navy and the air force signed a formal memorandum of agreement establishing a "Concept of Operations for USAF Forces Collateral Functions Training," including air force support in search and identification, electronic warfare, tactical deception, attack against surface and air units, and aerial mine-laying. In February

1977, the Strategic Air Command confirmed for the first time that USAF B-52s from Guam were conducting sea surveillance exercises with the navy.

Strong naval leadership was now needed to protect navy programs that were essential to establishing war-fighting superiority against the growing Soviet threat. Many of these programs began under the former CNO Adm. Elmo Zumwalt, and Navy Secretary John Warner in a supportive Nixon-Ford administration. Zumwalt's successors, Adm. James Holloway, and Adm. Thomas Hayward, had a much harder time in internal budget battles against the Defense Department bureaucracy, which tried to kill all programs linked to a naval offensive strategy. This was true despite the fact that Defense Secretary Brown favored developing, if not actually buying, these weapons. In both Republican and Democratic administrations, the vast Pentagon bureaucracy has its own priorities. During the Carter years, the navy lost many battles in the corridors of the Pentagon, then won most back in the halls of Congress with the support of a majority of Republicans and Democrats.

In 1981 the Reagan administration took office, and I was sworn in as secretary of the navy. Thanks to these men, including Harold Brown, I found that the full suite of weapons systems and sensors necessary to defeat the Soviet Navy had been developed and were ready for equipping the fleet. All that was needed was the funding to buy them.

In early 1977, the Soviets began their relations with the new American president with a dramatic deployment of land-based mobile SS-20 intermediate-range nuclear ballistic missiles in Europe, capable of destroying NATO bases in Europe with negligible warning. The West reacted by deploying U.S. Army Pershing II ballistic missiles and USAF Gryphon ground-launched nuclear cruise missiles as a counter. This issue would dominate NATO–Warsaw Pact relations for more than a decade.

In the name of détente and cutting the defense budget, Carter had been prepared to give away some of the crown jewels of Mahanian naval superiority. He initiated talks with the Soviets to limit naval deployments in the Indian Ocean, and he inexplicably offered to negotiate the removal of sonar detection and other submarine-killing weapons from large areas of the seven seas. Such an agreement would have ended American naval supremacy.

Under the shah, Iran had long been a reliable American ally. When demonstrations started against him in 1977, the U.S. administration quickly distanced itself from him, and as his support diminished, the administration expedited his departure on January 16, 1979.

On November 4, student supporters of the ayatollah seized the U.S. embassy in Teheran and held fifty-two hostages until January 20, 1981.

In December 1979, the Soviet Union invaded Afghanistan.

After three years of arms reductions and arms control initiatives, the Carter policies were not achieving the intended results. Carter finally bestirred himself and broke off his ill-advised talks with the Soviets aimed at limiting U.S. freedom of action in the Indian Ocean.

A month later, on January 23, 1980, President Carter in his State of the Union address proclaimed the Carter Doctrine, stating that the United States would use military force if necessary to prevent outside control of the Persian Gulf, an area of vital U.S. interest.

As Carter's fourth year in office unfolded, one setback followed another. Nevertheless, he continued to believe in turning the other cheek. Defense Secretary Brown, concerned with the withering of American credibility, again proposed challenging Libyan dictator Muammar Gaddafi's claim over the Gulf of Sidra, a large area of the Mediterranean Sea. Again Carter rejected Brown's recommendation. He ordered the Sixth Fleet to observe Qaddafi's claim, to not enter what were clearly international waters, and to operate only north of 32° 30′. By doing so, he granted implicit recognition to Libya's illegal claim.

The 1980 presidential election campaign got under way early in 1979. Ronald Reagan had been carefully planning and hiring staff, and national security was at the core of his campaign. On March 17, he made his initial campaign speech before the Chicago Council on Foreign Relations, calling for a "superior navy," one that must "stay ahead of the Soviet buildup . . . to enable the United States to command the oceans for decades to come."

That same month, I testified before the U.S. Senate Budget Committee. In response to questioning from Senator Henry Bellmon (R-OK), about my urging a new naval strategy and a much larger fleet, I responded, "The Kola Peninsula in the Soviet Union is probably the most high-value military real estate in the world today. It is the fleet headquarters and the naval strategic headquarters of the Soviet Union. It is within our capacity today, if we were to mass our forces—our naval battle groups and our land-based air—to actually take that area; this is assuming a conventional battle." I pointed out that being able to demonstrate NATO's capability and intention, if the Soviets attacked, to destroy by conventional means the Soviet Northern Fleet and sea-based strategic nuclear weapons would in itself be an enormous deterrent. Conversely, such a loss to the Soviets would mean certain defeat in a war against NATO.

As global deterrence continued to deteriorate, and the Persian Gulf slipped toward chaos, the Defense Department began to shift from sole preoccupation with the NATO balance of land forces to address southwestern Asia and other contingencies. For the navy, this would mean a new requirement to build or charter a fleet of cargo ships to be preloaded with weapons, ammunition, and supplies for marine, army, and air force units. The ships were then to be kept permanently at Diego Garcia, an island base in the Indian Ocean. This amounted to a major new stress on the existing fleet without any appreciable increase in resources. In 1979, Secretary Brown quietly dropped the unrealistic requirement to "swing" Pacific Fleet carriers to the Atlantic in the event of a NATO–Warsaw Pact war.

As an understanding of the changed priorities of the U.S. government reductions and negotiations began to sink in to friend and foe, the balance of deterrence became unsettled. Allies suddenly realized that the new policy of keeping NATO naval forces below the

GIUK Gap seemed to write off Scandinavia to Soviet occupation. Norway began to agitate against the policy and pushed hard to get the United States to commit navy and marine forces to its defense and to pre-position sufficient marine corps equipment for a major reinforcement.

As a result, the marines were able to participate for the first time in a major cold weather exercise, Cold Winter '77, a biannual NATO winter ground exercise in northern Norway (ongoing since at least the 1960s). The marines were shocked to find that they were not at all prepared for winter warfare. As a result, they found funding to rejuvenate the moribund Bridgeport Mountain Warfare Training Center in the High Sierras, which had been established during the Korean War. The corps rapidly produced large numbers of marines with thorough training in cold weather and mountain warfare.

Adversaries of NATO and the United States were also watching the rapidly changing "correlation of forces," as the Soviets referred to the shifting balance of power, and they took advantage of it.

On November 4, 1979, the American embassy in Teheran and some seventy American hostages were seized by students encouraged by the new Revolutionary Government of Iran. President Carter directed the secretary of defense to examine options for rescuing the hostages.

On December 27, 1979, Soviet military forces invaded Afghanistan and killed the Afghan president. In response, President Carter ordered the already stretched Seventh Fleet to increase its presence in the Indian Ocean.

On April 14, 1980, Operation Eagle Claw was launched. This was the hostage rescue operation chosen from the options presented to President Carter by the Pentagon. It was a catastrophic failure. It had been decided that for political reasons it must be a "joint" operation, so all U.S. services participated. Since they had so little time to train together, the joint requirement was a major contributor to the failure. The carriers *Nimitz* and *Coral Sea* launched aircraft and provided standby support.

Then in the Mediterranean, on September 16, 1980, two Libyan MiG aircraft fired missiles at a USAF RC-135 reconnaissance aircraft in international airspace. The aircraft escaped damage. The United States did not respond further.

Six days later eight Libyan fighters flown by Syrian pilots attempted to intercept another USAF RC-135, operating two hundred miles off the Libyan coast. This time, however, the spy aircraft was escorted by three F-14 Tomcat fighters from the *Kennedy*. The Tomcats immediately challenged the aggressors, who broke off and returned to base. Once again there was no U.S. response.

On that same day, September 22, 1980, Iraq invaded Iran, commencing an eight-year Iran-Iraq War in and around the Persian Gulf.

On July 14, 1980, the Republican National Convention met in Detroit to select Ronald Reagan as its presidential candidate. The week before, the platform committee met to draft the party platform. Chairman of the platform committee was Senator John Tower (R-TX), a strong Reagan ally. Tower selected me to oversee the drafting of the platform's national security planks. The final platform criticized the administration for having "cut President Ford's proposed shipbuilding plan in half, and vetoing a new aircraft carrier":

> This was done while the Soviet Union pursued an aggressive shipbuilding program capable of giving them worldwide naval supremacy in the 1980s unless current trends are reversed immediately. . . . We will build toward a sustained defense expenditure sufficient to close the gap with the Soviets, and ultimately reach the position of military superiority that the American people demand. . . . A more effective strategy must be built on the dual pillars of maintaining a limited full-time presence in the areas (Norwegian, Baltic, and Mediterranean Seas) as a credible interdiction force, combined with the clear capability to reinforce this presence rapidly with the forces necessary to prevail in battle. In addition,

the strategy must envision military action elsewhere at points of Soviet vulnerability.

It was an expression of the classic doctrine of Alfred Thayer Mahan. Party platforms are usually ignored, but this time candidate Reagan decided it would be his actual program. Not only would he campaign on defense issues, but he would actually pursue and accomplish these goals if elected.

On November 4, 1980, the American people overwhelmingly elected Ronald Reagan as president in a landslide victory. He won forty-four of the fifty states and 50.8 percent of the popular vote. Republicans also won control of the Senate for the first time in twenty-eight years. A key—and effective—Republican motto during the election campaign had been "Peace through Strength."

CHAPTER 2

Ocean Venture '81

A Bold New Strategic Operation

A CENTERPIECE OF Reagan's campaign had been naval rearmament and maritime superiority. After winning the election, he set about selecting his national security team to implement it: Richard Allen as national security adviser, Al Haig at State, Cap Weinberger at Defense, Bill Casey at CIA, and for the navy, me. This team was in place by the end of February 1981.

During the transition between the election and the inauguration, he met often with his team to be ready to implement his strategy immediately after being sworn in. He approved the navy launching a massive exercise to demonstrate his new policy before the end of his first year in office.

On July 16, 1981, Vice Admiral Lyons, on the deck of the command ship USS *Mount Whitney*, took command of the Second Fleet and the NATO Striking Fleet Atlantic. The U.S. Navy had established the Second Fleet after World War II, with responsibility for operations throughout the Atlantic Ocean, from the Arctic and the Barents Sea all the way south to the littoral of Antarctica, and from the east coast of the Americas to the shores of Western Europe and Africa. Thus the Second Fleet commander had responsibilities for Caribbean military contingencies, as well as for training navy forces

Vice Adm. James A. ("Ace")
Lyons, Commander
NATO Strike Fleet,
and Capt. Peter Swartz.
(U.S. Navy photograph.)

deploying to Europe to join the Sixth Fleet on permanent station forward in the eastern Mediterranean. It was the Second Fleet that President Kennedy had called upon to conduct the "quarantine" operations against the Soviets around Cuba during the 1962 Cuban Missile Crisis; and President Johnson had tasked it in support of the U.S. military intervention in the Dominican Republic in 1966.

When the NATO alliance command structure for the North Atlantic was set up in the early 1950s, the U.S. Second Fleet commander received an additional responsibility and designation (a "double hat," as they say in the navy): commander of the NATO Striking Fleet Atlantic. To carry out his different national and alliance functions, he was supported by a U.S.-only Second Fleet staff and by a multinational NATO staff, at separate headquarters in Norfolk, Virginia. Most of the time he operated in his U.S. capacity, but at least once a year in his NATO role as he assembled the alliance's striking force assets and operated across the Atlantic as far as the

Norwegian Sea in large multinational at-sea NATO exercises. Were war to occur between the Warsaw Pact and NATO, he would fight as NATO Striking Fleet commander, coordinating as necessary with other NATO Atlantic and European commanders and forces.

NATO had another striking fleet, the Striking and Support Force South, command of which was a double hat of the U.S. Sixth Fleet commander in the Mediterranean. Thus when the Second Fleet sent trained U.S. Navy forces across the Atlantic to join the Sixth Fleet, it also had to prepare them for operating within an allied force against Soviet forces invading southern Europe or supporting such an invasion. Sixth Fleet commanders invariably saw training naval units for these southern NATO (and Middle East) strike missions as the pre-eminent task of the Second Fleet. The Sixth Fleet resented Second Fleet activities focused on the Norwegian Sea and northern flank as a needless distraction from that primary Mediterranean theater.

Aggressive Second Fleet commanders, of course, saw things quite differently, considering Soviet forces in the Balkans, Mediterranean, Black Sea, and Crimea as of secondary importance to the enormous Northern Fleet that the Soviets had built up opposite northern Norway on the Kola Peninsula to threaten all northern Europe and the Atlantic. Balancing these two vital requirements was one of the basic conundrums of U.S. Cold War maritime strategy, and it was also part of the responsibilities of the secretaries of the navy and defense as well as the Joint Chiefs of Staff, including the chief of naval operations.

Lyons was my choice for the Second Fleet, and I was present at the ceremony where he took command. Lyons's navy, joint, and NATO boss, Adm. Harry Train, was also present. Train had experience as a navy planner, systems analyst, battle group commander, Sixth Fleet commander, and director of the Joint Staff. In his navy hat, Train was the commander in chief of the U.S. Atlantic Fleet. In his joint hat, he was commander in chief of the U.S. Atlantic Command, one of the nation's unified commands. And in his NATO hat, he was the Supreme Allied Commander Atlantic, equal in status and responsibility if not in publicity to the Supreme Allied Commander Europe, who at the time was the former U.S. Army chief of staff Gen. Bernard Rogers, at the Supreme Headquarters, Allied Powers Europe, at Mons in Belgium.

I had specifically selected Ace Lyons as Second Fleet commander because of the centrality of the Norwegian Sea campaign to deterring or fighting a global war with the Soviets, and the importance of using its exercises to send the Reagan administration's initial operational message to the Soviets and others. While Lyons had much more experience operating in the Mediterranean, he was one of the principal architects of the Northern Strategy and was anxious to get into the icy bastions that the Soviet sailors considered their domain. Over the next two years, Lyons would plan and lead three large, imaginative, and aggressive NATO naval exercises into the northern seas. The saga begins with Ocean Venture '81.

Vice Admiral Lyons was an unusually astute operational surface warfare officer with many years at sea, an extensive war col-

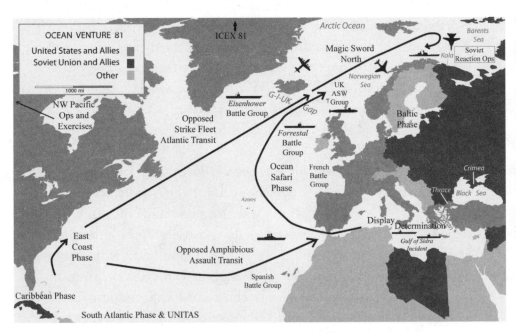

The Ocean Venture '81 exercise. (© *John Lehman*)

lege education, and even more extensive Washington experience in politico-military affairs and strategic planning. I had briefly served under Lyons and had worked with him on Sea Plan 2000 and in numerous think-tank and naval conferences on strategy. As I mentioned, I first met him when he was a captain and I was on active duty flying A-6 *Intruders* on the carrier *America*. But Ace was not actually aboard when I met him. The ship was in the harbor of the island of Rhodes in the Aegean, and he was under siege in the city hall by an angry mob of leftists. One of our search and rescue helos lifted him out just before the mob crashed through the gates. I am told that this occasionally happens to him now when he speaks on campuses.

We sailed away from Rhodes and resumed flight operations as part of a major NATO exercise. During the ensuing weeks, we spent a lot of time together, even though he was the exalted chief of staff of the battle group and I a lowly lieutenant. Ace's naval career had been evenly divided between operational sea duty and strategic planning ashore. I was impressed by his geopolitical grasp and his deep belief that our blue-water navy was the foundation of American security and world stability. His personal approach might best be described in words always attributed to aggressive military leaders from Frederick the Great to George Patton: *L'audace! L'audace! Toujours l'audace!* (Actually, it was guillotined French revolu-

Chief of Naval Operations Adm. Thomas Hayward. *(U.S. Naval Institute.)*

tionary Georges Danton, who said: "*De l'audace, encore de l'audace, toujours de l'audace, et la patrie sera sauvée!*")

Lyons, the chief of naval operations Adm. Tom Hayward, and I viewed Ocean Venture '81 as a transformational strategic operation, not just as a training event. Lyons was as focused on achieving its effect on the global balance of power between the West and the Soviet bloc as he was on testing his men and their equipment in the ice and storms of the northern seas. Consequently, his planning had focused not only on maintaining and improving the Striking Fleet's competence at sea but also on changing understanding and attitudes throughout the U.S. and allied navies and governments, and the rest of the NATO command structure, as well as at Soviet Navy headquarters and in the Kremlin.

Ace Lyons would reorient the primary concern of the Second Fleet from training battle groups for the Mediterranean Sixth Fleet to training them for their offensive role in northern seas as NATO Striking Fleet. His concepts included aggressive testing and demonstrating the offensive Reagan Maritime Strategy policies far forward, including around North Cape into the Barents Sea. He conceived of his fleet dispositions not only as training evolutions but as matters designed to elicit Soviet responses—which they did. At the same time, he anticipated capitalizing on Soviet reactions as further training opportunities for his own forces.

Operationally and tactically, Lyons was particularly knowledgeable in cover and deception operations and in leveraging U.S. Air Force and allied naval capabilities to enhance U.S. Navy forward operations and exercises. He was also an expert in electronic warfare (EW): in previous sea tours, he had conceived and practiced innovative EW tactics extensively and successfully, including dispersal, deception, concealment, and emissions control (EMCON) tactics, to simulate and hide carriers from Soviet satellite surveillance. To confound Soviet surveillance, he had designed a dispersed fleet disposition covering some 64,000 square miles—not really a formation at all. He knew that if he could avoid Soviet surveillance, their warships and aircraft would be unable to target his forces with their weapons and would also be vulnerable to his own attacks. Said Lyons, "Let me say that the only way the Soviets will be able to launch his weapons at two to three hundred miles away is if we let him. He cannot pick out a 'high value unit' without assistance. The Soviets need a strike coordinator—normally a 'tattletale' [a small intelligence ship]. . . . I have no intention of permitting a tattletale to perform this function—in fact it is nonsense. In Ocean Venture '81 [the Soviets] were not able to pick out priority targets."

Lyons had no qualms about integrating allies, the U.S. Air Force, the U.S. Coast Guard, and U.S. Army units into navy exercises. He routinely sought out and welcomed participation and support by land-based USAF F-15 fighters, the E-3 airborne warning and control system (AWACS), E-8 Joint Surveillance and Target Attack Radar System (JSTARS) aircraft, KC-10 tankers, B-52 bombers, and USAF space systems. Always in the past, a few parochial navy officers viewed the air force as a rival to be kept at a distance, but Lyons's long association with air force officers in joint matters led him to see that sister service as a valuable resource and an opportunity.

In particular, Lyons relied heavily on land-based air force tankers. "Our basic tactic is go after the missile platform," he said. "I have no intention of letting a hostile aircraft, submarine or surface combatant reach a weapons launch position unopposed—given the appropriate Rules of Engagement. The Outer Air Battle is to be conducted outside 250 nautical miles from the carrier. The key is a solid tanking plan. We need to be able to put large amounts of fuel in the air. When available we utilize all the land-based aerial tankers possible. This greatly increased the effectiveness of our outer Combat Air Patrol stations and our carrier-based tankers."

Our little team of Lehman, Hayward, Barrow (Gen. Bob Barrow, marine commandant), and Lyons believed that NATO's Striking Fleets needed to be well prepared to deploy rapidly and arrive quickly in far forward positions, to confront the Soviets at the first warning of a conflict, even at the cost of some risk: "We firmly believed that the Striking Fleet must always have the capability and be perceived as having the capability to strike the Soviet homeland. . . . There is always a lot of talk that the Striking Fleet will not go into the Norwegian Sea until the sub threat is brought under control. We will go where we have to go. . . . We do not believe we can afford to wait. . . . The Striking Fleet may have to accept a higher degree of risk and move into the area with its own inherent antisubmarine defenses."

To the navy leaders, "The key to the Battle of the Atlantic is winning the battle of the Norwegian Sea and maintaining the territorial integrity of the northern flank. In that regard, we do not view the Greenland-Iceland-UK (GIUK) Gap as any Maginot Line. The greater success we have in the Norwegian Sea, the less pressure there will be on the central region."

As Lyons said later, when he turned over command of the Second Fleet on his way back to work in the Pentagon, "The message we want any potential adversary to take back is that 'it just might be too hard.' In effect, if that message gets across, then we have raised the level of deterrence without firing a shot. That is what it is all about."

In the early fall of 1980, the Striking Fleet had participated in the annual NATO exercise, practicing keeping open the sea line of communication to Europe against Soviet strategy to interdict it. Poor weather at the end of the exercise had limited operations. Upon return from that event, Striking Fleet and Second Fleet exercise planners began preparing for the next year's routine evolution. Their plans reflected the conventional wisdom—with a few incremental changes—that had been guiding NATO exercises in recent years. Given the announced and predictable nature of NATO exercises, the Second Fleet and the allies—and the Soviets—expected the fall 1981 exercise to follow in the normal rotation of things, emphasizing testing the maritime defense of reinforcement and resupply shipping across the Atlantic. With the Royal Navy having announced the retirement of its last conventional aircraft carrier and with the shrunken American carrier fleet stretched thin across the globe, no more than one lone flattop was expected to be available to try to deter Admiral Gorshkov's swollen Northern Fleet.

With the arrival of Vice Admiral Lyons at Second Fleet headquarters, all that immediately changed. As he later recollected: "The first thing I did after taking command was to tear up the old canned Ocean Venture OPORD [operations order] that basically had been used for years. They were still using World War II carrier formations [FORM-40], which was a circular formation with the carriers in the center surrounded by support ships (a bull's-eye target). Such a formation was easily tracked by Soviet satellites. What we did was plot out Soviet satellite area footprints and time of exposure. We then went to dispersed dispositions. We used a num-

The navy's E-2C Hawkeye radar surveillance aircraft (U.S. Naval Institute). The air force's airborne warning and control (AWACS) radar aircraft. (*U.S. Air Force photograph.*)

ber of cover and deception decoys and tactics. For the first time ever, we integrated AWACS into fleet operations. AWACS is the U.S. Air Force four-engine Airborne Warning and Control aircraft carrying a large revolving radar able to see three hundred miles in all directions. The navy-carrier-based version is the E-2C Hawkeye. To make sure there were no tactical problems, we put navy air controllers into the AWACS to make sure the intercepts were run smoothly. One of the messages we intended to send was—you will never get to your missile launch point. And that's deterrence!"

Lyons and his staffs began furiously to plan a series of large, combined, interrelated naval exercises, building on but going way past earlier Second Fleet and Striking Fleet staff exercises. Weaving together a web of previously unrelated exercises into a coherent whole was intended to send a powerful message: "The war in the Atlantic will be an aggressive coordinated, well-thought-out, ocean-wide offensive campaign, with forward operations in the North Norwegian Sea and Barents Sea as its centerpiece targeted on the most valuable strategic assets in your homeland. You will lose any such war. So you'd better not start one."

The entire series was usually referred to as Ocean Venture '81, which technically was the name of only one of its phases. In Europe and Canada, it was referred to as Ocean Safari '81, which was its primary NATO phase. The operational planning area extended from the South Atlantic and Caribbean up through the North Atlantic and North Sea, to the Norwegian and Baltic Seas, and back down to the coast of Portugal. It would be the largest and most aggressive U.S. and NATO at-sea exercise within memory. It would be the leading edge of the new U.S. Maritime Strategy.

In January 1981, when Lyons was heading my transition into the navy secretary job, I told him that he was my choice to command the Second Fleet and take point in implementing the new forward strategy. Lyons quietly began assembling a staff of aggressive bright young strategist/operators to be his brain trust. First was Cmdr. Patrick Roll, an operational deception expert who had served under then-Captain Lyons on the staff of Carrier Group Four when I met them both aboard the carrier *America* in the Mediterranean several years before. Lyons valued his expertise, energy, imagination, and loyalty. Another was Cmdr. Philip A. Dur, a Ph.D. from Harvard who had written a dissertation on the evolution of employment of the Sixth Fleet, was fluent in French, and had been mentored in navy strategy and policy by Lyons as an action officer in the Pentagon just a few years before. He would participate in the exercise as commanding officer of the destroyer *Comte de Grasse*.

To send the intended message, Lyons needed at least two carriers, not just the one at his disposal in Norfolk. Accordingly, he managed to pry one of the Sixth Fleet's carriers loose from the Mediterranean. For carrier battle group commanders, he had two of the most aggressive and innovative admirals in the navy: Rear Adm. Hank Mustin, commanding the *Forrestal* battle group, and Rear Adm. Jerry O. Tuttle, commanding the *Eisenhower* battle group.

Mustin had been handpicked by Lyons to meet and take command of the *Forrestal* battle group when it outchopped from the Mediterranean to Lyons's area of responsibility in the Atlantic. A fellow destroyerman and a Vietnam War riverine combat veteran, Mustin had recent carrier battle group command experience in the Mediterranean, including operations approved by Reagan to challenge Gaddafi's famous "Line of Death" in the Gulf of Sidra that resulted in the shooting down of two Libyan MiGs. He well understood high-level policy and strategy considerations, having helped draft Adm. Elmo Zumwalt's master plan for his term in office as CNO, Project SIXTY. He also had served as executive assistant to the commander in chief of U.S. Naval Forces Europe.

Tuttle, for his part, was an attack aviator who had seen combat in the skies over North Vietnam and had been commanding officer of the carrier *John F. Kennedy* when she had operated in the Norwegian Sea above the Arctic Circle, training to operate an air wing in ice, fog, and gale-force winds. He was a Naval War College graduate and one of the navy's most forward-thinking experts in the arcane worlds of targeting and countertargeting, electronic warfare, and command, control, communications, and intelligence (C3I). Tuttle had used his deployment in Arctic waters to begin developing what would become the Joint Operational Tactical System (JOTS) for over-the-horizon targeting of enemy naval units. The cumbersome Pentagon procurement bureaucracy was at least five years behind the pace of digital technology, procuring new computers that were long obsolete when delivered. So Tuttle procured his own commercial desktop computers. (JOTS was also said to stand for the "Jerry O. Tuttle System.")

To ensure he got the air force participation he needed, Lyons reached out to his old boss on the Joint Staff, Gen. Richard Lawson USAF, with whom he had worked in the Pentagon on more than one occasion. Then-General Lawson had been the director for strategic plans and policy (J-5) when then-Rear Admiral Lyons was deputy director for political-military affairs. Lawson left the J-5 in July 1980 to become the U.S. representative to the NATO Military Committee in Brussels, earning a fourth star. In July 1981, when Lyons became Second Fleet commander, General Lawson became the Allied Command Europe chief of staff at NATO military headquarters and was in a position to help.

Not only was Lyons eager to bring the air force into his tent, but he welcomed his allied compatriots as well. He got on particularly well with Royal Navy admirals John Cox and John Fieldhouse. A big bear of a man, Rear Admiral Cox was the Striking Fleet's Anti-Submarine Warfare (ASW) group commander; he was also flag officer of the Third Flotilla and commander of ASW Group 2. His boss, in turn, was Adm. Sir John Fieldhouse RN, commander in chief of the Fleet, NATO commander in chief of the Channel, and commander in chief of the Eastern Atlantic.

Part of Ocean Venture '81, as devised by the three of them, had U.S. Navy attack submarines barreling north through the waters of the Greenland-Iceland-UK (GIUK) Gap, in which opposing Royal Navy submarines lay in wait. (Fieldhouse would go on the following year to command Operation Corporate, the mission to recover the Falkland Islands. Later he would be made an admiral of the fleet and chief of the UK's defense staff.)

Four days after taking command, Lyons took part of his fleet to sea to start practicing what he had been planning. He sailed with one submarine and thirteen surface combatants and auxiliaries, including destroyers and frigates from several alliance nations assigned to NATO's Standing Naval Force Atlantic. During this "workup" phase, he gave additional type training and practice in battle group operations to ships scheduled to participate in Ocean Venture '81.

Ocean Venture '81 involved fifteen nations, more than a thousand aircraft, and 250 ships, including *Eisenhower* and *Forrestal* and a Royal Navy jump jet carrier, HMS *Invincible*. It was the largest such exercise in anyone's memory.

In late August, Ocean Venture '81 moved into a new phase: exercising the procedures required for a battle group to support the reinforcement/resupply of northern Europe. The *Eisenhower* battle group was now joined by a substantial British force, including *Invincible* in ASW Group 2. Canadian units, the Standing Naval Force Atlantic, and U.S. Coast Guard forces also linked up, for an opposed transit from the U.S. East Coast through the Iceland-Faroes Gap. Following a scenario of increasing tensions, Tuttle's *Eisenhower* battle group conducted both cold and hot war sea control operations to counter hostile surface, air, and subsurface threats.

Capt. Edward Clexton, the commanding officer of *Eisenhower*, was a legendary fighter pilot whom I knew from Naval Air Station Oceana where we were both based in Virginia. He had flown F-4 Phantoms up here in the North almost exactly ten years before in September 1971, aboard *Independence*. They were operating with *Intrepid* (a forty-thousand-ton World War II vet and years later a museum ship in New York Harbor) and the Royal Navy carrier *Ark Royal*. The seas were so rough that the latter two carriers had to cease flight ops because of excess pitch and roll. The much larger *Independence*, one of the first 85,000-ton supercarriers, was able to continue operating throughout the exercise.

Now ten years later Clexton was in even worse weather. Even after the exercise, the weather continued foul. Back in the Atlantic, they hit a storm with eighty-knot winds. Everything was battened down, but Ed describes the force of the storm:

> The four helos just under my nose in front of the island, there to do the off-loading in the morning, had been tied down well, and all their blades were covered and sheaved alongside their body. However, in this wind, the sheav-

ing was torn/blown off and the tie-downs were loosened, so . . . I watched four helos destroy each other as their blades flew unabated through the night. . . . All four helos were "struck," which means taken out of service—ruined! Never to fly again.

As a key feature of the exercise, Tuttle's *Eisenhower* group was soon opposed by Mustin's *Forrestal* battle group, deploying from the Mediterranean under total radio silence. The commanding officer of *Forrestal* was Capt. Clarence "Skip" Armstrong. *Forrestal* had earlier participated in Gulf of Sidra combat operations against Libya. She approached in stealth, emitting nothing, to engage the *Eisenhower* group by surprise. Later the two groups formed a large, dual-carrier battle force for transit of a submarine barrier established in the Iceland-Faroes gap. By now the exercise participants were all operating using their previously agreed NATO tactical organization. The attack was under way.

In a total departure from previous exercises, Lyons was going to blow right through the NATO Maginot Line of the GIUK Gap with the entire NATO Striking Fleet. This was the heart of the new strategy. In preceding years, during the hopeful pursuit of détente and arms control by Presidents Ford and Carter, such robust NATO activity would have been unthinkable, as provocative to the Soviets.

To achieve maximum impact, Lyons had a trick up his sleeve. His intelligence staff knew well when Soviet signals intelligence satellites were to be overhead, as well as the large and easily tracked radar satellite specially launched to track the carriers. Lyons knew that there was always foul weather available in the North Atlantic to hide under, so he intended to make his entire strike fleet disappear.

First he specially equipped a small number of combatants with cover and deception technology, essentially simulating the radar, voice, and sonar emissions of an entire battle force. He sent them off on a southeasterly track consistent with previous exercises. At the same time, the main force went into total EMCON—emissions con-

F-18 (left) and A-6 (right) landing in a snowstorm. *(U.S. Navy photographs.)*

trol, that is, no radio or radar emissions—and headed north. The Soviets fell for the decoy, and the first they learned of the presence in the Norwegian Sea of the Striking Fleet was Lyons's thousand-mile air show near Murmansk, described in the preface.

When the Soviet Northern Fleet realized the massive NATO force was in their backyard, it surged Badger, Backfire, and Bear reconnaissance flights. Lyons personally directed the delicate conduct of the first F-14 intercepts of them. He also personally oversaw the equally delicate simulated air strikes into northern Norway in support of allied amphibious landings reinforcing NATO's Northern Norway Command, while simultaneously defending the battle force against simulated surface and subsurface attacks by the Soviets.

Upon completion of the last air strikes into northern Norway on September 4, the *Forrestal* group detached from the exercise to resume its transit from the Mediterranean to Norfolk. The carriers had gone up well above the Arctic Circle, but they did not go as far as or around North Cape. But U.S. surface combatants and submarines did. *Eisenhower* herself had reached seventy degrees north latitude—

An F-14 Tomcat fighter-bomber intercepting a Soviet Tu-22M Backfire bomber over the northern Norwegian Sea. *(U.S. Navy photograph, National Archives.)*

well north of Tromsø, Norway (and also north of the strategic Soviet bases on the Kola Peninsula, some few hundred miles to the east).

The exercise was a demanding one for the force's sailors and aviators. Said *Forrestal*'s Capt. Skip Armstrong:

> With the heavy seas and poor and rapidly changing weather during Ocean Venture '81, coupled with an end-of-the-cruise deck with slippery well-worn nonskid, my focus was on keeping my aviators alive. I had little time for "strategic thinking." The other carrier . . . had to recover several of our planes (and we theirs) when ceiling and visibility went to zero. I recall one time when turning to port into the wind for launch, I had to shift to full right rudder to prevent an S-3 from sliding sideways off the deck. Hank Mustin flew his flag on *Forrestal* and never once questioned my fly-don't-fly decisions. Darn near developed an ulcer during that exercise!

As part of an effort to improve sensor coverage for the Striking Fleet units operating off the coast of northern Norway, Lyons and his staff evaluated the tactic of placing an early warning picket ahead of the main body along the threat axis. The destroyer *Caron* was placed on a station approximately three hundred nautical miles north of Task Force 401, between the carrier battle groups and the principal Soviet threat from the Kola Peninsula area. Initial indications were that this stationing tactic proved its worth, and Lyons's staff began to develop doctrine and procedures for the use of an early warning ship as an extension of the battle group's organic sensor horizon for NATO-wide use. In addition, two navy "Clipper Troop East" electronic signals and voice intelligence-gathering aircraft were successfully employed in support of the Striking Fleet's units. These aircraft, together with USAF RC-135 and Royal Air Force Nimrod-R signals intelligence (SIGINT) aircraft, provided Lyons with a significant extension of the fleet's horizon and absolutely precious real-time intelligence.

Lyons was particularly pleased with the performance of the U.S. Air Force AWACS aircraft that he had introduced to support the Striking Fleet, including his provision of naval air controllers aboard to make a smooth transition during the exercise. He also experimented with introducing attack submarines in direct support of carrier battle groups, using simplistic "moving sanctuaries" in order not to conduct attacks on his own submarines. It proved to work so well that it has become standard practice.

On September 1, during the northernmost phase of Ocean Venture '81, I visited the fleet off northern Norway. I flew out to *Ike* in an A-6 from VA-65, my old squadron from Oceana, Virginia, with my friend and squadron mate Cmdr. Joe Prueher. (Prueher was later to become commander in chief Pacific and then President Bill Clinton's ambassador to China.) According to the ship's history, this was the first of seven visits I made to *Ike* during the three years when Clexton was skipper, three flying with VA-65 on active duty training and four as navy secretary.

This time I had two purposes. First, I sought to actually participate first hand in this historic first implementation of President Reagan's new Soviet strategy by flying a few operational missions in this very hostile environment and experiencing the Soviet reaction. Second, I believed it was very important to keep every sailor in the picture of how they fit into the larger strategic plan and what that plan was. Every time I visited a carrier I would address as many of the crew members as possible assembled in the hangar deck, reaching all 5,700 by simultaneously transmitting throughout the ship on the 1MC public address system. I encouraged the admirals to do the same. During this visit, I explained the simple logic of President Reagan's forward strategy. What they had been doing in these freezing waters, I said, was to demonstrate to the Soviets in no uncertain terms that if they started a war in NATO, "we would kick their ass at sea, and from the sea." Needless to say, the sailors loved it.

Secondary to boosting morale, the purpose of these pep talks was to magnify, through the sailors and their families, the public relations impact of press conferences, congressional testimony, speeches and newspaper articles ashore, and Reagan's message of aggressive deterrence.

The following day, September 2, I flew with VA-65 on a strike mission attacking targets around Tromsø. Then I continued northeast on a carefully planned route at about three hundred feet AGL (above ground level) to simulate penetrating the Soviet border to attack targets on the Kola Peninsula, which is at about the same latitude as Tromsø. The weather was so bad that we had to climb into the clouds and icing above the area's highest mountains. After completing the mission, we returned to *Ike* for one of the scariest landings I ever experienced. I was fully qualified in the A-6 as bombardier/navigator but not as pilot, so I was happily not at the controls. We were in the goo for the entire approach, experiencing worrisome icing. We did not see the pitching ship through the fog until we were less than a quarter mile from touchdown. I began to suspect that détente was not the only reason the fleet had not operated this far north.

After our debrief and lunch down on the mess deck with the crew, Joe Prueher and I launched in another A-6 and flew to Lossiemouth, the RAF base in northern Scotland, where after debrief we were treated in the officers' club to a badly needed wee dram of the house malt.

The next morning at zero dark hundred, we briefed for a flight back into the exercise in a brand-new RAF *Nimrod* maritime patrol aircraft equipped with the latest technology profiling surface search radar. This was a real breakthrough and better than we had in our P-3 Orions. The radar picture was such high definition that we could easily pick out Russian and allied ships by type and sometimes by actual name because of differing equipment and weapon configurations.

An important part of the operational plan was to leave no pause between each phase of Ocean Venture to show the Soviets that the NATO Striking Fleet could be relentless and enduring. All during September, in the Sharem 44 phase of Ocean Venture '81, the utility of passive towed-array sonar sensors in defense of a main body was demonstrated against allied diesel electric submarines. The Soviet Navy had large numbers of these difficult-to-detect U-boats. That phase was conducted in the southwestern approaches to the United Kingdom, with British, French, and Netherlands forces in support.

Magic Sword South, the next phase in the operation, was conducted in the North Sea. Rear Admiral Tuttle's *Eisenhower* battle group provided close air support to the European central region while defending itself against a multiple threat opposition provided by West German and Danish units. During two days of the exercise, long-range air support missions were flown from *Eisenhower* into southern Germany using air routes across France. Said Lyons with a wry smile, "We ran strikes on central Europe from carriers over Bernie Rogers's shaking fists."

Then came the Ocean Safari '81 phase, sponsored and conducted by all three major NATO commanders. It was held in the eastern Atlantic, in an area extending from the southwestern approaches of the UK to the waters off the Iberian Peninsula. It included eighty-three ships from nine countries, with Lyons commanding. The operation featured sea control operations in a scenario of transition from cold war to hot war. The forces tested three Naval Control and Protection of Shipping (NCAPS) tactics: area protection, barrier protection, and convoy escort. They also tested an antisubmarine Defended Lane Concept, which proved very effective.

France had for years stayed outside NATO's unified command structure, but for this event the French decided to play and play big. Admiral Train and the French Navy Atlantic Command commander had concluded a special military agreement for Striking Fleet operations in the French National Safety Area (FNSA). Now, for the first time, Lyons assumed responsibility as the overall coordinating authority. During that period of the exercise, he was responsible for coordinating all air and surface operations within the entire FNSA, and uniquely, a French Navy carrier battle group participated in joint and combined operations. The French Navy participated in strength: a maritime headquarters, the carrier *Clemenceau*, eight surface combatants, four submarines, and several mine warfare ships.

Meanwhile, in the portion of the exercise known as Botany Bay '81, Danish, West German, and British forces were engaged in a NATO exercise to defend the Danish Straits.

Also, U.S. amphibious and surface forces transited the Atlantic to Rota, Spain, and then to the Mediterranean to conduct type and intertype training in preparation for a war-at-sea exercise with elements of the Spanish Navy. It was to be a bilateral U.S.-Spanish exercise, since newly democratic Spain would not join the NATO alliance for another eight months. The operating area was in the vicinity of Spain's Canary Islands. The U.S. Navy force included Mediterranean Amphibious Ready Group 3-81, comprised of the helicopter carriers *Saipan*, *Guam*, and two other amphibious ships, full of U.S. Marines, with five U.S. Navy surface combatants. The Spanish force centered on the carrier *Dedalo*, three submarines, and two patrol boats. Then the Spanish practiced convoy escort roles. Overall command of this portion of the exercise rotated on a daily basis between the American and Spanish admirals.

In late September a smaller portion of the exercise was held off the coast of Dakar, Senegal. It was designed to bolster anti-Soviet nations in West Africa, who were worried by a new Soviet foothold developing in Guinea.

Throughout each of these many phases, which came to be lumped under the term *Ocean Venture '81*, a dumbfounded Soviet Navy shadowed closely with unprecedented numbers of submarines, surface ships, and reconnaissance and electronic-intelligence-gathering aircraft. They were most welcome and indeed a major part of the target audience.

This massive and continuing operation came as a thunderclap to the Soviets, who had never seen such a NATO exercise on their northern doorstep, in waters that they had come increasingly to think of as their own. Once they finally figured out where the dispersed and silent carriers really were, Ocean Venture '81 elicited the most extensive reaction from Soviet naval forces in memory. Many Tu-95 Bear and Tu-16 Badger surveillance and strike aircraft, over twenty Soviet surface warships, a large number of Soviet submarines, and many auxiliary general intelligence spy ships were detected. These operations, in turn, provided U.S. and allied forces, through the coordinated use of national, theater, allied, and organic surveillance assets, an ideal opportunity to monitor the reaction and assess the Soviet capability to conduct surveillance and target allied maritime forces.

The Soviet reaction was a coordinated evolution, involving long-range reconnaissance aircraft conducting surveillance from the Flemish Cap east of Newfoundland and from the coast of Spain all the way to the Kola Peninsula as the Striking Fleet's two-carrier battle force approached, entered, and surged up through the Norwegian Sea. In a traditional scenario for defense of their homeland, the Soviet reaction climaxed while the carriers operated off northern Norway, as scores of Badger strike aircraft conducted both reconnaissance and simulated strikes over a three-day period.

Eisenhower reported that Soviet Bears and Badgers intruded at least eighty times, as did nine shadowing warships, including the helicopter cruiser *Moskva* and numerous Soviet submarines. Battle force officers shrewdly crafted deception measures to thwart Soviet surveillance and were later chagrined to read media allegations that Russian submarines had penetrated the carriers' screen, generating heated controversy. They had, of course, penetrated the defenses but never undetected. In a war, they would have been sunk well before reaching launch points.

Noted Lyons, "The Soviets couldn't find us, because they went to the tracks in the old Op Order [that he had torn up]. It was at that time that I knew that they were reading our communications. I thought the leak was in NATO. This was four years before we found out it was the Walker spy ring who was selling them our codes."

Lyons was particularly pleased that he had intercepted Soviet strike bombers a thousand miles away, then simulated attacks on them (up to three times before they got to missile launch position). His proud message to the Soviet Northern Fleet was "You ain't never gonna get there," thereby demonstrating his readiness for combat and raising the deterrence level, which, of course, was the primary purpose of the huge operation.

Soviet naval headquarters got the message. Rear Adm. Boris D. Yashin wrote in the Soviet journal *International Affairs*:

> Between August and November 1981, large-scale joint naval exercises of the USA and some other capitalist countries were held. These maneuvers were the most extensive since the end of the Second War in their scope, areas of action and the total number of men and hardware (which involved up to 250 ships, some 1000 planes, and 120,000 men. Their conception, conduct, and thrust leave no doubt that the USA is not only trying to demonstrate its hostility towards the socialist and many developing countries, but also to establish naval leadership in the capitalist world, secure for itself numerous bases, and create a military-strategic regime in the World Ocean, that would

favor rapid deployment and support of the actions of the Task Forces of the U.S. Navy.

Ace Lyons wouldn't have put it much differently.

In March 1982, Atlantic Fleet commander Admiral Train and Striking Fleet commander Vice Admiral Lyons briefed Ocean Venture '81 to legislators and staff members on Capitol Hill. It was important that Congress learn firsthand what the navy had just done, and why and how. Congressional support for the Reagan shift in U.S. foreign and military strategy was essential, and here was a real-world example of the Reagan strategy in action. And the Congress needed to know what it was getting for the funds it was voting on and the policies it was being asked to underwrite.

Atlantic Command joint exercises named Ocean Venture would recur throughout the decade, but the name would never again be used for a pan-Atlantic or forward Norwegian Sea exercise. Other exercise names would be used, however, and other massive and even more imaginative forward exercises would pound home the same message: *Attack NATO, and you will lose.* Building on the foundations of Ocean Venture '81, they would continue through the end of the Reagan administration.

As 1981 ended, the U.S. Naval Institute's *Proceedings* and other professional journals published commentaries by participants from the U.S. and allied navies, pointing out mistakes made, tactical shortcomings, and some successes by the Soviet Navy against the exercise defenses. Unlike some other services, the navy has strongly encouraged critical commentary by serving officers since the founding of its professional journal, the *Proceedings*, in 1874.

While the principal purpose of Ocean Venture '81 was to debut the Reagan doctrine of Maritime Supremacy, it was also the opening round in an internal navy campaign to accelerate navy and allied tactics and operational art. It ushered the navy into a rapidly changing era of digital communications, precision munitions, and surveillance satellites, and into learning to counter the aggressive thinking and actions of General Secretary Brezhnev, Marshal Ogarkov, and Admiral Gorshkov.

In addition to these primary motives, the exercise had other important fish to fry, especially to reassure exposed allied governments and publics. In that sense, the Maritime Strategy exercises of the 1980s—starting with Ocean Venture '81—were primarily "real-world operations" with geopolitical impact and a continuation of politics by other means. They were also essential tactical development and training evolutions. As the leading NATO navy and a component of NATO's leading political, economic, diplomatic, and military power, the U.S. Navy bore special responsibilities in this regard that other NATO navies, even the Royal Navy, did not share.

Thus, while Ocean Venture '81, and its successors stressed real-world training and tactical development against actual Soviet units, "signaling," diplomatic, intelligence, and deterrent goals often trumped exercise training goals. The tactical lessons learned from Ocean Venture '81 continued to be dissected and used by the U.S. and allied navies—and the Soviets—as had been intended all along.

CHAPTER 3

Taking a New National Strategy to Sea

Sending a Message

THE DRAMATIC SUCCESS of Ocean Venture '81 sent a message to
the Soviets that there was a new game in town, and delivered it with
something like a two-by-four. But now, for the navy, came the hard
part. A critical task had to be accomplished without delay: explaining
the new strategy in layman's terms to important audiences within
the administration, within the navy and marines, to the American
public, to Congress, especially the key committees, and, of course, to
our allies, beginning with NATO, Japan, and Korea.

To educate and persuade the American public and Congress as
well as these other constituencies, the navy had to change its public relations strategy. In 1941, when President Roosevelt appointed
Adm. Ernest King to lead the navy in the war effort, King's subor-
dinates asked him what the public relations strategy should be. Only
half tongue-in-cheek, he replied, "Tell them nothing. When the war
is over, tell them who won." The navy and marine corps nevertheless
did an excellent job of public relations as part of the war effort. After
the war, President Truman remarked that the marine corps had a
better propaganda program than Stalin, a remark for which he later
had to apologize.

In the Carter years, the White House kept a tight rein on navy

PR. The navy did not cooperate with Hollywood, for instance, on movies that seemed to boost the services. The very successful 1982 film *An Officer and a Gentleman*, about naval aviation officer training, was made despite the navy's refusal of help. The marines, however, gave full support, including training Lou Gossett as a drill instructor, helping him to win an Academy Award.

We reversed course with Reagan's blessing and went on the offensive to sell the new strategy. We recruited a brilliant young public relations officer, Capt. (later Rear Adm.) Jimmy Finkelstein, ably assisted by a reservist, Cmdr. "Spike" Karalekas, to coordinate the navy-marine campaign. Finkelstein let it be known throughout the media that the top admirals and I were open and accessible. We treated media professionals as equals, regardless of their political leanings, which were overwhelmingly liberal, and as a result we were treated fairly.

When Jerry Bruckheimer and Don Simpson, accompanied by former CNO Adm. Jim Holloway, approached us to get help in making a movie about the Naval Fighter Weapons School, we made a deal with them that in return for full cooperation, they would give us the right to edit the script. We proceeded to give them at-sea availability on two aircraft carriers, modified two F-14s to carry the cameras, and put the principal actors through an orientation flight program and gave them continuing technical assistance. The result was the record-breaking 1986 smash hit *Top Gun*. We were fully reimbursed for all costs and never needed to change a single word in the script.

It was the highest-grossing film of that year, heightening public awareness of and interest and pride in the navy and naval carrier operations. Admiral Holloway was the lead technical adviser on the film. "Following the movie's release," he said, "the interest in navy flight training virtually exploded. Applications from fully qualified candidates exceeded the available training quotas by 300 percent. I was able to get [Weinberger's] authority to 'bank' these applications and spread the input out over the next three years

Tom Cruise, my star shipmate in showcasing American naval supremacy, and me at the premiere of *Top Gun*. *(Courtesy of Greg F. Mathieson.)*

to assure a full input of top quality aviation candidates well into the future."

We also needed to integrate and conform the governing naval documents, doctrines, and fighting instructions from the highest levels down and through fleet unit levels. The syllabus and tactical training for all fleet schools and units had to be modified and updated with the new strategy. New initiatives were taken to integrate American and NATO air forces' bombers and fighters into the strategy, providing training for their aviators and technicians in operating over the sea with naval forces, and helping to arm them with Harpoon antiship missiles.

The marine corps was well ahead of the navy in using cutting-edge technology for tactical development, training, innovation, and integration of new weapons. In Yuma, Arizona, it had over time created a fully integrated and fully instrumented ground and air warfare development and training center. Every summer in the huge desert restricted area, the corps conducts a six-week war involving land units of infantry, armor, artillery, air defense, and air units of fighters, bombers, and helicopters. Every movement of every infantry unit, tank, artillery round, rocket, and bomb, every surface-to air and air-to-air missile, and every action of every aircraft dogfight and bomb drop is accurately recorded by advanced radars on surrounding mountaintops, then played back for the participants in a specialized movie theater. There is no doubt about who shot whom. Lessons are learned, and innovation is constant.

In the navy's surface warfare and aviation communities, tactical development and advanced tactical training and education were little changed from the era of Korea and Vietnam. Admiral Hayward started the process of reforming tactics and training for the surface navy by the creation of Tactical Training Group Atlantic and Tactical Training Group Pacific.

The submarine community, however, was in very good shape, as its participation in those wars was minimal, and it had never lost its focus on the threat from the Soviet Navy and Air Force. It had established in New London a unit called Submarine Development Group 2 that was constantly testing and refining tactics and training in the real world under the surface.

Drawing partially from that submarine training model and from the cutting-edge Marine Air Warfare Training Center in Yuma, we completely overhauled tactics, training, and education for naval aviation. We established Naval Air Station Fallon Nevada as the tactical training center. We moved the famous *Top Gun* fighter weapons school from San Diego to Fallon and established what came to be known as "Strike University, or "Strike U" for air-to-ground attacks. We provided both units with authority to develop and promulgate new tactics based on the latest technology and to input directly to the budget priorities being prepared in the Navy Department. We invested more than $300 million in installing the latest technology and fully instrumented air-to-air and air-to-ground tactical air combat training ranges that recorded and validated which tactics and weapons actually worked and which did not.

IRANIAN HEZBOLLAH KILLS 241 MARINES AND OTHER SERVICEMEN IN BEIRUT

On October 23, 1983, we lost 241 marines to an Iranian Hezbollah attack on the barracks in Beirut, Lebanon. President Reagan immediately ordered the joint chiefs to plan retaliation. The Pentagon dithered until the frustrated Reagan ordered an air strike against Syria, which took place on December 4, 1983. It was not a success. Two carrier aircraft and their pilots were shot down.

After that disappointing performance, we realized that embedded in the naval aviation community was a decade of Vietnam tactics and training that was obsolete. Starting in World War II, each carrier air group (CAG, now called carrier air wing) had been commanded by an aviator who was junior to the carrier's captain and reported to him. But since then technology and intelligence had moved so far that there was an urgent need for our wing commanders (still called CAGs) to have more experience and training in the intelligence products and technologies and enemy capabilities that were now available. That meant they needed more time to train and learn before they commanded a wing, and that they must be equal not subordinate to the carrier skipper, who had enough on his plate. In short, a CAG must be a senior captain in rank. The Reagan strategy depended on the confidence that a broad array of new technology weapons, far more advanced than the Soviets had, would soon be flowing into the fleet thanks to the foresight of defense and navy leaders in the Nixon, Ford, and Carter years (including defense leaders James Schlesinger, Donald Rumsfeld, Harold Brown, William Perry, and John Foster and navy leaders John Warner, Graham Claytor, and Adms. Elmo Zumwalt, James Holloway, and Thomas Hayward). At the beginning of the Reagan administration most of these systems were either nearing or beginning production. All that was needed was the money to buy them. The first Reagan budget amendment put sufficient money behind the best programs to start equipping the fleet.

Major technical developments had occurred in antisubmarine warfare and strike warfare. These new weapons and electronics made possible an attack on the heavily defended Kola complex. The new *Los Angeles*-class of nuclear attack submarine would be proven in undersea antisubmarine and intelligence operations. They were

A *Los Angeles*–class attack submarine. Later 688s were equipped with underwater-launched Tomahawk precision-strike cruise missiles. *(Official U.S. Navy photograph.)*

equipped with new torpedoes, advanced sonar, and the ultimate in submarine stealth.

The fixed passive-listening sonar arrays (SOSUS) lying on the ocean floor provided continuous intelligence on ship and submarine (and whale) movements in the area. A particularly valuable break-through was the development of the Captor mine. Anchored on the sea bottom, it carried a secret design homing torpedo that was deadly against any enemy submarine while completely safe for friendly subs.

P-3 patrol aircraft with new sensor systems gave wide area sur-veillance. Many were concerned that carriers could not survive so close to the Soviet homeland, but the vastly improved surface-to-air missile systems on Aegis cruisers and destroyers provided game-changing defense against the supersonic Backfire bombers and sea-skimming antiship missiles when combined with carrier based

E-2 surveillance aircraft and the F-14 interceptor with its Phoenix long-range missiles. Analysis and simulation left little doubt that the carriers would survive and launch wave after wave of long-range all-weather A-6 *Intruders*, each carrying up to twelve thousand pounds of precision-guided bombs and missiles.

From fleet submarines and surface ships would come hundreds of fifteen-hundred-mile-range Tomahawks, each with a thousand-pound warhead able to hit tiny precision targets. When fully modernized, the fleet could simultaneously project power ashore against submarines and ships in port, air bases and aircraft, radars and missile launchers, and all support facilities in the Kola Peninsula. The capability also made possible nonnuclear attacks on ballistic missiles in silos. All the technical pieces were in place to make the offensive strategy that had been developed on the Black Pearl napkin into a reality.

The submarine hunter/killer P-3 Orion patrol aircraft had new sensor systems providing wide area capability. (*U.S. Naval Institute.*)

A Captor mine dropped from a USAF B-52 parachutes into the sea. They also serve who only stand and wait. *(U.S. Navy photograph, National Archives.)*

Still more new systems began to arrive in the fleet, needing to be integrated into fleet exercises imaginatively and aggressively, in order to realize their war-winning potential: *Ohio*-class ballistic missile subs, *Kidd*-class destroyers, Phalanx Gatling gun missile defense systems, *Iowa*-class battleships, *Ticonderoga*-class Aegis cruisers, Tomahawk cruise missiles, air cushion high-speed assault landing craft, Skipper laser-guided missiles, high-speed antiradiation missile (HARM), anti-SAM homing missiles, vertical launch systems for a variety of missiles, Pioneer UAVs, improved *Los Angeles*-class submarines, fleet communications satellites, etc.

Although Ocean Venture '81 was carried out without those essential technological and weapons advantages, the exercise was planned and executed as if they were fully operational in the fleet. In other words, in early years of the strategy, while we modernized the fleet, a certain amount of bluff was necessary. The absence of new-technology radars, electronic countermeasures, missiles, and jam-proof communications in that first operation would have meant

The Aegis cruiser *Bunker Hill* and the destroyer *Sampson* steaming together. *(Official U.S. Navy photograph by Michael Russell.)*

that if war had actually broken out, the outcome would have been far less certain than it would be a few years later, as these new systems reached the fleet in numbers.

In addition to the massive task of conforming actual global war plans to the new strategy, we had the closely related task of reorganizing all the exercises on the five-year calendar with our allied navies. The huge forward exercises in the North Atlantic and North Pacific took precedence, as we intended to keep the pressure on the Soviet Union and improve and increase each year as new technologies, weapons, and lessons learned came into the fleet. Marine amphibious operations were added in northern Norway, Denmark, the Aleutians, and Hokkaido.

In addition to the northern exercises, operations in the eastern Mediterranean, the Black Sea, the high Arctic, the Caribbean, the Persian Gulf, the Indian Ocean, and Southeast Asia, with our traditional allies including the Australian, Thai, and Philippine navies, all required attention and updating.

Four years after Ocean Venture '81, Northern Wedding '85 returned to the same northern waters with even more ships and aircraft. They were fully equipped with Aegis cruisers, electronic jammers with cutting-edge technology, the latest torpedoes and missiles, adequate numbers of aircraft equipped with the newest radars, and

An A-6 Intruder fighter-bomber over Norway. The Intruder's motto was "We go deeper, stay longer, and deliver a bigger load." *(U.S. Naval Institute.)*

many other technologies that would almost certainly have enabled success if war had broken out.

The massive challenge for the Navy Department outlined above was a very full menu to carry out. But of course, on top of this, the real world kept intruding. With fleets and marines deployed around the globe, crises erupted regularly, and decisions had to be made about protracted challenges from the Soviets, Cubans, and Sandinistas in Nicaragua; Iranian Hezbollah terrorist attacks in the Middle East; a civil war in Lebanon fomented by Syria and the PLO; constant friction and recurring crises between Greece and Turkey and between Pakistan and India; North Korean attacks on South Korean ships; the war against the Soviet occupation of Afghanistan; the Falklands War; Libyan terrorist attacks and harassment of U.S. aircraft; The Soviet/Cuban coup in Grenada and subsequent U.S. invasion; a new war on drugs that assigned navy ships and aircraft

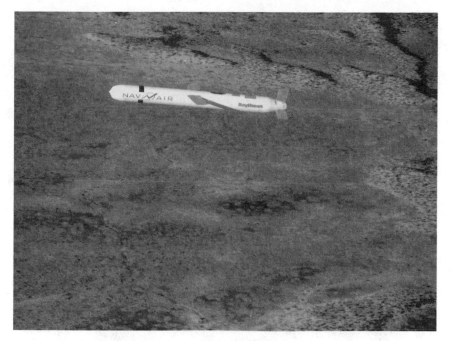

A precision-strike Tomahawk cruise missile. *(Official U.S. Navy photograph.)*

to interdict the flow of drugs into the United States; and countless lesser crises in Southeast Asia, West Africa, and the Caribbean. I don't remember a single uneventful daily intelligence briefing during my six years in the Pentagon.

President Reagan was inaugurated on January 20, 1981, and I was sworn in as secretary of the navy on February 5. As recounted above, the president wanted no time wasted in executing the new naval strategy he had campaigned on, as well as the secret psychological campaign he had approved during the transition. We got under way immediately on both.

On March 30, Adm. Harry Train, Supreme Allied Commander Atlantic, testified before Congress:

> In the event of war with the Soviets, I intend to carry the fight to the Soviet home waters. Strong early action in the forward areas is necessary to defeat the Soviet Navy

in the Atlantic area. It is important to remember that the Soviet Navy has never won a naval war. Early Soviet losses will certainly prove demoralizing and cause them to reduce out of area deployments. With remaining forces, I will assure the resupply and reinforcement of Europe and support the operations of adjacent allied and national commanders.

On March 3, I held an initial press conference, intending to focus on the new strategy and the importance of forward naval operations against the Soviet Union. The media asked about little else, and it was widely reported.

The next day the president submitted a supplemental to the FY81 defense budget that had been sent to Congress by President Carter, adding 11 percent for the navy, and an amendment to the FY82 defense budget, adding another 15 percent for the Navy Department. These Reagan amendments enabled reactivation of two battleships and substantially increased ship construction.

On March 6, Defense Secretary Caspar Weinberger and I went to the White House to read President Reagan into the most sensitive submarine intelligence operations that were critical to our forward strategy. The briefers we brought along included the vice-chief and later chief of naval operations, Adm. Jim Watkins; the current CNO, Rear Adm. John Butts; and his special assistant, Rich Haver. Toward the end of the briefing, the president made it clear that he approved the continuation of the operations and strongly endorsed an aggressive forward naval maritime strategy.

During March and April, we sent a specially outfitted amphibious ship, *Fairfax County*, to conduct research and surveillance operations on Soviet Northern Fleet activities in the Norwegian and Barents Seas. A Russian *Kashin*-class destroyer trained its guns on her. When *Fairfax County* attempted to retrieve a torpedo during a Soviet exercise, the Soviets protested.

In implementing the new strategy in the Pacific, President Reagan met with Japanese prime minister Suzuki in Washington, on

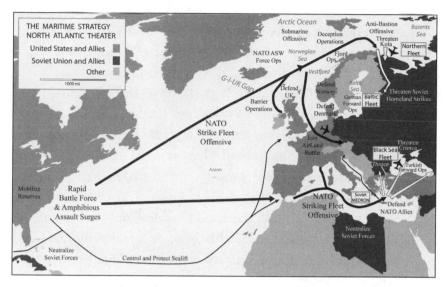

The North Atlantic strategy. (© *John Lehman*)

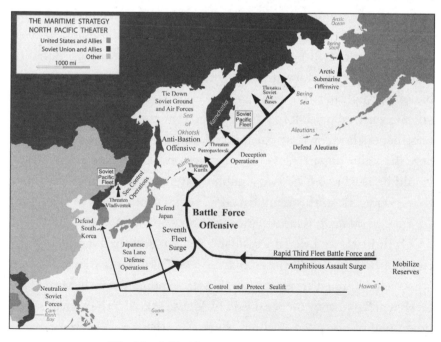

The North Pacific strategy. (© *John Lehman*)

May 3. As a result, Suzuki publicly committed Japan to the defense of sea-lanes out to a thousand nautical miles from Yokosuka, a move that greatly vexed the Soviets, who viewed the move as a major expansion of the threat from Japan, the biggest "aircraft carrier" in the western Pacific. Only a week later the Seventh Fleet sailed a task force of three destroyers and an oiler into the Sea of Okhotsk, further raising Soviet blood pressure. A few weeks later, continuing the psychological warfare, the Second Fleet sent the destroyer *Connolly* through the middle of a Soviet antisubmarine warfare exercise in the North Atlantic, forcing several smaller ships to scatter.

A few days later, we had the U.S. Marine Corps commandant, Gen. Bob Barrow, make public his plan to greatly increase and improve the marines' Arctic warfare center in Bridgeport, California, in the High Sierras.

During the summer of 1981, as we prepared with allied navies for our big event, Ocean Venture '81, I published an explanation of our new strategy in *Strategic Review*. The article emphasized linkages among strategy, operations, and programs. "The U.S. Navy of the near future will be visibly offensive in orientation . . . global in reach. It will stress forward deployment, including operations capable of war-fighting and winning in areas denoted as 'high risk.' Such an approach should force the Soviets, historically dominated by continental horizons, to concentrate more resources on homeland defense—and possibly less on interdiction of U.S. sea lanes." This would be the basic U.S. Navy public statement on strategy for more than two years, until we published a special supplement to the *Naval Institute Proceedings* issue of January 1986.

On July 31, we briefed President Reagan and the National Security Council on the proposed Sixth Fleet exercise off Libya. Reagan approved it. "The President said we will respond instantly, should we be shot at." Attorney General Edwin Meese asked, if the Libyans shot down one of our planes, would we pursue them into their airspace? "The President said we would chase them right into the hangar."

On August 19, the exercise began. As soon as the American carriers *Forrestal* and *Nimitz* penetrated Gaddafi's self-declared "Line of Death," Libyan fighters rose to attack: a Sukhoi Su-22 Fitter-J fighter fired a missile at them. Under the new Reagan administration "hot pursuit all the way into the hangar" rules of engagement (ROE), Nimitz F-14s from VF-41 shot down two Fitters with Sidewinder air-to-air missiles over the Gulf of Sidra, in international waters, about sixty nautical miles off the Libyan coast. Under Carter administration ROE, the F-14s would not have been permitted to shoot at the Fitters. Word of "President Reagan's ROE" spread throughout the Sixth Fleet and gave a big boost to morale. Thereafter the fleet would exercise regularly in the Gulf of Sidra without Libyan opposition. Libya would not challenge the fleet again until 1986. Reagan wrote in his memoir, "I also wanted to send a message to others in the world that there was a new management team in the White House, and that the United States wasn't going to hesitate any longer to act when its legitimate interests were at stake."

The same day elsewhere in the Mediterranean, a Soviet destroyer reported that it was buzzed by an American S-3 jet and an SH-2 helo. (Today positions seem to be reversed: in the spring of 2016, the United States lodged a protest when an American warship was buzzed by Russian helicopters.)

Shortly before President Reagan was inaugurated, the CNO, Adm. Tom Hayward, had the foresight to establish a Strategic Studies Group (SSG) at the Naval War College, made up of a dozen of the most outstanding operational navy and marine commanders, captains, and colonels most of whom had just completed their operational command tours. They were assigned to spend a year thinking about and debating the new strategy and its operational implications, with the benefit of their recent experience in the fleet, the latest intelligence, war games, and analysis of our exercises and new weapons and systems.

In my first meeting with them, I reminded them that a key factor in developing our strategy for the navy was to ensure that the rest of the world perceived the navy as capable of coping with the Soviet threat to American and allied interests. For that, the navy would need innovative, coherent, and institutional thinking about how a six-hundred-ship navy could be used. "We need to focus on the battle of, say, the Norwegian Sea, rather than the battle of the budget," I said, and "the United States should cut back its sights in terms of how much should be invested in the Persian Gulf area during a major U.S.-USSR war." In reporting on my remarks, one author highlighted that I had said I "felt it would be a great mistake to be overly involved in a ground war in that region."

The establishment of the SSG completed the orbit of strategy planning at navy headquarters, beginning with the actual exercise by the fleet, followed by operational analysis and critique by the Center for Naval Analyses then global war gaming at Newport based on those results, and then the SSG for new tactical ideas and critique, to be tested in the next year's exercises. The CNO, the marine commandant, and I came to depend on this virtuous circle to keep our strategy constantly evolving and incorporating the latest technology, lessons learned, and intelligence for the remainder of the Reagan administration.

Once the success of Ocean Venture '81 set the course in the Atlantic, attention turned to strategy in the Pacific. President Reagan's concordat with Prime Minister Suzuki was bearing much naval fruit: Japan assumed responsibility for a zone a thousand miles out from Yokosuka. The Japanese Maritime Self-Defense Force (JMSDF) began to receive ninety-four P-3C Orion long-range antisubmarine aircraft, equipped with the very latest technology to find Soviet subs. It began holding major air and sea exercises every two to three years, growing in size and effectiveness.

The North Pacific counterpart to Ocean Venture '81 was planned to be an even bigger departure from past practice. The Norpac series of bold exercises would last from January through May 1982 and include much expanded participation by the Japanese and South Korean naval forces. Taking a leaf from Ace Lyons, the series began with a dash by the Seventh Fleet carrier *Coral Sea* and thirteen other warships, in complete radio and other emissions silence, into and through the South China Sea and then into the Sea of Japan.

Cmdr. Denny McGinn, the skipper of the A-7 attack squadron VA-27, aboard *Coral Sea*, which operated throughout the exercises, described his experience thus:

> We made the transit from the South China Sea up to the Sea of Japan east of Korea. One of the clearest memories was of the dramatic temperature and weather changes. We went from really nice flying weather, warm air and sea temperatures, to really cold conditions. We regularly had snow showers and ice on the flight deck, everyone was wearing cold weather gear, including aircrew exposure suits, and we regularly encountered heavy seas, high winds and low visibility conditions that made flight operations quite challenging. We were very careful and deliberate in our launch and recovery operations, but we flew day and night and maintained a round the clock alert posture to intercept Soviet aircraft that were coming out to take a look at us. It was very sensitive in that we really wanted to test our ability to transit undetected for days at a time and then show up ready to conduct full operations.

Cmdr. Vance Morrison participated as skipper of a fast frigate, conducting related surveillance ops of the Soviet Pacific Fleet in Vladivostok. Said Morrison:

> The annual joint U.S.-South Korea display of military ability to deter North Korea known as exercise *Team Spirit* held in the late winter of 1982 occurred while I was in command of an Anti-Submarine Warfare frigate, *Francis Hammond*, operating from Yokosuka, Japan, as an element of the *Midway* carrier battle group. The ship received orders to detach and sail independently to the

Flight operations on *Coral Sea* in the northwestern Pacific during Norpac '83 illustrate the extreme challenges involved in implementing the forward naval strategy. *(U.S. Navy photographs from the 1980s USS Coral Sea tribute, National Archives.)*

vicinity of Vladivostok harbor to detect and report Soviet Navy reaction to the Team Spirit exercise ongoing in the Sea of Japan and ashore in South Korea, well to the south of our assigned station. The ship had new SH-2F LAMPS helicopters embarked.

After transiting thorough the Tsugaru Strait under cover of a heavy snowstorm and arriving without incident, we were soon met by our uninvited "shotgun," a Soviet *Kashin*-class guided-missile destroyer who stuck with us for the week or so that we were on station. While there, a *Juliet*-class cruise-missile-equipped Soviet submarine surfaced near us once, and we were overflown at least daily by Soviet Badger or, occasionally, Bear reconnaissance bombers. Alone, we were very much in the midst of the Cold War in more ways than one—the temperature was often below zero outside the ship.

As we departed, the *Kashin* came close aboard our starboard side, and the ship's skipper saluted me from their bridge. Our LAMPS flew daily and heavily photographed all the surface units and the submarine for our intelligence experts to ponder. We believed we had accomplished our mission well. Our transit home was uneventful as we thawed out along the way back to Yokosuka for our local "Hot Wash Up" debriefing. This event clearly met two

objectives of the Maritime Strategy's principles: *forward defense* and *alliances*. It was a few more years, however, before I began to relate consciously to that *strategy*.

THE FALKLANDS WAR

On August 2, 1982, Argentine troops landed to seize the British Falkland Islands, but by June 14, the Royal Navy had taken them back. In this Falkland Islands War, the U.S. Navy quietly but significantly supported the Royal Navy and later studied the war's operations for lessons learned, so as to improve future U.S. Navy operations and exercises at sea and to incorporate some new programs in the navy budget.

The Soviets also followed the war closely and were amazed by the will and effectiveness of British combat capability. It forced them to recalculate their "correlation of forces," which had given little credence to the fighting worth of UK and other European NATO navies.

As winter 1982 became spring, the operational tempo of the western Pacific maritime exercise steadily increased until it became the largest held since World War II. A phase of the exercise began in the Philippine Sea with a three-carrier battle force including *Midway*, *Constellation*, and *Ranger*. The force included a marine amphibious group that carried out an assault on Iwo Jima. The opposing exercise force included USAF B-52 and F-15 aircraft. A little later the United States and Japan, after a lapse of ten years, resumed conducting joint naval drills in the Sea of Japan.

These exercises not only developed confidence in the navy and air force that we could fight forward in hostile icy waters in close coordination with our allied navies; they also demonstrated to the governments of our northern exposed allies, particularly Japan, South Korea, Norway, and Denmark, that the U.S. government was committed to defending them. It was time now to turn to our exposed allies on NATO's southern flank, including Greece and Turkey.

In June 1982, we deployed four carriers to exercise with our Mediterranean allies: *Eisenhower*, *Kennedy*, *Forrestal*, and *Independence*. In addition to raising our allies' confidence, the air wings' operations made clear to the Soviets that carrier strikes from the eastern Mediterranean could reach deep into the Soviet heartland.

Only slightly less shocked than the Soviets by the dramatic naval activities of the first year of the Reagan administration were the congressional and media supporters of the Carter policies of détente and defense reductions. After the publicity around Ocean Venture '81 and resulting Soviet protests, the criticism from some quarters, including some former Carter officials, became quite loud. The old campaign slogans of Reagan the cowboy were resurrected. When the president sent up his new budget for the navy with substantial increases across the board, including a request for not just one but two new nuclear aircraft carriers (for the first time since World War II), the critics became strident. In February 1982, I presented the budget to Congress, laying out the elements of the president's call for a six-hundred-ship navy and its strategic rationale, and calmly declaring, "Clear maritime superiority must be reacquired." The rumor mill then spread that the new navy secretary was a loose cannon and was off on a frolic of his own. We soon squelched that.

During his spring testimony, the chief of naval operations, Admiral Hayward, was asked whether he endorsed Secretary Lehman's description of naval strategy and the six-hundred-ship navy policy. He forcefully replied "I endorse unequivocally his views."

Soon afterward Secretary of Defense Caspar Weinberger testified, "The most significant force expansion proposed by the administration centers on the navy, particularly those components of it that have offensive missions. . . . We are determined to restore and maintain maritime superiority over the Soviets."

Some of the damaging rumors were floating out of the vast bureaucracy of the Joint Chiefs of Staff (some five thousand souls). We recommended to the White House that the president let it be known that this was his strategy, not just that of the navy. On May 18, President Reagan discussed the navy, as well as Norwegian and Barents Seas and Iceland strategy issues, at lunch with Secretary Weinberger and all the joint chiefs. He confided in his diary that he "lunched with Joint Chiefs of Staff and Cap W. It was a good meeting with a sound discussion of strategic problems— for example—the importance of the sea above Norway and what Iceland means in the navy strategy should there be conflict on the NATO front."

President Reagan had approved our keeping the pressure mounting indefinitely lest the Soviets get the impression we were one year and done. In one theater after another and often simultaneously, we went, as the Royal Navy likes to say, from strength to strength.

In August 1982, Rear Adm. Jerry Tuttle led the carrier *America* battle group into the Baltic for Bold Guard '82, the largest amphibious assault exercise ever landed in Jutland, Denmark. It included two amphibious landings supported by USAF F-15s flying out of Norway (allowed by the Norwegian government for the first time), USAF B-52s, and AWACS early warning and control aircraft. To Tuttle's delight, the assault triggered a major Soviet aviation response, enabling U.S. Navy forces to test the targeting of 102 incoming Soviet aircraft sorties against NATO forces. During the exercise, Tuttle secretly sent the nuclear cruiser *South Carolina* north off Norway in total emissions silence to practice vectoring and controlling

Norwegian Air Force F-16s. It was a total success, once again confounding Soviet expectations.

From September through October 1982, we ran near-simultaneous
exercises in the northeastern Atlantic, the Mediterranean, and the
northwestern Pacific. From September 13 through 21, we conducted
Annualex '82 with Japan in a combined naval exercise from the northern Sea of Japan to the Bonins, with more than eighty ships and
ninety aircraft participating.

Then from September 29 through October 9, we conducted Norpac '82, a two-carrier eighteen-ship strike exercise with *Enterprise*
and *Midway*, running from southwest of Attu Island in the Aleutians
to the Sea of Japan through the Tsugaru Strait, to three hundred
miles southeast of the Soviet nuclear missile submarine base at Petropavlovsk, and then to the East China Sea and South China Sea.
Ships transited under strict EMCON conditions. It was the largest
naval force off Alaska since World War II.

The Soviet reaction was unprecedented (129 aircraft reacted to
the exercise): "the apparent surprise appearance of two U.S. carrier
battle groups off Kamchatka probably prompted a tightening of
Soviet surveillance practices." The Soviets' surveillance was intense,
including the heavy use of supersonic long-range Backfire bombers.
It was the first-ever use of such bombers in a simulated strike against
a U.S. carrier battle group. By forcing them to exercise their actual
attack modes, we were much better able to calibrate our own systems
and tactics against them. Lt. Cmdr. Paul Giarra, assistant navigator
on *Midway*, recalled:

> Norpac '82 was right up [our] alley—innovative, maneu-
> ver warfare using every trick in the book. . . . I'm not cer-
> tain of the overall Soviet reaction—there was no running
> commentary provided to the crew, and I saw none from
> my Navy Department perspective. I do remember being
> overflown directly overhead (or so it seemed) by a large

[Soviet Navy] bomber with what looked like an impossibly large air-to-surface cruise missile slung underneath.

Other officers recalled:

> four Backfires approached the carriers. . . . At a distance of 120 miles the aircraft simulated release of their cruise missiles. The following day, four more Backfires approached the fleet in another simulated air strike.

> I think that everyone knew that something special was going on—trailing screws and EMCON Alpha were good indicators [that something big was afoot] for us. Also, it was unusual to sortie and head north. But there was very little indication that this was part of a conscious push by the navy and the Reagan White House to pressure the Soviets. Later (when Navy headquarters made a major effort to explain the strategy to all hands in the fleet) it became obvious, but not at the time. We went for long periods without any news—if we were lucky, yellow teletype printouts might be tacked up outside Main Comm— and there was no such thing for us as "the Big Picture."

> While *Enterprise* and *Midway* were at flight quarters, somehow the weather closed in on *Enterprise*, and an F-14 crew had to recover aboard *Midway*. This was quite exciting for several reasons. First, *Midway*'s Airwing-5 flew F-4's, not Tomcats. Second, the aircrew had only the flight suits on their backs, which were orange (*Midway*'s were green), and they stuck out like a sore thumb during their overnight stay aboard *Midway*, to everyone's amusement. (Normally it is tradition, when this happens, that the visiting fighter is covered with graffiti identifying it as an air force airplane.) Third, their departure was quite

memorable, because *Midway*'s jet blast deflectors (JBDs) were not large enough for an F-14's engines and could not withstand the Tomcat's exhaust. So *Midway* conducted a full airborne re-spot, launched or struck below all aircraft on deck, and launched the *Enterprise* F-14 (suitably festooned with all sorts of Midway and CVW-5 marks) from an empty deck with the JBD stowed. It was quite a sight.

This first major aggressive North Pacific exercise of the Reagan administration was in fact a very big deal. Along with the nearly simultaneous North Atlantic and eastern Mediterranean naval exercises, it demonstrated a global coordinated air and naval threat to the Soviets from three axes. *Enterprise* and *Midway* would build on this experience the following year, with the same commanding officers, in FleetEx '83-1.

These northern exercises were a new experience for most of the fleet since political sensitivity had kept the navy from northern latitudes for years. These first experiences reminded the navy that Arctic seas are dangerous and unforgiving, so increased training was essential. As part of this realization, the Pacific Fleet, from October 15 through December 15, conducted Icex '82, training in Arctic operations and cold weather drills. On November 2, the nuclear attack subs *Tautog* and *Aspro* surfaced together at the North Pole, to demonstrate to the Soviets that they could face missile attacks from any azimuth at any time of the year.

When a fighter lands on a carrier not its own, it must be suitably decorated before being allowed to leave for its own. *(U.S. Navy photograph.)*

A B-52 bomber operating with the carrier *Enterprise* in the North Pacific. *(U.S. Navy photograph.)*

While the media treated these exercises as navy only, in fact they were fully joint in operations. On October 25, the secretaries of the navy and air force and their chiefs of staff signed a memorandum of understanding fully integrating the training exercising and equipping of the services for war at sea and in the air. The USAF participated in virtually all our forward exercises and added a powerful dimension of capability.

The following month, from November 16 until December 17, 1982, the Kernel Potlatch '82 exercise provided the perfect test. The U.S. Third Fleet, with substantial Canadian, U.S. Coast Guard, and U.S. Air Force participation, deployed from southern California to the Aleutians. It made the first amphibious landing in the Aleu-

My A-6 Intruder fighter-bomber from USS *Eisenhower* operating in Egypt during Bright Star '82.*(U.S. Navy photograph.)*

tians (on Amchitka, in the western Aleutians) since World War II. Soviet Bear aircraft overflew the exercise and were intercepted by USAF F-15s. This represented a sea change in the U.S. Pacific Fleet and Third Fleet exercise posture. The long-forgotten lessons from operating ships with ice-caked radars, snow-covered decks, and sub-zero temperatures had to be relearned as northern operations now became frequent.

So that the world understood the context of these exercises, on November 22, President Reagan gave a major televised speech on strategic arms reduction and nuclear deterrence:

> The world has also witnessed unprecedented growth in the area of Soviet conventional forces. The Soviets far exceed us in the number of tanks, artillery pieces, aircraft, and ships they produce every year. What is more, when I

arrived in this office, I learned that in our own forces we had planes that couldn't fly and ships that couldn't leave port mainly for lack of spare parts and crewmembers. The Soviet military buildup must not be ignored. We've recognized the problem, and together with our allies, we've begun to correct the imbalance.

Rubbing a little salt in the Soviet wounds, from December 4 to 9, we carried out the third major joint exercise with the recent Soviet ally Egypt in Bright Star '82.

The year 1982 ended on a triumphal note for the navy. On December 28, we recommissioned the *New Jersey*, in Long Beach, California. The first of four *Iowa*-class battleships to join the Reagan fleet, it was equipped with the most advanced electronics, air defenses, and Tomahawk and Harpoon cruise missiles as well as

The battleship *New Jersey* firing a Tomahawk cruise missile.
(U.S. Navy photograph.)

President Reagan and me at the recommissioning ceremony for
USS *New Jersey* at Long Beach, California, on December 28, 1981.
(National Archives, Ronald Reagan Presidential Library and Museum.)

their famous long-range sixteen-inch guns. President Reagan used
the occasion for a major speech: "Maritime superiority for us is a
necessity. We must be able in time of emergency to venture in harm's
way, controlling air, surface, and subsurface areas to assure access to
all the oceans of the world. Failure to do so will leave the credibility
of our conventional defense forces in doubt."

CHAPTER 4

Soviet Panic;
Misreading the Message

The Mobilization of 1983

THE DRAMATIC CHANGE in America's global national security posture by the Reagan administration took the Soviets by surprise. They had spent more than a decade dealing with presidents and administrations mired in Vietnam, coping with internal strife, and striving for détente with the Communist world. Ronald Reagan's aggressive rhetoric on the 1980 campaign trail was reminiscent of that of Richard Nixon's a dozen years earlier, and the Politburo assumed that once in office, Reagan too would soften and seek accommodation with the Soviets. They were, of course, quite wrong. Reagan thought his predecessors had allowed America's military power to slip dangerously behind that of the Soviets—and therefore had diluted its guarantees to the rest of the free world and its credibility as a deterrent to Soviet aggression and adventurism. Once in office, he told his national security establishment, including the military, that it was time to surge back.

The military deterrent offensive he launched was on many fronts. He increased the defense budget. He rebuilt the armed forces with new army divisions, a new strategic bomber, and intercontinental ballistic missile. He reactivated battleships. And he bought four new nuclear aircraft carriers, to name the most visible. He revised the

rules of engagement. He engaged with and backed up key allies—
who responded by backing him up. He supported anti-Communist
forces all over the globe. And he sent the U.S. Navy forward.

Instead of choke point barriers and convoys, the Soviets now
faced offensive naval strike forces off all their major naval bases.
Instead of scripted exercises and stale scenarios, the Soviets now
faced imaginative new U.S. and allied operational concepts and tactics. And instead of a western naval posture centered on resupply
of armies in Germany, the Soviets now had to face major concen-
trations of naval power in the Norwegian Sea, northern Norway,
the eastern Mediterranean, and the Arctic and western Pacific
Oceans—while America's allies expanded their own roles in protecting the sea-lanes.

Soviet KGB defector Oleg Gordievsky and Christopher Andrew
later wrote:

> During the American presidential election campaign in
> 1980, Moscow had expected the anti-Soviet rhetoric of the
> victorious Republican candidate Ronald Reagan to mel-
> low once he had been elected, much as Nixon's had done a
> decade earlier. Not till Reagan entered the White House
> did the Kremlin fully grasp that his hostility to the Soviet
> Union derived not from campaign tactics but from deep
> conviction. . . . The Reagan administration was convinced
> that as a result of the growth of Soviet military might
> over the past decade "the American deterrent had been
> placed in doubt." The defense budget was increased by
> 10 percent—double Reagan's campaign promise. Reagan
> took a much tougher line than Carter on arms control,
> publicly condemning the SALT treaties, and showed him-
> self in no hurry to return to the negotiating table until the
> U.S. nuclear strike force had been strengthened. Carter
> had suspended work on the MX missile and B-1 bomber.
> Reagan reinstated both.

The Soviets didn't like what was going on and didn't understand it. They began to realize that their game was up, and some in the leadership also began to fear that the United States would somehow irrationally attack them first. In this respect, they were mirror-imaging their own thought processes, since surprise and achieving the "first salvo" were cornerstones of their military doctrine. They had seen the West as a rich, succulent beast that they would eventually gobble up when given the chance. But the West had little interest in returning the compliment. As President Reagan noted, "What the h—l do they have that anyone would want?"

And the Soviets were particularly fearful of being attacked under cover of a forward U.S. exercise. Why? Because their own doctrine was to use military exercises to mask surprise invasions. They had done exactly that in an exercise in Poland in 1981. Launching an attack under cover of an exercise had been a long-standing tenet of Russian military doctrine, and the Soviets had recently incorporated it into their new strategy, developed in the 1970s, to defeat NATO with conventional forces alone. Its central concept was a high-speed offensive launched under the cover of military exercises in East Germany and Czechoslovakia.

The initial Soviet reaction to the new forward naval strategy was all over the map. They tried intimidation. They tried analysis. They scrubbed our internal communications that—unknown to us—they were reading by the thousands. They countered with big—and small—exercises and operations of their own. They extended themselves even farther into the seas that surrounded them and into the far reaches of the world. They tightened up their own coastal security laws and railed indignantly and publicly against our actions. Some of them even began to panic, bizarrely fearing a U.S. nuclear first strike. At arms control negotiations—when they weren't walking out of them—they hung tough to their positions on intermediate-range nuclear missiles in Europe, seeking to maintain their recently achieved superiority (while stirring up "peace movements" in Western Europe, to gnaw at the will of our allies from within).

But most of all, they redoubled their efforts to outdesign, out-build, and outspend us—despite the handwriting on the wall that such a policy would inevitably seal their fate.

First, the Soviets sought to intimidate America's sailors by sending waves of bombers and numerous surface ships and submarines out whenever a U.S. forward exercise was held. Soviet reaction to Ocean Venture in the fall of 1981 had been fierce, as we have seen, although somewhat confused, since they often couldn't figure out exactly where the Striking Fleet actually was on any given day. The Soviets did not surge large numbers of warships into the Mediterranean to counter U.S. Navy buildups there during Lebanon crises in 1982–83, as they had in 1967 and 1973. But against the NATO Striking Fleet conducting Northern Wedding '82 in the North Atlantic and the North Sea, they launched some 120 air sorties

In the fall of 1984, during the exercise Fleetex '85-1, the Soviets again threw a big Soviet Naval Aviation raid against a U.S. Navy carrier—this time at our newest deployed flattop, *Carl Vinson*.

Following Fleetex, *Vinson* and other battle groups, supported by an air force AWACS aircraft, entered the Sea of Japan and staged mock battle force attacks fifty miles off Vladivostok. This drew repeated Soviet aircraft and warship sorties. U.S. Navy strategist Cmdr. Kenneth McGruther participated in this exercise, as CO of the frigate *Knox*:

> I was on Kennel Freelance, which was the patrol off the Soviet port of Vladivostok, basically intelligence gathering, show the flag, and be a pain in the ass but outside twelve-nautical-mile limit, in November–December 1984. We came off that patrol and joined a major exercise that involved three carriers entering the Japan Sea (as I recall, two from the north and one from the south). Naturally the Soviets went batshit, and we had Badgers all over us. (Thanks for the targeting services, guys.) Having always been deployed in Westpac [western Pacific] before, I had

never known of any such exercise in scale, scope, or near-
ness to the USSR. So I suppose that was a legacy of the
Maritime Strategy way of "thinking forward."

All through this period, the U.S. Navy periodically maintained
a ship, an amphibious landing ship tank (LST), on station in the
northern Norwegian Sea, to monitor Soviet naval activity. The Soviets, in turn, periodically harassed the LST, often with *Petya*-class
patrol craft.

Soviet intimidation operations, however, weren't intimidating
anyone. They were just giving the Americans and our allies free
targeting services, intelligence opportunities—and an audience for
perception management. American Navy commanders had long
had to deal with Soviet tattletales and reconnaissance aircraft. Now
they were building them into their own exercises, targeting not just
"Orange"—the exercise enemy—but "Red"—the real one. In 1982,
for example, during Norpac '82:

> From the time she neared her NorPac operations area on
> 23 September 1982, until she departed the Sea of Japan,
> *Enterprise* proved "the subject of extensive Soviet air, sur-
> face, and subsurface surveillance." Of particular note was
> the unprecedented use of Backfire bombers, on 30 Sep-
> tember and 2 October, to "reconnoiter" the [*Enterprise/
> Midway* battle groups]. . . . The operations . . . provided
> the airwing with excellent opportunities to train against
> Soviet surveillance aircraft, submarines, and surface com-
> batants, conducting dual CV [carrier] operations includ-
> ing air wing coordinated strikes.

Often U.S. Navy commanders and their political leaders used
exercises to signal to the Soviets, since they were there anyway providing an audience. As I noted in a speech in mid-1983 and an article
in early 1984:

Recently, there were four Soviet spy ships among our Second Fleet Readex [readiness exercise] in the Caribbean. Their presence was publicly welcomed by Strike Fleet Commander, Admiral James A. Lyons, Jr. As missile after missile took down drone after drone—as eleven Harpoons had eleven direct hits—Admiral Lyons sent his now usual message to the Soviet participants in the exercise. It could well serve as the maritime theme for U.S.-Soviet relations in the decade ahead. That message again read, "Admiral Gorshkov, eat your heart out."

In March 1984 testimony on the navy's Maritime Strategy, CNO Watkins told the U.S. Congress:

These exercises are extremely important because, unlike any other service, the Navy runs eyeball to eyeball with the Soviets daily, either in the air, on the surface, or under the water. . . . These exercises, then, bring out the Soviets and in many cases the Soviets actually act as our target forces. . . . They provide very effective exercise services to our forces because we can really see what we are up against.

In 1985, the Russian aircraft carrier *Kiev* and her group transited through the Bosporus and the Strait of the Dardanelles and entered the Mediterranean via the Aegean Sea. The *Kiev* was for vertical and short takeoff and landing (V/STOL) aircraft, not a conventional carrier. It could operate only aircraft that could take off and land vertically, like the Yak-36 Forger. *Kiev*'s crew behaved very boldly toward the U.S. Navy carrier *Eisenhower* and at one point conducted a strike exercise in proximity to the Americans. The latter noted, however, that although the Soviet Forger pilots flew practice strafing and bombing runs against *Kiev*'s wake, they never flew more than fifty nautical miles out of range from their carrier, demonstrating a lack of capability of that aircraft type in comparison to U.S. capabilities.

The Soviet *Kiev* V/STOL carrier recovering one of its Yak-36 jump jets. (*Courtesy of the Naval History and Heritage Command.*)

American skippers turned the tables on their counterparts whenever they got the chance. *Enterprise* made simulated strikes on another V/STOL carrier, the *Minsk*, in the Indian Ocean. The Sixth Fleet conducted targeting exercises with our new Harpoon missiles against the Soviets' new *Slava*-class cruiser in the Mediterranean and later against their helicopter carrier *Leningrad*.

In October 1981, a Soviet Baltic Fleet Whiskey-class submarine ran aground on rocks in Swedish territorial waters, in a restricted military zone, two kilometers from the main Swedish naval base at Karlskrona. Most regarded this "whiskey on the rocks" incident as proof of Soviet infiltration of the Swedish coastline and a violation of Swedish territorial waters. Other Soviet submarine intrusions in Swedish waters were reported all through the decade.

A few years later, during exercise Team Spirit '84-1 in the Sea of Japan off Korea, near Tsushima Strait, a Soviet Victor I-class submarine rose up under the carrier *Kitty Hawk* and got run over during night operations. The collision embedded pieces of a propeller and chunks of anechoic coating in the carrier's hull, from scraping the hull of the submarine (an accidental intelligence coup for the U.S. Navy, which was able to gain valuable information from the Soviet materials). The Soviet submarine had significant damage and required a tow to Vladivostok. The Soviet task force flagship cruiser *Petropavlovsk* refused to respond to flashing light signals from *Kitty Hawk*. During the eight-day U.S.-Republic of Korea annual exercise, there had been heavy Soviet reconnaissance: Soviet aircraft had overflown the *Kitty Hawk* battle group forty-three times, while six Soviet surface units and the Victor I had also appeared.

During the official debrief back at the Pentagon, it was pointed out that "during the course of three days' exercising, the sub had been 'killed' more than 15 times and was ignored thereafter." CNO Admiral Watkins reflected, "The reason behind the submarine captain's slip in judgment is the only mystery here. He showed uncharacteristically poor seamanship in not staying clear of *Kitty Hawk*. That should cause concern in Moscow."

In jest, *Kitty Hawk's* crew considered her therefore the U.S. Navy's first "ASW carrier weapon." A red submarine was painted on her island near the bridge.

The Soviets also redoubled their efforts to figure out what we were really up to and to learn our secrets. We knew, of course, about the ubiquitous Soviet Navy spy ships, spy submarines, spy aircraft, and spy satellites that sought to monitor our every move and intercept our every message. Soviet Navy "tattletails" were everywhere. And we knew how to counter them through deception operations, radio silence, and innovative maneuvering and tactics. Examples abounded: they routinely surveilled our movements in the Mediterranean and in the Atlantic, Indian, and Pacific Oceans. In one particularly blatant example, they planted an intelligence-gathering ship off Camp Pendleton, California, in 1984 to monitor our exercise Phalanx Sound II. This was the largest U.S. Marine Corps Reserve exercise and amphibious landing since the Korean War, simulating a landing in Europe against a Soviet thrust into Denmark from Germany.

Our navy, in turn, routinely intercepted their surveillance aircraft and maneuvered our ships to stay out of the way of their specialized intelligence-gathering ships and surface combatants. The *Enterprise* command histories, for example, are filled with instances of Bears, Mays, and Cubs overflying the carrier and her escorts as they plied the world's oceans.

SPIES AMONG US

What we did not know, however, was the massive extent to which they were receiving our secrets from our very own people, who were being paid with cold hard cash. These spies in our midst had been at it for a very long time, and it only slowly emerged how much damage they had been doing to us—and were continuing to do. Typically, they were not foreign agents or ideologically driven "true believers" who infiltrated into our ships and offices. Rather, they were home-grown Americans who lacked any shred of loyalty to their fellow Americans or the country that had nurtured them but were consumed by greed—and petty greed at that. They themselves had initiated contact with the Soviets; the Soviets hadn't come looking for them. The damage they did was incalculably costly, while the blood money they sought and received from the KGB was relatively paltry.

John Walker, a U.S. Navy warrant officer, had been spying for money since as far back as 1967, providing secret cryptographic codes; operation orders; data on operations, exercises and secret technological equipment; and much else. One particularly valuable function he performed for the Soviet Navy was to inform them of just how noisy their submarines were and how easy it was for the U.S. Navy to know where they were. Walker enabled the Soviets to understand the seriousness of the U.S. Navy buildup and strategy, requiring them to expend even more military and naval resources and funds to counter them. They learned, to their chagrin and probable shock, that the United States was far more advanced than the Soviet Union in certain maritime technologies, which enabled the Soviets to better focus their research institutes to produce new countertechnologies to deal with American advances. The results of the better-targeted research and development soon appeared in the Soviet fleet. It took the Soviets decades, but by the early 1980s, U.S. Navy antisubmarine warfare forces realized that the Soviets' Victor III and subsequent submarine classes were indeed far quieter than previous classes and were increasingly difficult to find—and potentially to kill.

Along the way, Walker roped in his brother, his son, and his best friend, Jerry Whitworth, a navy radioman. Whitworth's biggest scoops came when he was assigned to *Enterprise*. During its 1982–83 western Pacific and Indian Ocean cruise, photographing millions of pages of internal navy secret documents pertaining to freedom of navigation operations (FONOPS) against Soviet client state Vietnam, intelligence operations against the Soviet carrier *Minsk*, interceptions of Soviet tattletale ships and surveillance aircraft, and northwestern Pacific exercises Team Spirit '82 and Fleetex '83-1. John Walker passed this treasure trove to the KGB in 1984, a year before he was finally apprehended by the FBI.

The U.S. Navy's Fleetex '83-1 exercise in the northwestern Pacific was intended to stimulate Soviet responses. But "overt Soviet reaction was less than expected, especially in light of their reaction during 1982's 2-CVBG operation."

> When the navy studied the Soviet reactions to the exercise, they were puzzled. While the Soviet air monitoring was heavy, the surface surveillance was "nearly non-existent," [Capt. Robert "Barney"] Kelly noted in one [USS *Enterprise*] report. Another commander recalled that despite the unique nature of the exercise—the only

one using three carriers in decades—"the Soviet reaction was mild." The Soviets sent their standard Bear and Badger aircraft by every other day.

The Soviets, of course, knew that Walker family spy Jerry Whitworth was now aboard *Enterprise*. Whitworth and Walker would pass data on *Enterprise*'s Kuril flyover to the Soviets in June 1983. The entire exercise—and much more—was compromised by a data transfer in April 1984. According to one keen reporter:

> When the three-carrier operation ended, the Pentagon tried to determine whether it was successful. Its immediate reaction was mixed. While the exercise had given the Navy a chance to train its commanders, the Pacific Fleet headquarters was dissatisfied and frustrated because, strangely, the three carriers had not generated as much intelligence information about the Russian response to a three-carrier threat as the Pentagon had anticipated. Pentagon analysts couldn't figure out why the Soviets hadn't done more to monitor the fleet exercise. It seemed somewhat odd, especially since the Russians had paid close attention to smaller exercises in the past that were less important. Years later, Pentagon officials wondered if Jerry Whitworth hadn't been the reason for the Russians' lack of interest. "Jerry copied everything he could about the operation," John Walker confided after his arrest.

The Walker family weren't the only traitors in whom the U.S. government had mistakenly placed its trust and confidence. Ronald Pelton, an NSA employee, contacted the Soviet embassy in Washington with information to sell. For a pretty modest amount, he told the KGB—among other things—that U.S. Navy submarines had been tapping one of its undersea communications cables since 1971 in an operation known as Ivy Bells. When a submarine showed up to resume the tap in late 1981, it discovered the operation had been compromised. Pelton went undiscovered until 1985, when Soviet defector KGB Colonel Vitali Yurchenko identified him. Yurchenko then quickly re-defected to the Soviet Union, where he was decorated by the KGB. The KGB's motives for "burning" Pelton are not known. He was eventually convicted and sentenced to life in prison. He was released from prison in 2015.

Arresting the Walkers and Pelton went only so far, unfortunately. A month before the FBI snared John Walker, CIA officer Aldrich Ames began betraying U.S. intelligence sources to the Soviets. Among the sources he betrayed was the U.S. Navy's single best source of tactical intelligence on the Soviet Navy. Ames was not arrested until 1994.

Meanwhile, unknown to any U.S. government agency, another well-placed government employee, FBI agent Robert Hanssen, was continuing to spy for the Soviets, as he had since 1979. Hanssen was a member of the FBI's own Soviet analytical unit, charged with studying, identifying, and capturing Soviet intelligence agents in the United States. Accordingly, he briefed the U.S. Navy's Strategic Studies Group (SSG) on Soviet ways of thinking, as part of its study on improving navy capabilities to deter the Soviet Union and its navy. He may well have also briefed his KGB handlers on SSG ways of thinking as well. Hanssen would continue to spy for the Russians long after the Warsaw Pact unraveled and the Soviet Union imploded. He would not be arrested until 2001.

Our closest and most important allies were penetrated too, and again the motivation was greed, not ideological fervor or Soviet infiltration. The Japanese Toshiba Machine Company and the Norwegian Kongsberg Vaapenfabrikk began selling advanced milling machinery and accompanying numerical control equipment to the Soviet Union for use in manufacturing very quiet propellers for Soviet Navy submarines, in clear violation of legal export restrictions. This technology gave a big help to Soviet efforts to quiet their submarines, to remedy the vulnerabilities made known to them by the Walkers. This orgy of espionage complicated and slowed U.S. Navy efforts to surpass the Soviets in strategy, operations, tactics, and systems. There was, however, a certain silver lining. Their own espionage made clear to the Soviets that the Americans were not planning any surprise attack, and that the Reagan forward maritime strategy was meant to deter the Soviets from using their preponderance of land power in central Europe to intimidate or attack NATO.

Sometimes Soviet surveillance and harassment turned ugly. Soviet police and intelligence workers were often little more than thugs. In August 1984, a U.S. Consulate-General Marine security guard sergeant was dragged from a car and beaten by Soviet police in Leningrad. In a much more heinous incident less than a year later, Soviet soldiers shot and killed Army Maj. Arthur D. Nicholson, an unarmed official observer of Soviet military facilities in East Germany. This incident so incensed Secretary of Defense Cap Weinberger that he imposed across-the-board freezes on U.S.-Soviet military-to-military relationships. Even the annual U.S. Navy-Soviet Navy Incidents at Sea (INCSEA) meetings became distinctly frosty, at Secretary Weinberger's orders.

Of course, every once in a while we wound up being too careful. At Christmastime in 1984:

> A stranger with a Russian accent delivered a package to the gatehouse of the Washington Navy Yard, addressed to Vice Admiral James A. Lyons. A military bomb squad, called to investigate, saw an X-ray picture of "two liquid-filled canisters," and the package was duly destroyed by a small explosive device. The remains disclosed that it had contained two bottles of premium Russian vodka, a present from the Soviet naval attaché's office to Admiral Lyons, who had headed the U.S. Navy delegation to the annual U.S.-Soviet meeting on preventing incidents at sea that year.

Cold War espionage wasn't a game of solitaire. We got to play, too. In 1978 a brilliant but disgruntled Soviet radar engineer named Adolf Tolkachev began selling us Soviet secrets, especially about the radars and avionics in state-of-the-art Soviet fighter and interceptor aircraft. This was just what we needed to ensure that our naval aviators going through the rigors of Strike U and Top Gun training at the Naval Aviation combat training center in Fallon, Nevada, knew what would be in front of them over the Norwegian and other seas and how to shoot them down. Our successes in the air in the 1980s against the Libyan Air Force's Soviet-built aircraft—and our even greater successes in the skies over Iraq in 1991 against Saddam Hussein's similar aircraft—were attributable in part to information from Tolkachev. Soviet general secretary Gorbachev himself complained at a Politburo meeting that "American intelligence paid [Tolkachev] generously. He was caught with two million rubles," while his KGB boss confirmed that "this agent handed over very important military-technical secrets to the enemy."

Unfortunately, in 1984 a fired and vengeful former CIA trainee, Edward Lee Howard, began betraying American agents to the Soviets, probably including Adolf Tolkachev. The following year Aldrich Ames began betraying U.S. agents as well, again probably including Tolkachev. Tolkachev was arrested as an American spy in June 1985, and his execution was announced the following year. Meanwhile Howard escaped and defected to the Soviet Union in late September 1985. Ames, of course, was unfortunately not apprehended until 1994.

In the late 1970s, as the Carter administration deemphasized the U.S. Navy, the Soviets became ever more confident that they were soon to achieve naval supremacy to match their numerical dominance in army, air force, and nuclear forces. They continued to develop larger more sophisticated naval combined exercises, improving their own capabilities and readiness and signaling their determination to keep U.S. naval forces far from Eurasian waters and from aiding forward U.S. allies and forces.

In the spring of 1980, the Carter administration was preoccupied with coping with the Mariel Boatlift of refugees and others from Communist Cuba, as well as launching Eagle Claw, the failed attempt to rescue our diplomats and others held hostage by Iran. Meanwhile the Soviet Navy was exercising in waters critical to the solidity of the NATO alliance: the eastern Atlantic, the UK approaches, the western Baltic and North Seas, the English Channel, and the Norwegian Sea. They also ran an amphibious exercise on Socotra Island, South Yemen, in the Arabian Sea, demonstrating their interest in and capability for distant-area power projection. In September they were at it again in the Baltic, trying to intimidate the captive but rebellious Poles and the West in the exercise Comradeship in Arms '80, with Soviet, Polish, and East German forces practicing amphibious landings.

In the spring of the following year, in Soyuz '81, the Soviets and their Warsaw Pact allies exercised yet again in the Baltic to intimidate the Poles and hone their own skills, including antiship and amphibious assault operations. In the summer of 1981, the Soviet Northern Fleet put to sea for a major fleet exercise in the Barents, heavy with aircraft sorties. In that same summer, Soviet Navy warships landed a thousand of their naval infantry on the Syrian coast, the first event of its kind in the eastern Mediterranean, demonstrating again their interest in and capability for distant-area power projection. More ominously, as summer turned to fall, the Soviet Pacific Fleet deployed a surface combat task group, including one cruiser and two frigates, far forward to within 230 nautical miles off the U.S. Oregon coast, and a Soviet naval task force steamed through the channel separating the islands of Maui and Hawaii. A year and a half later, two Soviet warships deployed as close as fifty miles off the Mississippi Delta, including the nuclear-armed *Kresta II*-class guided-missile cruiser *Admiral Isakov* and the *Krivak II*-class guided-missile frigate *Rezvyy*. The U.S. Navy said this was the closest that Soviet warships had come to the United States since they began deploying to the Caribbean in 1969.

The fall of 1981 saw the crisis in Poland starting to boil over, threatening once again the iron Soviet grip on its captive Eastern European–Warsaw Pact allies. To cow the Poles, warn the West, and test their new anti-NATO strategy, the Soviets launched Zapad '81, one of the biggest exercises in the history of the Soviet Armed Forces and Warsaw Pact and the largest armored Soviet military exercise since World War II, with one hundred thousand ground troops. It included the largest peacetime Soviet military exercise in the Baltic Sea area, centering on amphibious naval infantry assault operations in Lithuania, fifteen miles from the Soviet-Polish border. Unlike earlier, smaller such exercises, no Poles or East Germans were allowed to participate. The exercise featured amphibious assault use of air-cushion vehicles and helicopter vertical envelopment. It also included as a theme an invasion of neutral and NATO Scandinavia.

The Soviet Baltic Fleet carried out major maneuvers, including the Soviet V/STOL carrier *Kiev* (which acted as exercise flagship), the helicopter carrier *Leningrad*, and the new large amphibious ship *Ivan Rogov*. Over eighty vessels participated, including warships from other Soviet fleets. The exercise demonstrated the concept of fast-moving Soviet Operational Maneuver Groups (OMGs) as part of Soviet offensive doctrine, and it gave a powerful impetus to the U.S. Army's nascent AirLand Battle concept and NATO's Follow-On Forces Attack (FOFA) concept. The exercise was widely criticized in the West for violating the Helsinki Final Act on notification of military exercises.

In 1982, with Poland now firmly under martial law, the Soviets and their Baltic allies went to sea again for a small exercise, reaching into the North and Norwegian Seas. The emphasis was on practicing antisubmarine warfare, antiair warfare, and underway replenishment. Half a dozen surface ships and submarines participated. They practiced antisubmarine warfare in the North Sea, then shifted up to the Norwegian Sea for antiair warfare against attacking Badger strike bombers from the Soviet Northern Fleet. In 1983, the Soviets and their Baltic allies again joined in an exercise, Soyuz '83, including an amphibious assault on the East German coast involving one hundred or so ships and thirty combat aircraft. And in March 1984, the Soviets practiced an attack on the Turkish Straits in the exercise Soyuz '84.

That same month the Soviets began Springex '84, a large-scale exercise with the Northern and Baltic Fleets out into the western approaches to the Soviet Union, including the Greenland, Barents, and Norwegian Seas, and well out into the Atlantic, larger than any exercise the previous year (but still smaller than Okean '75). The exercise included substantial air activity, including the farthest Backfire bomber strikes yet conducted out into the Norwegian Sea. More than 148 surface ships, close to fifty submarines, and fifty aircraft participated, with 150 aircraft sorties counted. The scenario called for antisubmarine warfare, antiair warfare, and antisurface warfare defense of the Norwegian Sea approaches to the Soviet homeland; protection of Soviet nuclear-powered ballistic missile submarines; and gaining control of NATO's northern flank. At one point, approximately twenty-three nuclear-powered ballistic missile submarines were deployed, making it the most extensive dispersal of its kind ever detected. The Northern and Baltic Fleets conducted dispersals, defensive maneuvers, antisubmarine operations, simulated reactions to nuclear attacks, and offensive nuclear strikes. Following that exercise, the Baltic Fleet ships returned to their home waters and conducted amphibious operations with Warsaw Pact allies in the Bay of Lübeck.

That exercise had some global outliers. In the Caribbean, a Soviet Navy surface action group including the helicopter carrier *Leningrad*, a *Udaloy*-class destroyer, a Foxtrot-class diesel submarine, and a logistic ship deployed. *Leningrad* was the largest Soviet warship ever to operate in the Caribbean, conducting exercises for seven weeks, once within seventy-five miles of Louisiana. On the other side of the world, in the Gulf of Tonkin, the carrier *Minsk* and the Soviets' second Ivan Rogov-class amphibious warfare ship conducted the first Soviet Navy amphibious exercise ever on the Vietnamese coast.

One of four 28,000-ton Soviet *Kirov*-class nuclear-powered battle cruisers. *(Defense Intelligence Agency, U.S. Navy photograph by Mitsuo Shibata.)*

In the fall of 1985, the Soviets ran another large naval exercise in the northwestern Pacific, featuring control of the Kuril Islands and possibly Hokkaido, and to protect the Sea of Okhotsk nuclear-powered ballistic missile submarine bastion. It included antisubmarine warfare operations and an amphibious assault on the southern Kuril island of Etorofu (claimed by Japan but illegally occupied by the Soviet Union), possibly simulating an attack on Hokkaido. This was said to be the first Soviet amphibious landing exercise in the Pacific since 1978. The carrier *Novorossiysk* participated, as well as twenty other ships, Backfire bombers, and MiG-23 Flogger tactical aircraft.

We didn't know it at the time—and perhaps neither did they—but 1985 would prove to be the last year of the great Soviet Navy global exercise series. We saw a continued buildup of the Soviet fleets, especially in Soviet Far East bases, exemplified by one *Kirov*-class nuclear-powered battle cruiser joining the Pacific Fleet that autumn. The Soviets and Admiral Gorshkov had achieved their dream of global reach: at the end of 1985, the Soviets maintained about one hundred ships forward: three or four ships in the Caribbean; five to eight off West Africa; twenty-five to thirty in the South China Sea; forty-five to fifty in the Mediterranean; and twenty to twenty-five in the Indian Ocean.

This had been a massive effort and a historic achievement, but as Soviet economic difficulties worsened, it was clear that the Soviet Navy had reached the crest of its tide and that such naval growth could not continue or perhaps even be sustained. More ominously for them, the results of the new Reagan forward naval strategy were everywhere apparent. Year after year aggressive exercises using new tactics and technologies were taking place in the USSR's oceanic approaches. American shipyards were turning out an average of twenty-eight new naval combatants per year. The Soviets' hope of prevailing at sea if war came was fading rapidly into the northern mists.

Despite the restiveness of the Poles and others under Soviet occupation in Europe, the USSR continued to seek client states and influence even farther abroad. A month before the 1980 American election, it signed a Treaty of Friendship and Cooperation with Syria, tightening a long-standing relationship. A few months after President Reagan was sworn in, its Marxist Sandinista proxies in Nicaragua seized control of the government there, and the Soviets accordingly ramped up their military and economic aid. In the summer of 1981, the Soviets began deploying Il-38 May land-based anti-submarine warfare aircraft from airfields in Libya and Syria. These marked the first Soviet naval aircraft deployment from Mediterranean bases in ten years, since they were expelled from Egypt in 1972. Thereafter the Soviets would deploy Mays, Badgers, Cubs, and Classics from Syria, all looking for and gathering data on the U.S. Sixth Fleet and other NATO forces. In November 1981, Soviet Tu-95 Bear reconnaissance aircraft began working out of Cuban airfields, and the next year a four-ship Soviet Navy flotilla deployed to the Caribbean for more than two months—the longest stay in those waters by a Soviet squadron since 1978.

In 1983, the Soviets began periodic deployments of Tu-142 Bear F long-range ASW aircraft to the Caribbean; delivered SA-5 long-range SAM systems to Syria, the first non-Warsaw Pact country to receive these weapons; and began to deploy Badger C strike aircraft from the Cam Ranh Bay air base in Vietnam. In May 1984, their long-time client the North Korean Communist leader Kim Il-Sung visited Moscow. The Soviets promised him MiG-23 Floggers and received in return overflight rights for Soviet military air traffic to Vietnam.

In 1985, Soviet warships began visiting North Korean ports. Being allowed into North Korean harbors enabled them to bypass Japanese and South Korean choke points and improved Soviet access to—and potential ability to mine—the Tsushima Strait. In January of that year, a squadron of Soviet Flogger fighter-bombers arrived at Cam Ranh Bay, the Soviets' first fully developed overseas operating base, and they later started flying intercepts on U.S. reconnaissance aircraft over the South China Sea. Also in 1985, the Soviets delivered the first SA-5 long-range SAM systems to Libya—the only other non-Warsaw Pact country to receive these weapons besides Syria.

Soviet naval doctrine had long called for total Soviet naval control over waters adjacent to the Soviet homeland and for keeping U.S. and allied forces well beyond those waters. In Western parlance, these ocean areas were termed *sea control* and *sea denial* zones (*Sea control* means control to operate freely in a sea area with unquestioned ability to prevent hostile operations there. *Sea denial* means the capability to prevent enemy naval forces from controlling a sea area.) Over time it had been Soviet naval policy to so improve their capabilities as to extend the sea control zones farther and farther out to sea and to extend the sea denial zones out even farther. The result by the early 1980s was a Soviet operational concept of sea control and sea denial out to some two thousand kilometers from the Soviet Navy's bases. If the Soviets had been able to achieve that capability in time of war, not only would they have kept U.S. and NATO forces at a considerable distance from their country, but they would have totally severed U.S. transoceanic links to NATO's European flanks, including Norway, Denmark, Greece, and Turkey and to U.S. and allied forces stationed in Japan and Korea—a calamitous outcome totally unacceptable to the West.

Moreover, U.S. intelligence agencies had determined that the Soviets had no plans to stop where they were but intended to continue extending their sea control and sea denial zones out even farther over the next several years. Unless their plans were disturbed—and the U.S. Navy under President Reagan had every intention of disturbing them—the Soviets would eventually achieve the war-stopping capability of denying U.S. military support to much of Western Europe, including the entire United Kingdom and Iceland, as well as a huge swath of the North Pacific, encompassing all the waters surrounding western Alaska, the Aleutians, and Taiwan, and barring access to the Arctic.

Throughout the 1970s and into the first half of the '80s, the Soviets continued to develop the concepts, doctrine, tactics, and systems needed to execute this plan. For as long as they could, Soviet planners ignored the implications of the aggressive new U.S. and allied forward naval exercise program, which, if successful, would send all their intentions to Davy Jones's locker.

The Soviets weren't stupid. They figured out what we were up to and were mightily displeased. They began to worry that if they could not get massive budget increases to counter the NATO buildup and new forward strategy, they were going to be checkmated. Realizing this, they started to crank out incessant complaints in all their propaganda organs that the U.S. Navy—the glue that held the Western alliance together—was instead a threat to world peace. Here's a typical example (there were lots more): writing in the *Naval Digest* in May 1983, Capt. 1st Rank V. Strelkov contended that

> all of these "risky, unprincipled plans" of the American leadership to establish and maintain "command of the sea" are officially served up by the leadership of the Navy as a "new" U.S. naval strategy. This is especially clear during the multilevel exercises of NATO Unified Naval Forces that are conducted each year. Their main distinguishing feature is their anti-Soviet orientation, working through provocative missions. . . . The principal means of implementing the "new" naval strategy of intensifying the threat to the Soviet Union from the oceans and seas is activating the everyday activities of the American fleet directly off the Soviet coast. This is seen in the intensifi-

cation of reconnaissance, and moving the regions of exercises and maneuvers close to the Soviet coast.

The Soviets were particularly concerned with the attention we
were paying to them in the North Pacific. Soviet deputy foreign minister Mikhail Kapitsa told the Mongolian foreign minister, "We will
push on Japan. . . . The situation is difficult, militarization of East
Asia and the Pacific Ocean is under way. . . . The crux of the matter is that Imperialism is creating a global military coalition, which
has linked three fronts of forward deployment of the first strike:
Western Europe, Near East [and] the Indian Ocean, and East Asia
[and] the Pacific. . . . Japan is becoming a part of the global system of
Imperialism, it is being integrated."

The Soviets' concern deepened, and some of the leadership
started to panic. American shows of force to counter their own mis-
chief across the globe alarmed the top Soviet leadership and the
KGB. Soon the Soviets gave in to their worst bouts of paranoia and
began to think President Reagan was about to attack them. As one
study of the KGB described it,

> In his sometimes simplistic denunciations of the Soviet
> Union as the "evil empire," Reagan overlooked one dan-
> gerous Soviet vice: its tendency to paranoia in interpret-
> ing the West. Andropov saw the policy of the Reagan
> administration as based on an attempt to give the United
> States the power to deliver a successful nuclear first strike.
> During the early 1980s Reagan's evil-empire rhetoric
> combined with Moscow's paranoia about Western con-
> spiracies to produce a potentially lethal mixture. In May
> 1981 Brezhnev denounced Reagan's policies in a secret
> address to a major KGB conference in Moscow.

In May 1981, the Soviet leadership initiated Operation Ryan
(Raketno-Yadernoye-Napadeniye), an unprecedented KGB and

GRU effort to collect indicators of U.S. preparations for a nuclear first strike attack on the Soviet Union. The Soviets had become skittish at Reagan administration rhetoric and naval and air force deployments along Soviet borders. By 1983, following U.S. missile deployments to Europe, the announcement of President Reagan's Strategic Defense Initiative ("Star Wars"), the KAL-007 shoot-down, and the NATO exercise Able Archer, Ryan accelerated.

> In May 1981, Soviet KGB Chairman and future Communist Party Chairman Yuri Andropov announced to his KGB employees that Reagan was preparing for nuclear war. He told them that the possibility of a nuclear first strike by the U.S. was a real one. Andropov announced that, for the first time ever, the KGB and GRU (main intelligence directorate of the Soviet Armed Forces general staff) were ordered to work together. Collection of indicators continued well into 1984 and continued to fuel Soviet paranoia for three more years.

NEGOTIATING FROM STRENGTH . . . THEN NOT NEGOTIATING AT ALL

During the 1970s era of détente, the Soviets had achieved more than strategic nuclear weapons parity with the West. (By some counting measures it was a clear superiority.) They then embarked on achieving—and maintaining—theater nuclear weapons superiority in Europe and the Far East by introducing SS-20 intermediate-range ballistic missiles.

In September 1981, they agreed to sit down with the Reagan administration to negotiate force levels for intermediate-range missiles in Europe. They would be negotiating from strength, since their missiles had already been in place and operational for four years, while NATO's missiles—in response—were still being designed, argued over, and picketed against. Arms control negotiations with détente-seeking Americans had been a useful arrow in the Soviet strategic nuclear quiver for years, and they intended to use them to maintain their theater nuclear superiority as well. The talks would yield little and be terminated in 1983, not to be restarted until 1985. Their hearts were still not in it, and even the resumed talks would drag on for a while with no real end in sight.

In November 1983, with no possibility of an intermediate-range nuclear missile arms control agreement with the Soviets in sight, NATO deployed its own U.S. nuclear ground-launched cruise missiles (GLCMs) and nuclear intermediate-range ballistic missiles (Pershing II) at bases in various NATO European allied countries. That they had done so only in response to the Soviets' deployment of SS-20 missiles a half-dozen years before seemed lost on the Soviets.

The Communists were furious—especially since they had spent much time, effort, and money organizing and supporting "peace" movements all over Western Europe in a vain attempt to build pressure from within on NATO governments against hosting the Pershings and GLCMs. They walked out of ongoing arms control talks in a huff. Then in 1984, they began to deploy their submarines toward America's coasts in what they called an "analogous response" to the NATO action. The new Soviet deployments were by Delta-class nuclear-powered ballistic missile submarines and Echo II-class cruise missile submarines. They augmented the normal patrols of three older Yankees off the U.S. East Coast and two off the West Coast. Said the Soviets, "Corresponding Soviet weapons will be deployed, in view of that circumstance, in ocean areas and in seas. By their characteristics, these weapons will be commensurate with the threat which the United States missiles deployed in Europe are creating for us and our allies." They cited the U.S. Army and Air Force land-based missile deployments as the reason for these ship movements, not the U.S. Navy's actions at sea.

But the redeployment of Soviet submarines took place in the midst of the navy's own forward operations, and it responded. To the Office of Naval Intelligence (ONI) in particular, this was the "ultimate experience" for its operational intelligence professionals. They began to track with zeal the unprecedented numbers of Soviet nuclear-powered ballistic missile submarines that appeared off America's seaboards, as well as the Soviet nuclear-powered attack submarines that congregated off the U.S. Navy's own ballistic missile submarine bases at Kings Bay, Georgia, and Puget Sound, Washington. President Reagan backed them up: "The message to the Soviets is that if they want an arms race, the U.S. will not let them get ahead.... Their choice is to break their backs to keep up, or agree to reductions."

TOP: A Soviet Delta II-class ballistic missile submarine.
BOTTOM: An Echo II-class cruise missile submarine.
(U.S. Navy photographs.)

At first the Soviet Navy carried out its redeployments without much fanfare. Later, in May 1984, when the Soviets thought we weren't paying enough attention, they announced it publicly, hoping to scare U.S. public opinion. In this they would be disappointed.

"Analogous Response" deployments ended in 1986, as the Soviets

TOP:
A *Balzam*-class
armed spy ship.
MIDDLE:
An *Udaloy*-class
antisubmarine
destroyer.
BOTTOM:
A *Sovremenny*-
class guided-
missile destroyer.
*(Official U.S. Navy
photographs by Jeff
Hilton [Balzam and
Sovremenny] and
Jason R. Zalasky
[Udaloy]).*

decided to try other tacks. The military budget and economy that supported them faltered badly as a result of the collapsing price of oil and in the face of the policies of the Reagan administration and its allies on Capitol Hill and overseas.

The most noticeable thing the Soviets did in reaction to the Reagan navy's global forward pressure, however, was to continue their naval buildup program. The program's breathtaking momentum continued. It was difficult—indeed often impossible—for Western intelligence professionals and decision makers to believe in a panicky and fearful and retreating Russian bear at the same time that a considerable number and variety of sophisticated new and lethal weapons systems were being sent to sea.

An entire new generation of naval weaponry entered the Soviet inventory in the early-to-mid-1980s. In 1980, while Governor Reagan was running for president, the Soviet Navy had commissioned its first new *Sovremenny*-class antiship guided-missile destroyer. Fourteen would be commissioned between 1980 and 1991—a potent force, although suffering from engineering plant problems. At the same time, the Soviets commissioned their first of twelve *Udaloy*-class antisubmarine destroyers. They also introduced the first of four big *Balzam*-class armed spy ships into their fleet, and new Helix A shipborne antisubmarine warfare helicopters.

At the end of that year, they commissioned the first of four 28,000-ton *Kirov*-class heavy guided-missile nuclear-powered battle cruisers, and the first Kilo-class quiet diesel attack submarine. The *Kirov*'s SS-NX-19 antiship cruise missiles and SA-N-6 surface-to-air missiles made it a fearsome antiair warfare and offensive antisurface warfare platform. The Kilo gave the Soviets a very quiet blue-water submarine able subsequently to launch the latest supersonic SS-N-27 antiship cruise missile. The Soviets would commission more than a dozen Kilos throughout the 1980s, and provide several to Poland, Romania, India, and Algeria.

Major Soviet naval warships already had numbered well over five hundred in December 1980, at the start of the decade. These had included over 350 submarines (70 nuclear-powered ballistic missile submarines, 50 nuclear-powered cruise missile submarines, 20 conventional-powered cruise missile submarines, and 160 diesel electric attack submarines); two carriers; more than 120 cruisers, destroyers, and frigates; and some twenty large amphibious ships. Not included in these numbers were more than a thousand auxiliary submarines, small amphibious ships, small frigates and corvettes, mine warfare ships, patrol ships, missile boats, and auxiliaries.

As 1986 began, the U.S. government and the navy were continuing to press forward at sea with their global Maritime Strategy but had little reason to believe that their opponent was giving any ground. The Soviets had just completed another massive round of at-sea exercises, the Soviet fleet was expanding its reach into adjacent waters and buttressing its own as well as its nation's position in the far corners of the world, and a flood of sophisticated and deadly new ships and aircraft types were entering the Soviet naval order of battle.

The number of major Soviet combatants in 1985 now exceeded 560, according to the Office of Naval Intelligence. While the number of conventionally powered antiship missile submarines had declined somewhat, the count for their more lethal nuclear-powered undersea replacements had risen from 55 in 1980 to 77 in 1985. The number of large Soviet amphibious ships had gone up by a fifth during that same period. The fleet of large surface combatants—cruisers, destroyers, and frigates—had also grown, as had the number of carriers. And again these figures don't include the continuing deployment of more than a thousand auxiliary submarines, small amphibious ships, small frigates and corvettes, mine warfare ships, patrol ships, missile boats, and auxiliaries that also were included in the Soviet fleet. Moreover, the Soviet Navy's air fleet had grown from 1,430 active aircraft in 1980 to some 1,635 in 1985.

While some of their most important espionage sources had recently been choked off, Soviet intelligence offices were awash with purloined documents that had already bared some of the U.S.

Navy's most valuable secrets, and other avaricious spies were still very active. The U.S. Navy knew what it had to do to win, however, and was determined to press on. It had a winning strategy, which it continually practiced and refined, implemented by a potent, flexible, and balanced fleet fast approaching six hundred ships. It continued to work hard at neutralizing the clouds of tattletales, surveillance aircraft, strike bombers, and satellites that incessantly dogged it as it pursued its mission of bonding America's alliances together and holding her enemies at risk globally and far away from our shores.

What we did not yet fully realize was that our efforts were in fact achieving the desired effect and that our enemy's days were truly numbered.

Using data as of November 1985, the CIA's Office of Soviet Analysis concluded in a recently declassified secret analysis that the Soviets had perceived a marked U.S. increase in emphasis on sea power and an increased and rapidly developing threat to the Soviet Union from the sea. In the CIA's analysis, the Soviets viewed U.S. aircraft carriers as increasingly capable and survivable systems in the Norwegian Sea and northwestern Pacific. The Soviets were even more concerned, however, with U.S. Navy strategic nuclear capabilities, in which they included nuclear cruise missiles as well as nuclear ballistic missiles (Cruise missiles are essentially jet-powered drones with low altitude navigation and pinpoint accuracy with a range of about fifteen hundred miles. Ballistic missiles are rocket-powered missiles with ranges of more than six thousand miles and pinpoint accuracy. Both can be fired from submerged submarines.) CIA analysts judged that the Soviets' ground-centric leaders did not yet believe that combat at sea would be decisive in a conventional NATO–Warsaw Pact war, and they still saw the NATO maritime flanks as secondary to ground operations in Central Europe. They did, however, view U.S. Navy nuclear systems as able to be decisive in a nuclear war.

At a conference in Bodø, Norway, in August 2007, which I attended, Vitaly Tsygichko, one of Moscow's leading defense analysts, discussed how the Soviet Union responded to the new U.S. strategy:

In Moscow, the "Lehman strategy" was perceived as a serious offensive threat to the USSR. The Kremlin's view was that the U.S. Navy now challenged and directly threatened the Soviet Union's second-strike capability. At this time its capability to strike back in a massive nuclear showdown depended on its strategic submarines, and in the northern hemisphere the submarines at Kola played a very important role because of their ice-free access to the North Atlantic. The balance of terror was at risk if these submarines could be eliminated by the U.S. Navy in an early phase of the war. In this perspective the new American strategy left the Soviets with a strong feeling of being locked in. . . .

Countermeasures were initiated by the Soviets. As early as January 1985, the Soviet Navy launched Project 949, which became the Oscar-class SSBN submarine designed to attack U.S. carrier groups. At the same time, the Soviet Navy designated its own attack submarines to defend the strategic ones (SSBNs) in the Barents Sea.

Attack submarines (SSN) were designed to hunt and kill other subs and surface ships. They do not carry nuclear-armed ballistic missiles. Strategic missile submarines (SSBN) are designed to carry nuclear-armed intercontinental ballistic missiles as part of the strategic nuclear deterrent. Hence, Soviet air forces had to take care of wartime attack operations against allied sea lines of communication (SLOCs).

This momentous decision was forced on the Soviet General Staff, who opposed it because it would and did shift the balance immediately in the calculus of a land war in Central Europe by largely eliminating the heretofore serious threat of Soviet submarines cutting the wartime supply lines from the "arsenal of democracy."

However, the Reagan administration's comprehensive strategy, including the Maritime Strategy, [and "Star Wars,"] made the Soviet military realize the significant technological gap that was widening between the USSR and the U.S. Gradually the Soviet military acknowledged that there was no way to close it, an acknowledgement that had huge implications.

Soviet Naval Modernization in the 1980s

By 1981, the Soviet Air Force was introducing its new F-14-like MiG-31 Foxhound supersonic interceptor aircraft, to defend against attacking U.S. Navy, U.S. Air Force, and NATO aircraft and cruise missiles. U.S. satellites photographed the Soviet Navy's first Typhoon-class ice-capable nuclear-powered strategic ballistic missile sub deployed in the White Sea. Between 1981 and 1989, the Soviets introduced a half-dozen of these Arctic-capable submarines—the world's largest and the first designed specifically to operate under the ice. At about the same time, the Soviets commissioned their first Oscar I-class nuclear-powered cruise missile attack submarine, designed to attack U.S. Navy carriers from long ranges (up to three hundred nautical miles) with SS-N-19 Shipwreck cruise missiles. And early in 1982, the first of three new *Slava*-class antisurface warfare missile cruisers was commissioned in the Soviet Navy.

Later in the year, they commissioned their third *Kiev*-class carrier, *Novorossiysk*, and began construction of what they anticipated would one of their crown jewels—a new class of 65,000-ton multimission aircraft carriers, to be named *Riga* (later named *Leonid Brezhnev*, then *Tbilisi*, finally *Admiral Kuznetsov*). They would be the third generation of Soviet Navy "aviation ships," following the *Moskva* and *Kiev* classes. In 1981, the Soviets also laid down the first of seven quiet Delta IV-class nuclear-powered ballistic missile sub-

CLOCKWISE FROM TOP LEFT:
Typhoon-class under-ice nuclear-powered SSBN. (*Courtesy of the Bellona Foundation, Oslo, Norway.*)
Oscar I-class nuclear-powered cruise-missile attack submarine. (*U.S. Navy photograph.*)
MiG-31 Foxhound supersonic interceptor aircraft. (*Official U.S. Navy photograph, Combined Military Service Digital Photography files, National Archives.*)
Slava-class antisurface warfare missile cruiser. (*Official U.S. Navy photograph by Paul D. Goodrich, Combined Military Service Digital Photography files, National Archives.*)

marines and launched their second *Kirov*-class nuclear-powered battle cruiser, *Frunze*, building since 1978. *Frunze* would be followed the next year by the launching of the first two *Slava*-class cruisers, with a third launched the very next year.

Nineteen eighty-three saw even more new Soviet naval weaponry go to sea: the first of four Yankee Notch-class SSGNs, rebuilt from SALT-limited Yankee-class nuclear-powered ballistic missile submarines to include a new "notch-waisted" central section, their ballistic missiles replaced by sea-launched cruise missiles (SLCMs);

SS-N-21 cruise missiles, similar to U.S. Navy Tomahawk cruise missiles; and SS-N-19 Shipwreck antiship cruise missiles, to be launched by Oscar II-class nuclear subs, *Kirov* battle cruisers, and new Soviet Navy aircraft carriers. Also, a Delta II-class nuclear-powered ballistic missile submarine conducted the world's first under-ice ballistic missile launch, firing two submarine-launched ballistic missiles while operating under the ice pack. A third *Kirov*-class nuclear-powered battle cruiser—*Kalinin*—was laid down that year, as well as the fourth *Slava*. And the Soviets created "a unique Soviet naval infantry brigade on the Kola peninsula to repel amphibious landings—probably a direct response to the U.S. Navy's new forward maritime strategy."

In 1984, the Soviet Navy commissioned its first deep-diving Sierra-class titanium-hulled nuclear-powered attack submarine—another quiet Soviet Navy submarine type benefiting from the Walker family spy ring's espionage since 1967. They also introduced the new SS-N-21 Sampson submarine-launched antiship cruise missile into the fleet, to be carried on Akula-class and other submarines. Meanwhile the Soviet Air Force introduced the Il-76 Mainstay air control aircraft, similar to the U.S. Air Force AWACS, to control air defense interceptor fighter aircraft against attacking U.S. Navy, U.S. Air Force, and NATO aircraft. By the end of the year, the Soviet Navy had also commissioned its first Delta IV-class nuclear-powered ballistic missile submarine. (A total of seven would be commissioned

A 65,000-ton Soviet carrier now in the Chinese Navy. Another carrier of the class is currently operational in the Russian Navy. (*U.S. Navy photograph from "China's Aircraft Carrier Ambitions: Seeking Truth from Rumors," U.S. Naval War College Review 57, no. 1 [Winter 2004].*)

TOP:
Soviet Akula-
class nuclear
attack subma-
rine. *(Official U.S.
Navy photograph.)*
MIDDLE:
Mike-class
deep-diving
nuclear-powered
attack subma-
rine. *(Official U.S.
Navy photograph.)*
BOTTOM:
Sierra-class
nuclear-powered
attack submarine.
*(Royal Norwe-
gian Air Force.)*

by 1990.) The Delta IV carried the SS-N-23 strategic nuclear missile, the Soviets' first hard-target-capable sub-launched strategic missile. They also commissioned the first of seven quiet Akula-class nuclear attack submarines to be commissioned in the 1980s. Again, the continued Soviet focus on quieting was a result of data that the Walker spy family had passed to the Soviets since 1967. Finally, closing out the year, they commissioned their only Mike-class deep-diving nuclear-powered attack submarine.

Nineteen eighty-five brought even more new Soviet Navy systems into their fleet, greatly enhancing Soviet at-sea aviation capabilities: the Yak-38 M carrier-based strike-fighter—an upgraded Yak-38 Forger A—entered service with Soviet Naval Aviation. A total of fifty would be produced. And at the end of the year, the Soviets launched their new 65,000-ton conventionally powered *Riga*-class aircraft carrier, which they had been building since 1982. And yet another was under construction, to be launched later in the decade.

All of this was a continuation of Admiral Gorshkov's quest for naval superiority, and very much out of sync with the official Soviet policy pursuing arms control.

CHAPTER 5

Gaining Global Velocity, 1983–1985

By the beginning of 1983, the institutional machinery for taking the new Maritime Strategy from theory to reality was in place and operating smoothly. The navy strategy planning office (OP-603) was in place, and navy headquarters was staffed by some of the most experienced and well-educated operators in the navy; weapons programmers and budget experts were busily shaping navy weapons procurement and funding to conform to the new priorities drawn from the new strategy. The Strategic Studies Group of bright young operational commanders was in place at the Naval War College; the new fleet commanders were busily conforming their training programs, their war plans, and their classified fighting instructions to the new strategy, and the new tactical training and development groups were fully engaged.

The exercises of the two previous years, beginning with Ocean Venture '81, were being thoroughly analyzed by the Center for Naval Analyses and the operations analysts in each of the fleet headquarters. Lessons learned and new ideas were being incorporated into the global war games as well as being tested at sea and on the instrumented air warfare test ranges.

Our NATO naval allies were well integrated into the NATO staffs in Norfolk, Virginia, and were excitedly working with their own naval staffs to integrate into the new forward strategy, which they welcomed.

And the all-important new weapons were finally reaching the fleet and making operational the huge technology advantage over the Soviets that underlay the new strategy. One of the most important was the Aegis cruiser program, to build twenty-seven of these phased-array radar-equipped ships that could track hundreds and destroy dozens of incoming supersonic missiles or aircraft simultaneously. The first of these, USS *Ticonderoga*, was christened by Nancy Reagan and joined the fleet on January 22, 1983, with the others to follow at the rate of four per year.

In addition to the large international exercises, a new series of more focused exercises was initiated to test out and implement parts of the strategy. A good example was Arctic Sharem, to test out and develop antisubmarine tactics in the marginal ice zone (MIZ). A destroyer, three frigates, a U.S. Navy nuclear submarine, and a U.S. Coast Guard icebreaker operated in the marginal ice east of Greenland and north of Iceland and found it to be a dangerous and difficult area, which led to modifications of both equipment and tactics. Others were Cold Winter '83, demonstrating a Fourth Marine Amphibious Brigade assault in northern Norway; and Distant Drum '83, to demonstrate command of the seas in the Mediterranean by integrating three different carrier air wing operations with the *Eisenhower* and *Coral Sea* and the French Navy's *Foch*.

But we also increased the size and tempo of the really big exercises. In March and April, we conducted Fleetex '83, the first time since World War II that such a large force had been assembled in the North Pacific. Forty ships, three hundred aircraft, and three carrier battle groups—*Midway*, *Coral Sea*, and *Enterprise*—carried out long-range strike operations off the Aleutian Islands, keying off Royal Navy experiences in the Falklands War. The exercise tested U.S. Navy and U.S. Air Force's ability to coordinate strikes against Petropavlovsk and Alekseyevka in the Soviet Far East, as well as the navy's ability to detect and kill quiet Soviet Victor III-class subma-

Seventh Fleet operations in Fleetex '83 off the Aleutian Islands. *(U.S. Navy photograph by David B. Loveall, Department of Defense Imagery, Combined Military Service Digital Photography files, National Archives.)*

rines. It was also an opportunity to train and demonstrate to the Soviet observers our ability to operate in cold and stormy weather.

THE STRATEGIC DEFENSE INITIATIVE (SDI)

While Fleetex '83 was under way with the full knowledge of President Reagan, he chose that time to launch a major psychological warfare rocket. On March 23, in an "Address to the Nation on Defense and National Security," he proposed the creation of a Strategic Defense Initiative (SDI), dubbed "Star Wars" by its critics, to develop technology to intercept enemy nuclear missiles with beam weapons in earth orbit. The Soviets reacted negatively, even hysterically, fearing their own military obsolescence and the terrible economic stress it would bring to them if they tried to keep up. Many scientists doubted that "Star Wars" could be done, and even if it could, they thought it would take decades to develop and would be staggeringly expensive. The idea had started as part of Reagan's psychological warfare program, but it gradually took on a life of its own. The Soviet military, however, could not take the chance that it would not work and immediately demanded huge budget increases to launch its own SDI program.

In June, three large exercises began in sequence; United Effort '83, followed by Ocean Safari '83, and then Magic Sword '83, together involving ninety ships from ten nations practicing antisubmarine, antiair, and long-range carrier air strikes into the United Kingdom, France, and Germany—the longest being a thousand nautical miles.

Only one U.S. Navy carrier participated, *John F. Kennedy*, but three allied carriers did: the Royal Navy carriers HMS *Illustrious* and *Hermes*, and the French Navy carrier *Foch*. Turning the public relations heat up on the Soviets, we encouraged as many of our senior navy leaders to testify publicly to explain the purpose of the new strategy in blunt, nonbureaucratic terms.

On March 10, 1983, the Atlantic commander Adm. Wesley McDonald, testified to Congress in open session:

> Quickly establishing military superiority is of utmost importance. Early in any conflict, we must put at risk as much of the Soviet naval forces as possible. The majority of Soviet forces must be contained. This can be accomplished by offensive actions that keep the Soviet Navy focused on the threats to their own forces in the Norwegian and Barents Seas. . . . We must be able to carry the fight to the enemy—to deny him sanctuaries, to threaten key elements of his war fighting strategy—instead of reacting to his actions.

Meanwhile back at the Pentagon the senior executive committee, then called the Defense Resources Board, was meeting daily to put together the next year's defense budget. The newly confirmed deputy defense secretary, Paul Thayer, led an assault on the navy strategy and programs, proposing to transfer large sums from the navy and marines to the army. This would mean canceling one aircraft carrier and many other warships, essentially returning the navy to the Carter program. He was, of course, energetically supported by the permanent defense bureaucrats, who had essentially written the Carter program. Thayer, former head of one of the army's largest contractors, LTV Corp., had been in the job for only a short time and could be excused for not understanding how Washington works, so I was happy to take on the task of educating him. Our boss, Cap Weinberger, was on a long trip, and after checking with him, I went to the White House.

A few days later on August 2, in a letter to Weinberger, who had approved it in draft, President Reagan strongly endorsed U.S. naval superiority, including the firm requirement for fifteen carriers and six hundred ships. Reagan wrote: "We . . . dedicate ourselves to achieving the requisite naval superiority we need today, by building a fifteen carrier, 600 ship Navy."

A chastened Thayer did not challenge the navy again, but our personal relations were at best frosty until years later.

The year 1984 continued and slightly increased the pace of our global exercises, as lessons learned were shared throughout the U.S. and allied fleets and air forces. They included Team Spirit and Sojex in the northwestern Pacific, Cold Winter in Norway, National Week XXXIII and Dasix in the eastern Mediterranean, Fleetex '84 in the northwestern Pacific, and Sea Wind in the eastern Mediterranean.

In August 1984, in a strategic move planned by Secretaries Shultz and Weinberger and approved by the president, I led a delegation to Beijing to negotiate a formal agreement of cooperation between our two navies and air forces. During several days of negotiations, we agreed in principle to periodic reciprocal port visits, sale to China of modern antisubmarine weapons concentrating on modernizing their destroyers with sonars, and antisubmarine Mark 46 torpedoes and training to enable them to deal effectively with Soviet submarines. We also agreed in principle to modernize their air force and navy fighter planes up to an F-16 standard, to cope with state-of-the-art Soviet fighters and bombers. We established working groups to negotiate details and set a deadline for Adm. Liu Hua Qing, a savvy Long March veteran and chief of the Chinese Navy, to come to Key West early in 1985 to formally sign these agreements. Needless to say, the Soviet leaders viewed this event as disastrous.

Some Cassandras in the administration worried that Reagan continued to sound too aggressive and anti-Soviet as he campaigned for reelection. His forward strategy was so challenging to the Soviets that they were already making every effort to stop his reelection in

Reagan's policy to help China modernize its navy to deal with the Soviet threat is kicked off by my official visit hosted by Adm. Liu Hua Qing, head of the People's Liberation Army Navy. *(U.S. Navy photograph.)*

1984. As we have seen from the Soviet efforts in the U.S. election of 1976, cited earlier, Putin's alleged efforts in the U.S. election of 2016 election are not unprecedented.

On April 12, 1982, Yuri Andropov, the chairman of the K.G.B., ordered foreign-intelligence operatives to carry out "active measures"—*aktivniye meropriyatiya*—against the reëlection campaign of President Ronald Reagan. Unlike classic espionage, which involves the collection of foreign secrets, active measures aim at influencing events—at undermining a rival power with forgeries, front groups, and countless other techniques honed during the Cold War. The Soviet leadership considered Reagan an implacable militarist. According to extensive notes made by Vasili Mitrokhin, a high-ranking K.G.B. officer and archivist who later defected to Great Britain, Soviet intelligence tried to infiltrate the headquarters of the Republican and Democratic National Committees, popularize the slogan "Reagan Means War!," and discredit the President as a corrupt servant of the military-industrial complex. The effort had no evident effect. Reagan won forty-nine of fifty states.

But on November 6, he was overwhelmingly reelected by an even more lopsided landslide vote, defeating Jimmy Carter's vice president, Walter Mondale. Republicans retained control of the Senate and gained seats in the House. Reagan won forty-nine of fifty states, and 58 percent of the popular vote, and received 525 electoral votes to ten for Mondale. It was the largest electoral vote landslide in U.S. history. Both the Soviet Union and the White House saw it as a strong public endorsement of Reagan administration policies and a very clear mandate from the American people.

We finished up 1984 with a massive three-phase exercise involving the entire Pacific Fleet. It began off southern California and surged to the northwestern Pacific. Ninety-one ships, three hundred aircraft, and five carrier battle groups participated: *Vinson*, *Enterprise*, *Constellation*, *Midway*, and *Independence*. Three significant multicarrier battle group operations were conducted: two battle groups, *Vinson* and *Constellation*, in the mid-Pacific; two battle groups, *Midway* and *Enterprise*, in the South China Sea; and a Seventh Fleet three-carrier battle force, *Midway*, *Vinson*, and *Enterprise*, in the Philippine Sea. Among many phases targeted at the Soviets was a successful defeat of a multiwave regimental-size Backfire raid.

Lt. David Winkler, the senior naval officer in charge of the civilian-manned oiler USNS *Navasota* during the exercise, had an amusing experience:

[We] had a Soviet minesweeper alongside and I stood on the Signal Bridge with my Canon AE-1 waving to attract the CO to snap his picture. I was wearing a green reefer and black beany and these guys were in sable coats! So he

Rough seas in the north Pacific. *Midway* taking green water over the bow. *(U.S. Navy photograph, National Archives. DN-ST-92-04057.)*

Iowa leads its battle group, the *Coral Sea* on the left and the *Saratoga* on the right. *(U.S. Navy photograph, National Archives. DN-SC-90-11747.)*

and his XO [second in command] are waving and then he looks at the waterline and sees an open porthole where I stationed my Snoopy team, which was snapping [high-resolution pictures of the new Soviet minesweeping technology], and the CO turns and points at the offending camera, slugs his XO, waves his fist at me, and they scramble to put covers on topside gear and haul out of there.

Meanwhile Cmdr. Kenneth McGruther, who had been part of our strategy team in the Pentagon and at Newport, was now back at sea in command of *Knox*, a fast frigate that participated in the exercise. His log, written during the exercise, gives a good sense of the action. According to the log for December 3:

The U.S. frigate *Knox* off Vladivostok during Kennel Freelance. *(Official U.S. Navy photograph, National Archives.)*

- Back with the battle force again it was business as usual: Hurry up and wait.
- Refueled but had a rig break (rough seas) when transferring stores so have to go back again.
- Then we headed back to the carrier in radar-silent mode and joined at 1250, we were tasked to:
- Relieve Joseph Strauss (DDG16) as counter-tattletail [a Soviet spy or surveillance ship] against the Soviet Kashin DDG; he is capable of 38 kts, we of 27.5 but it's my job to out-maneuver him to keep him away from the battle group.
- Right now it is 2100 and so far so good: Typically Russian, he made 2 blatant efforts to run past—once trying to outrun us and a 2nd by bearing in on us to within 200 yds.
- But I had right of way, held course, and blew 5 shorts and he turned away.
- A couple more efforts to swing around astern of us have also come to naught and now it appears he has settled down for the night.
- No rest for the weary, I'll be up from 2300 to 0300, and still tired from fighting last night's water problems and being challenged by our own ships on the way in, then silent approach to underway replenishment.
- What the heck, I haven't slept the night through since KF (Kennel Freelance) started so why start now?
- Still, all in all it is fun, and I am glad they gave us a chance to operate once we are back into the battle group.

Log notes for December 4:

- Journey's end. Last night out after a taxing month. I am exhausted, but it's the good feeling that you went flat out and did a hard and important job well.
- Not only was Kennel Freelance super, but we came back to the BG and acted as if we'd been here all along—underway replenishments, counter-tattle tailing, station-keeping, plane-guarding.

- The only thing missing would be for *Knox* to find the Foxtrot [Russian sub that reportedly is stalking the exercise] tonight.
- Today we even out-maneuvered the *Kashin* DDG to the point that he went DIW [dead in the water] not once but three times. I loved it—full rudder turns at 27 kts, cutting close across the carrier's bow. He could neither out-run nor out-ship handle me: I have a good ship under me.
- I am so tired I'm not even sure I can sleep tonight. Ha!

As 1985 began, an editorial cleared by senior Soviet officials in the January–March issue of *Far Eastern Affairs* (Moscow) accurately worried that "in fact the aim is to attach China to the U.S. Asian policy, which is aimed at encircling the Soviet Union and other socialist countries from the Eastern flank."

In his State of the Union address to Congress on February 6, 1985, President Reagan laid out his policy of confronting Soviet-supported governments throughout the world, including providing overt and covert support for anti-Communist regular and irregular military forces, to impose further costs on the Soviet Union for its aggressive activities. Charles Krauthammer, in one of his syndicated columns, first used the term *Reagan Doctrine* to characterize the policy. The term stuck.

In April, we held our annual Team Spirit exercise with our South Korean allies. These had been going on since 1976, and by now were the free world's largest military exercise, with over two hundred thousand personnel participating. But this one would be different. Changing the rules, Rear Adm. Mike McCaffree conducted the first nighttime Team Spirit amphibious landing. His concept was a high-speed nighttime fifteen-knot launch by LST amphibious ships of fifty-three armored landing craft off the coast of Pohang, South Korea. The use of "quiet landing procedures" meant minimal use of radios.

For years I had chafed at the set-piece way in which our navy and marine corps conducted amphibious exercises. They lacked realism. They seemingly placed a greater premium on what I would call showmanship, conducting landings from nearly stationary amphibious ships during daylight hours before crowds of VIPs in viewing stands. This was not even as challenging as many of our World War II amphibious operations. It had long been my belief that our navy should train as we would fight by *injecting deception and speed and using the cover of darkness in amphibious exercises*. I intended that I would do as much as I could to incorporate these qualities in the amphibious operations for which my command would be responsible during my tenure.

The Soviets howled.

Moscow appeared to view *Team Spirit* as one part of a growing threat to the Soviet Union and to pro-Soviet states in Asia. The Soviets stated that if *Team Spirit* incited a military incident with North Korea, the incident would likely develop into a full-scale war, and although they were not explicit about committing forces to such a war, they indicated that they would protect their security interests and those of their allies.

GORBACHEV, GLASNOST, AND PERESTROIKA

On March 13, 1985, Mikhail Gorbachev became general secretary of the Communist Party of the Soviet Union, following the death of Konstantin Chernenko (in office for only thirteen months), continuing the turmoil in the Soviet government. (At fifty-four, Gorbachev was young and healthy, unlikely to die soon.) Faced with Soviet political and economic stagnation, he advocated and began to implement policy reforms based on perestroika (restructuring) and glasnost (openness). Glasnost meant giving publicity to problems, issues, and proposed solutions to generate support for perestroika, which meant restructuring the government bureaucracy and rebuilding the economy and industry.

In his first dramatic foreign policy move, he suspended deployment of Soviet SS-20 intermediate-range nuclear ballistic missiles in Warsaw Pact states. He then began to cut back on resources to the Soviet Armed Forces, including the navy. This was the beginning of a major effort to lower U.S. and global perceptions of the Soviet threat through unilateral force reductions, a series of arms control initiatives, and an aggressive campaign promoting a new Soviet "defensive" doctrine. He also tried to strengthen Soviet relationships and weaken U.S. relations with China, South Korea, and Japan.

Gorbachev also dumped Andrei Gromyko, "Mr. No," as his foreign minister, replacing him with the less obdurate and more open-minded Eduard Shevardnadze.

President Reagan watched these moves closely and was optimistic that his strategy was beginning to succeed and to bring close the possibility of substantive negotiations. He believed that Gorbachev was really someone different. Nevertheless he was not yet convinced that the Soviet drive for hegemony was in fact over. The success of the president's defense buildup of his first term had enabled him to flatten out the U.S. defense budget in his second term, and there was a concern that with so many Soviet ships and aircraft already funded and under construction, Gorbachev was simply portraying the reduced funding as a policy change when it was not. President Reagan wanted to maintain the pressure of the forward strategy. The navy and marines were only too happy to comply.

From March 15 to 22, 1985, another Cold Winter exercise was carried out 150 miles north of the Arctic Circle. This time, in addition to the Fourth Marine Amphibious Brigade, it included Norwegian, British, Canadian, and Dutch troops.

Marine elements were airlifted into central Norway, and prepositioned equipment was transported to northern Norway within five days. Combined US/Norwegian infantry, artillery, and helicopter training took place, and all infantry forces were on skis, supported by helicopters, prepositioned artillery, and snow vehicles. The exercise culminated with the marine/Norwegian force defeating an attack by a British/Netherlands amphibious force.

This exercise . . . demonstrated a level of training and mobility comparable to that displayed by the Finnish Army in their war against the Russians in 1939.

The U.S. Navy, meanwhile, was conducting an unprecedented Surgex exercise, a "submarine flush" of forty-four nuclear attack submarines deploying all at once from East Coast ports into the North Atlantic with full weapons loads, in a short (twenty-four hours)-

Marines in Norway during the Cold Winter exercise. (*U.S. Navy photograph, National Archives.*)

The U.S. nuclear-powered cruiser *Mississippi* during Operation
Snap Lock. *(Courtesy of the Naval History and Heritage Command.)*

notice readiness exercise. TASS obligingly reported this evolution
publicly in September 1985.

I helped them to understand what the exercise was all about on
May 13, when I was quoted as saying that U.S. attack subs would
attack Soviet missile subs "in the first five minutes of the war."

In May and June, one of our nuclear-powered cruisers, *Mississippi*, deployed on twenty hours' notice to Norwegian and Barents
Seas for Operation Snap Lock in response to the Soviet Navy's Summerex '85 exercise, to conduct surveillance ops and simulated strikes
against the NATO Striking Fleet. *Mississippi* greatly complicated the
Soviet exercise by operating in the middle of it for seven weeks without logistics support.

Aggressive navy operations like this were approved at the White
House but were not publicized because we knew the media would
accuse the navy and administration of being reckless and irresponsi-

ble. What they did not know, of course, was that we were reading the Soviets' mail and knew exactly what their rules of engagement were and how they would react. We never crossed that line.

DR. ROBERT BALLARD, "BOTTOM GUN"

Bob Ballard was the senior oceanographer at Woods Hole Oceanographic Institute working with very highly classified programs for the navy involving our deep-diving nuclear submarine, the *NR-1*, and our deep submersible *Alvin*. He was also a commander in the Naval Reserve. He was to lead a secret mission in northern latitudes during the summer of 1985. There was to be a practice mission early in the year in the deep ocean trench off St. Croix. At his invitation, I went with him in the tiny cockpit of *Alvin* to understand more about the complexity of the mission. The descent of five thousand feet into the depths and the return took a total of ten hours, during which Bob, who truly loves his work, never stopped talking. After indoctrinating me in the details of the mission, he moved smoothly into a new sales pitch.

He wanted approval to take as long as two weeks during the trip back to the United States to look for the *Titanic*. He had made previous expeditions to search without success, but now with our classified sonar and robotic equipment, he was sure he could find it and then video the ship inside and out. Further, he wanted us to allow him to release all the footage in a major PR extravaganza. Now Bob was privy to some of the most sensitive secrets in the navy underwater world and to the Reagan strategy. He knew of the special committee overseeing psychological warfare and argued that revealing our ability to operate at depths of more than two miles and making public such fabulous footage to a global audience would drive the Soviets' paranoia just as "Star Wars" was doing. Finally to shut him up and redirect his attention to the weird monsters in the floodlights outside the porthole, I told him that I would recommend approval to Weinberger and the president.

Dr. Robert Ballard is officially named the navy's "Bottom Gun." *(U.S. Navy photograph by Harold J. Gerwein.)*

On the last day of the allotted two weeks, Bob found *Titanic*. We gave him a few more days for video filming, and the rest is well known. At the press conference announcing the discovery back in Washington at the National Geographic Society, I formally designated him the navy's "Bottom Gun." And he was quite right; it did indeed cause much vexation in the Kremlin.

To distract and fuel the Soviets' paranoia while Ballard was at work, we arranged to have two of our nuclear attack subs, *Queenfish* and *Aspro*, surface together at the North Pole. Lest the lesson be lost on the Soviets, we simultaneously commissioned the *Providence*, the first of thirty-one nuclear-powered attack subs equipped to launch the fifteen-hundred-mile-range Tomahawk cruise missile, able to carry a nuclear or conventional warhead, from the North Pole or anywhere else.

OCEAN SAFARI '85

With four years of refinement and innovation after Ocean Venture '81, the Norwegian Sea again began to swell with warships on August

24 as Ocean Safari '85 began a month of naval operations. A rising tide of new technology and weapons systems was arriving in the fleet, along with interesting findings from previous years' exercises, and war games. New tactical ideas were coming from the Newport Strategic Studies Group, and the new Striking Fleet commander, Vice Adm. Hank Mustin, promised to provide the Soviet Navy with many surprises.

Ten NATO nations provided 157 ships, including the American carriers *Eisenhower*, *America*, and *Saratoga*, and the Royal Navy jump jet carrier HMS *Illustrious*. For the first time, the battleship *Iowa* was used, as well as the new Aegis cruisers *Ticonderoga* and *Yorktown*. Also for the first time, the large helicopter carrier *Nassau* participated with an air wing including U.S. Marine AV-8A Harrier vertical take-off and landing fighter-bombers.

Mustin reoriented the exercise to focus on early forward deployment and operations in the Norwegian Sea to defend Norway from Soviet attack, including a U.S. Marine Corps landing. This was also to be the first testing of Norwegian fjords as "haven" and "radar shadowing" concepts with *America* flying its full air wing in Vestfjord. "I got a hold of the best new intel I could. I discovered that the Soviet Naval Aviation bombers and fighters couldn't get close enough to target our carriers without being within range of USN surface combatant antiair systems, which could take them down (not to mention F-14 interceptors). I demonstrated that this would work. The Norwegians were delighted."

Mustin discovered that Soviet air-to-surface antiship missiles wouldn't work if targets were in fjords. Like most naval officers, he and Lyons were deeply interested and well read in history. Both admirals had studied the use of the fjords in World War II, where the Germans successfully protected navy ships like *Tirpitz* from determined British and Allied attack throughout the war.

Mustin made imaginative use of the geography of Norway's Vestfjord to provide radar masking for *America*. The fjord was seventy miles long, very deep, with vertical mountains up to three

America operating in Vestfjord during Ocean Safari
'85. *(Official U.S. Navy photograph by John Meore.)*

thousand feet along both shores. The operational concept involved dashing from the North Atlantic at flank speed using full cover and deception until well into the fjord after an attack sub had fully cleared it of any Soviet subs. Captor mines would then seal off the fjord entrance, and the carrier would begin strike operations shielded from detection or attack by staying in the radar shadow of the high mountains. We had successfully tried out such tactics in previous years in the Aegean Sea and other exercises, but never in such confined space and terrible weather. The accepted wisdom in the fleet had been that such operations were much too confining and dangerous to be effective.

Ticonderoga used and built on her 1984 eastern Mediterranean experience off Lebanon in tracking targets over land. *Iowa* fired full broadsides in western approaches to the English Channel giving its Soviet "tattletail" quite a show. While *America* was operating above the Arctic Circle, her airwing commander, Captain Jay Johnson (later CNO) launched a reconnaissance mission and located a Soviet *Kynda*-class cruiser with a *Krivak*-class frigate in the English Channel eight hundred miles away despite poor visibility.

As luck would have it, this time *America*'s skipper Richard "Sweet Pea" Allen was a good friend whom I had flown with in years past. He had been a role model because like me "Sweet Pea" was both a pilot and a rated Intruder bombardier-navigator. I flew aboard on September 19, 1985, and while we were in the fjord, I spent a lot of time with him on the bridge. According to my log, I flew two operational strike missions, one of 2.1 hours and one of 2.5 hours, and I remember them well. The first hop we catapulted off in the very early morning darkness, with the dawn just emerging, carrying four unarmed laser-guided bombs. Staying at one thousand feet above the terrain until the visibility improved, we then descended and flew nap of the earth (nap-of-the-earth low-level high-speed flight uses terrain to prevent detection of the attacking jet by enemy radar) eastbound through the

The battleship *Iowa* firing a broadside during Ocean Safari '85. (*U.S. Navy photograph.*)

snow-covered mountains at about one hundred feet above ground level at about 450 knots toward the Swedish border.

About thirty minutes into the flight, we saw the "enemy" fighters, in this case Norwegian Air Force F-16s guided by a NATO AWACS radar control aircraft that were hunting us. They passed about ten thousand feet above us and never got a sniff. We were flying so low that their radars could not detect us against the mountain ground clutter. Soviet fighters had far less capability. We proceeded on to our designated target, which in actual combat would have been inside the Soviet Union. After a simulated attack, we popped up into the overcast with transponder on to make sure the Soviets saw us. Then with transponder off, we headed back toward *America*, dealing with some rather severe icing along the way, which is typical in those latitudes even in late summer.

The second hop was a similar mission, except we never saw the opposing fighters although they were aloft trying to find us. After hitting the target on time, we were vectored out to sea by our E-2C controller to do some hunting on our own. With so many Soviet surface combatants looking for the carrier, we soon found a *Kara*-class cruiser and set up to run mock attacks on her. We practiced several run-in tactics, and the *Kara*'s radars were fully exercised. They did not show us their best tricks, and we reserved our best countermeasures as well, but it was invaluable training for both sides.

We then were directed to proceed to "marshal," a layered holding pattern astern of the carrier organized to set each different aircraft up to "push" toward the carrier at a precise time to land in a tight sequence, one right after the other, only seconds apart. We were held in marshal for a while in thick clouds while *America* proceeded through a snow squall, until we finally got a push time and proceeded toward the carrier. When we broke out of the goo and saw the carrier, we were in for a shock, for *America* was well into the fjord, and it looked like it was proceeding along a thousand-foot cliff. At about two miles out, we saw the "ball," the Fresnel light that moves up or down showing the correct glide path. We realized to our relief that the carrier was nearly a quarter mile away from the cliffs and we proceeded to an okay three-wire (perfect arrested landing).

Of course, the exercise, as usual, garnered considerable Soviet attention: Bears, Badgers, Cubs, Mays, and Coots flew 180 sorties in *America*'s vicinity. The Soviets denounced the exercise publicly as "clearly provocative in nature." Mustin crowed that the "Soviets could not locate the *America* at sea, nor could the great professional aviators of the Royal Air Force." But we had no trouble locating them. Later Soviet TV quoted Mustin as saying, "The task dictated by naval strategy lies in projecting forces to forward positions and, if need be, waging combat on the territory of the enemy, that is on the territory of Warsaw Pact countries."

Meanwhile early in 1985, President Reagan appointed Mustin's mentor, now four-star Adm. Ace Lyons, to commander in chief of the Pacific Fleet. As soon as he took command, Lyons did what he had done four years previously as a new commander of the NATO Striking Fleet. He immediately launched into planning a furious succession of exercises, often unprecedented or deviating from their predecessors, especially in their predictability. By this time, however, Pacific Fleet exercises had already become more aggressive, more forward, more innovative, and less predictable. Under Lyons, these characteristics all intensified. He aggressively tested and demonstrated the Maritime Strategy forward, including into the Bering Sea, the Sea of Okhotsk, and the waters off Vladivostok and Petropavlovsk.

He intended them to be shows of force and signals of serious intent as much as training evolutions. His exercises were designed to elicit Soviet responses—and he got them. He meant to demonstrate to the Soviets that the United States and NATO were going to "pin their ears back," at sea and from the sea, if they tried anything. Lyons's skill with electronic warfare was practiced extensively and very successfully, including cover, deception, and emissions control (EMCON), to simulate and hide carriers from Soviet satellite surveillance. Lyons required the full integration of U.S. Air Force,

A Pioneer UAV targeting drone launching from the battleship *Missouri*. *(U.S. Navy photograph.)*

Coast Guard, and Army in these navy exercises, especially USAF F-
15 interceptors, AWACs radar surveillance aircraft, KC-10 tankers,
and B-52 bombers.

Lyons used the Third Fleet as his primary force for North Pacific
operations and exercises, making it more like the Second Fleet in the
Atlantic. The Seventh Fleet was busy supporting real-world contingencies and presence operations in the Indian Ocean and the western Pacific, and its commander spent a great deal of his time as a
naval diplomat routinely sailing from port to port on his flagship and
conferring with regional leaders.

Back in the Atlantic, we had another little escalatory surprise
for the Soviets. During September and October 1985, we took an
entirely new approach to the annual NATO Baltops exercise in the
Baltic Sea. In addition to the substantial European navies' partici-

pation, we included a six-ship surface action group (SAG), including the battleship *Iowa*, the new Aegis cruiser *Ticonderoga*, three frigates, and an oiler in support. This was an unprecedented introduction of an American capital ship—armed with long-range cruise missiles— and a powerful new Aegis antiair capability—into the Baltic Sea. The Soviets saw this as a really big deal and denounced the exercise as "provocative," which, of course, we intended it to be.

The year ended with a dramatic development in the Soviet Union. On December 8, 1985, President Gorbachev sent ashore Admiral of the Fleet Sergei Gorshkov and replaced him with Admiral of the Fleet Vladimir Chernavin as deputy minister of defense and commander in chief of the Soviet Navy. (Admiral Gorshkov had headed the Soviet Navy since 1956—a month shy of thirty years.) The Soviet Navy thus lost its most highly influential and articulate spokesman for independent and offensive naval operations.

CHAPTER 6

The Beginning of the End

Northern Wedding, 1986

THE MOST DELICATE period of the Reagan naval strategy began in 1986. The steady and increasing pressure from the exercises and operations had demonstrated beyond a doubt to both sides that the Soviet forces could neither cope with nor keep up with the growing and modernizing NATO and American navies. The "correlation of forces" had been reversed, and American intelligence knew that the Soviet leadership knew it. The removal of Admiral Gorshkov, the most unrelenting and credible advocate of matching the United States and never accepting American naval superiority, confirmed that Gorbachev was in charge and knew that the ideology of Communist victory over capitalism was a fantasy.

The opportunity for Reagan diplomacy was at hand. The challenge was to continue to deploy and demonstrate the growing strength in ships, aircraft, missiles, tanks, and technology that the Reagan buildup had funded and that were now flowing into the forces in huge numbers, without humiliating the Soviet military and thus risking a coup. We had to tamp down the triumphalism that was everywhere visible in all levels of the U.S. Armed Forces. For the first time in twenty years, sailors were sure that they could win a war at sea with the Soviets.

We had planned to start the year off with a jolt when on New Year's Day 1986 we conducted our first modest exercise with the Chinese Navy in the South China Sea. But we decided to make no announcement that would aggravate the Soviets. We knew that they would be observing it firsthand. We also played it very low key when Admiral Watkins paid a formal visit to China later in the spring, the first chief of naval operations ever to do so.

We decided to both set the tone and yet reinforce to the public our confidence in achieving maritime supremacy by publishing an authoritative unclassified version of the Maritime Strategy as a special supplement to the *U.S. Naval Institute Proceedings*, with the commandant of the marine corps, Gen. P. X. Kelley, CNO Admiral Watkins, and I all providing detailed essays. (In an amusing illustration of the arrogance of the bureaucracy, even though I had cleared the insert with Secretary Weinberger, I received a stern letter from a senior defense bureaucrat rebuking me for not seeking the bureaucracy's approval for the publication.)

In Admiral Watkins' essay, he made clear that:

> I also have confidence in the maritime strategy because we test it in exercises . . . In 1984, for example, the navy participated in 106 major exercises, 55 of which involved our allies. Such exercises are an integral part of our deterrent strategy and a major source of my confidence that, should deterrence fail, maritime forces will have the skill, capability, and experience to prevail.

In a sidebar article on naval reform, he declared:

> For too many years, our fleet exercises suffered from a lack of realism and focus, and our routine operations seemed to be lacking in purpose. But the Maritime Strategy now forms a framework for planning realistic, purposeful exercises, and provides a strategic perspective for daily fleet

operations in pursuit of deterrence. Largely as a result of the Maritime Strategy, we have begun emphasizing exercises with multiple carrier battle forces, which would be required in a major war. We have increased our exercises in the Northern Pacific and Norwegian Sea, to build our base of experience in these key areas. We have begun exercising our submarines in Arctic waters, where they might be called upon to execute portions of the Maritime Strategy.

General Kelley and Major Hugh K. O'Donnell, in their essay on the amphibious warfare strategy, noted that "where once Marine participation in NATO training exercises was only thinly tolerated, we now have Marine air-ground task forces (MAGTFs) exercising in Norway, Denmark, Italy, and Turkey, on a regular basis."

In my essay on "The 600-Ship Navy," I stated:

We also train as we intend to fight. A full-scale general war at sea would rarely find a carrier battle group operating alone. So we train often in multiple carrier battle forces in such exercises as *Fleetex*, *Readex*, and NATO exercises, like *Northern Wedding*, which we conduct in the North Atlantic and the Norwegian Sea. . . .

Sea-based air of [the Sixth Fleet] can be added to [NATO'S land based air forces] to improve air superiority and to strike targets deep in Warsaw Pact territory. . . . The sea control forces . . . will be used to defeat the Soviet Mediterranean Fleet. This is ideally an offensive task, one in which the enemy is sought out and destroyed, rather than countered by defending convoys, harbors and choke points along the routes of supply and reinforcement.

That same week NATO Striking Fleet commander Vice Adm. Hank Mustin gave an interview to *Newsweek*, published on February 3, 1986: "We have to be a threat to [the Soviet Navy] in their own backyard. We have to tell them: It's a good thing you have those forces to defend your country, cause you're gonna need them. You're going to be so busy keeping us out of the Kola that if you've got enough forces left over to do something else, be my guest."

From the beginning of 1986, we saw a remarkable shift in Soviet strategy. Their naval operations began to highlight defensive operations more and to move closer to home. They reduced deployments and the number of exercise sea days and changed their operating patterns. This was a significant decline from the level of activity in 1983–85, from 456 operating sea days in 1985 to 207 in 1986.

That major policy change was accompanied by an equally dramatic diplomatic offensive. On March 26 came the opening salvo of Soviet leader Gorbachev's naval arms control propaganda campaign. Gorbachev's speech condemned U.S. Navy attacks on Libyan forces and proposed U.S.-USSR talks to withdraw Soviet and U.S. naval forces from the Mediterranean. Soviet naval arms control proposals would come thick and fast for the remainder of the decade, accurately portraying the U.S. Navy as an offensive force.

As the year unfolded, seriously bad news for Gorbachev piled up. On April 26, a disastrous and lethal nuclear power plant disaster occurred at Chernobyl in the Ukraine. The accident contaminated Northern Ukraine and Southeastern Belarus, reminding Gorbachev of the fundamental incompetence, callousness, and inefficiency of the Soviet socialist economic system. As one wag said at the time, "They pretend to pay us and we pretend to work."

Another body blow to the Soviet economy hit in July, when the world oil price dropped to a new post-1973 low, seriously degrading the Soviet economy. The Soviet economy was utterly dependent on oil revenue. The price recovered somewhat but remained low for the remainder of the decade.

ARCTIC OPERATIONS

From February 23 to March 12, we carried out Operation Anchor Express, a more ambitious cold weather winter exercise to reinforce northern Norway. It included 20,000 men from eight NATO countries. The Fourth Marine Amphibious Brigade (MAB) participated in the amphibious landing phase. Elements of the Fourth MAB took USAF C-141s, deploying directly to Evenes, an airfield in northern Norway. Equipment from Camp Lejeune and Cherry Point, North Carolina, was loaded onto a roll-on/roll-off ship and transported to Bogen Bay, twenty miles from Evenes. Concurrently, fixed-wing squadrons were deployed to Bodø air station, about ninety air miles south of Evenes. Forces that needed to pick up prepositioned weapons and supplies were flown into Trondheim, then moved with Norwegian assistance up to Bodø, to Bogen Bay, to Evenes, and to the deployed troops.

The northern strategy carried with it an enormous new level of difficulty in operating. At sea there were howling gales, fog, snow, ice, and huge waves. Ashore it was the same minus the waves and plus the mountains. Lubricants, hydraulics, electronics, and humans all required specialized modifications and protections. To deal with these challenges, we established the Applied Physics Laboratory Ice Station 180 miles north of Prudhoe Bay, Alaska. It was the largest navy ice camp ever.

We had 189 scientists and engineers representing thirty-nine research and development programs. It also included three submarines operating under the ice. They went on to surface together at the North Pole on May 6, 1986. We launched, tracked, and recovered torpedoes, tested P-3 aircraft-to-submerged submarine communications, and did other projects unique to Arctic operations. Occasionally Soviet Bear bombers flew over the camp to keep tabs on us. I went up to spend a few days at the camp and boarded one of the attack subs that broke through the ice near the camp to pick me up and spend some time operating under the ice. Later, on the flight back to Washington, I approved a new U.S. Navy Arctic Service Ribbon.

In March, we focused on integrating the antisubmarine warfare (ASW) forces of all the NATO navies with a large U.S.-led exercise in the Norwegian Sea lasting about two weeks. The operation was commanded from Northwood, the Royal Navy headquarters in the UK. The operation used combined arms ASW including attack submarines, maritime patrol aircraft, surface ships, and other classified sensors. This was quite a precedent at Northwood, with big staffs involved from each of the NATO participants.

One of our top strategists, Naval Reserve Cmdr. John Hanley, was brought back to active duty for the exercise and recalls:

> Either our [secrecy] was good or the Soviets thought their submarine deployment schedules inviolate, but they did provide target services on two occasions during [the operation]. . . . Sharing long-range contact data from surface ships and submarines with towed arrays and using negative [Bayesian] search techniques to vector [aircraft] to targets and high probability areas for finding simulated Soviet submarines, including their new, quiet Oscar-class nuclear [antiship missile attack subs], the detection rates exceeded the availability of [aircraft] to prosecute targets. This reversed the normal situation of attack assets waiting for a contact, as there were not enough [attack aircraft] in the exercise to prosecute the adversary submarines as they were localized. Actual Soviet submarines also transited through the exercise area, which covered the Norwegian Sea, providing actual target data. . . . This was the peak of the U.S. acoustic advantage over the Soviets.

As spring began, we launched Operation Shooting Star and Operation Coyote, with Adm. Ace Lyons, now commander of the Pacific Fleet, planning to demonstrate to the Soviets how powerful

The historic 1986 rendezvous at the North Pole with the *Ray*,
the *Hawkbill*, and the *Archerfish*. (*U.S. Navy photograph.*)

and flexible naval aviation had become in the northwestern Pacific.
Staging out of Adak, in the Aleutians, A-6E Intruder attack aircraft
flew toward the Soviet Pacific Fleet base at Petropavlovsk in a mock
attack, turning away one hundred miles from Petro. This happened
on "two dozen occasions" as the year unfolded.

Then, in response to increased Soviet air activity, on two days'
notice Lyons scrambled F-14s from Miramar, in southern California, to deploy and then operate out of Adak, intercepting Soviet surveillance flying in the vicinity of the U.S. Aleutian Islands. There
were many of these operations for the rest of Lyons's tenure.

In May, Operation Kernel Potlatch '86-1 was begun with a major
amphibious landing on Adak. For the first time since World War II,
the Third Fleet was commanded from a command ship at sea, the
cruiser *Horne*.

On May 6, Icex '86-1 was conducted. Three of our nuclear-
powered attack subs, *Ray*, *Hawkbill*, and *Archerfish*, were sent under
the Arctic ice to the North Pole, surfacing there together. It was

the first time three submarines were ever on the surface simultaneously at the pole. It was intended to remind the Soviets that their new strategy of hiding their nuclear missile subs under the Arctic ice was not a problem for us. A picture of the rendezvous was released on June 28 and showed up in the Moscow papers on July 7.

President Reagan did not want us to reduce the pressure as he shifted into serious diplomacy, but he did not want to be reading about provocations at sea. So with White House approval, we did not reduce our naval operations at all but ceased the public affairs offensive against the Soviets that had been part of the strategy for the past five years—that is, the policy of announcing forward operations and exercises, making public testimony before Congress, holding frequent press conferences, and inviting journalists aboard ship to participate. We went silent with regard to operations in the North but not those involving other troublemakers in other geography.

Thus on March 13, without any publicity, we went ahead with another freedom of navigation operation in the Black Sea. The cruiser *Yorktown* and the destroyer *Caron* asserted their right of innocent passage in the Black Sea within Soviet territorial waters south of Crimea, passing within six miles of the Soviet coast, eliciting a Soviet protest. The Soviets massed forces. A Soviet frigate notified the U.S. warships that they had violated Soviet territorial waters and requested they depart immediately. The U.S. vessels acknowledged receipt of the warning but did not change course. *Yorktown* and *Caron* stayed in Soviet territorial waters for approximately two hours. The U.S. Navy had operated in the Black Sea before, but this was the first time it had entered Soviet territorial waters, asserting a right of innocent passage. At the time, Gorbachev was resting nearby at a Crimean dacha in Livadia, and some Soviets saw this as a deliberate U.S. slap at him—they believed he was being too trusting of Reagan. We in the navy, however, did not know he was there. The Soviets were quick to condemn the U.S. maneuvers, calling in the U.S. chargé d'affaires in Moscow. We said nothing.

184 | JOHN LEHMAN

LIBYA OPERATIONS

American and allied intelligence was picking up increasing evidence
that Libyan dictator Muammar Gaddafi was planning terrorist
attacks against U.S. citizens. On October 7, 1985, the Palestinian
Liberation Front, with support and planning by Libyan Intelligence,
hijacked the Italian cruise ship *Achille Lauro* and killed a disabled
American, Leon Klinghoffer. The hijackers escaped to Egypt, where
they boarded an Egypt Air flight. That flight was intercepted by F-
14s from *Saratoga*, which forced them to land in Italy, where they
were taken into Italian custody. Three of the four soon escaped.

Then on December 17, 1985, Libyan Intelligence set off bombs in
the airports in Vienna and Rome, killing five Americans. President
Reagan ordered the Sixth Fleet, commanded by Vice Adm. Frank
Kelso, later CNO, to "the shores of Tripoli" with his previous rules
of engagement (ROE) to attack if threatened.

From March 23 to 27, Kelso led Operation Prairie Fire in the Gulf
of Sidra against Libya with the *Saratoga*, *America*, and *Coral Sea* battle groups. This twenty-six-combatant, 250-aircraft battle force—
Battle Force Zulu—conducted preannounced sorties including three
large surface combatants led by the Aegis cruiser *Ticonderoga* that
crossed the so-called Libyan "Line of Death." (The carriers stayed
north of the line; their aircraft crossed it, however.) Reagan's ROE
in effect, allowed on-scene commanders to respond to hostile threats
more forcefully and with less provocation.

The Libyan Air Force fighters flew intercepts, Libyan ground
missile batteries fired Guideline and Gammon missiles and locked
radars on U.S. Navy aircraft. Sixth Fleet A-6E, EA-6B, and A-7E
fighter-bombers attacked Libyan ground-based radars and missile
batteries and sank two corvettes. No air-to-air combat ensued. USAF
F-111s were on standby alert in the United Kingdom if needed.

Several new U.S. weapons systems—Aegis, the F/A-18 *Hor-
net*, *Harpoon* antiship missiles, HARM radar-homing missiles, and

LAMPS MK III helicopters—performed flawlessly in a combat environment. This was the first U.S. Navy combat operation for the F/A-18.

In a message to Sixth Fleet personnel, President Reagan told them, "You have sent a message to the whole world that the United States has the will and, through you, the ability to defend the free world's interests."

A Soviet ship remained in port in Tripoli in order to relay information to the Libyans and other Soviet ships shadowing each U.S. carrier.

On April 5, Libyan Intelligence detonated a bomb in a West Berlin disco frequented by American servicemen, killing an American soldier and a Turkish woman and injuring two hundred others. President Reagan ordered a retaliatory attack on Libya.

EL DORADO CANYON

On April 15, Admiral Kelso launched Operation El Dorado Canyon with Sixth Fleet battle force. The carrier battle groups *Coral Sea* and *America* launched air strikes, coordinated with USAF F-111 strikes from the UK, on Libyan ground targets in Tripoli and Benghazi. Strikes were made at night, under strict radio silence, to avoid problems incurred with daylight strikes over Lebanon in 1983. Since only the U.S. Navy and Marine A-6Es from the carriers and USAF F-111Fs had the appropriate night strike capability, nearly one hundred aircraft of all three services were used.

It was a very successful close navy/marine-USAF coordination and collaboration, including liaison officer exchanges and coordinated planning, the operational fruit of previous collaboration in the 1970s and '80s. Navy strike performance benefited from advanced strike warfare training at Strike U, which we established in 1984 to improve the navy's strike warfare tactics in the wake of mediocre performance—including losses—over Lebanon in December 1983.

The EA-6B, F/A-18A, and A-7E from *Coral Sea* and *America* suppressed Libyan radars electronically, and HARM and Shrike anti-radiation missiles homed in on and blew up the SAM radars. F-14s from *America* and F-18s from *Coral Sea* flew fighter support.

Two U.S. Navy attack subs were positioned to block Libya's six Soviet-built Foxtrot-class submarines from reaching the battle force. NSC staffer Capt. James Stark, who had helped craft Sea Plan 2000 and the Maritime Strategy, had traveled to France in January 1986, attempting to get French permission for the F-111s from the U.S. base in the UK to overfly France on the way to Libya. Remembering our abandoning them in the Libyan retaliatory strike, the French said no. As a result, the F-111 crews had to fly a round trip of seventeen hours. One F-111 was lost, killing the two-man aircrew, either by malfunction of its terrain-following radar when it went back over water after the strike, or by Libyan fire. I later traveled to Lakenheath RAF base in the UK, where the American F-111s were based, and gave the squadron a navy unit citation, the first ever given to an air force squadron. The air force awarded the unit nothing.

With much fanfare, on May 9, the USSR formally proposed mutual naval arms control measures at the United Nations. The initiative quickly disappeared among the bureaucrats in Turtle Bay (UN headquarters) but was accompanied by a media campaign.

On May 16, *Red Star* published an important interview with the longtime first deputy commander in chief of the Soviet Navy, Adm. Nikolai I. Smirnov: "The U.S. navy, together with its allies, is intentionally rehearsing the provisions of this Maritime Strategy in exercises and maneuvers both in Europe and in the Atlantic, as well as the Far East and has concentrated strike forces commensurate with wartime dispositions in close proximity to the Soviet Union's territory."

Unfortunately our efforts to "speak softly" were not entirely successful. Our four-year effort to go public and loud about the rebirth of the navy and its new strategy was bearing fruit, and Hollywood especially could not be expected to respond to our diplomatic needs. On the same day as the *Red Star* article, the movie that we had worked so hard on, *Top Gun*, was released. The enemy in the movie, while not named, was obviously the Soviet Union, and the swashbuckling, confidently professional naval aviators kicking their ass was exactly the message we had intended to project, but it was not quite the nuanced approach conducive to diplomacy.

TOP: Navy/Marine A-6E Intruder fighter-bomber. *(U.S. Naval Institute.)* BOTTOM: USAF F-111F all-weather night fighter-bomber. *(U.S. Air Force photograph by David S. Nolan.)*

Now in our sixth year of refining and improving our strategy in operations and exercises, we felt that we were ready to show the Soviets how we would go about defeating them simultaneously in the Atlantic and the Pacific and then using that "command of the seas" to project power into their homeland from all azimuths. President Reagan firmly believed that his nuclear arms control diplomacy would be empowered by the shadow cast by that naval power.

THE PACIFIC

The campaign began on June 5 with Rimpac '86, with the U.S. Navy and four allied navies totaling sixty warships in two carrier battle groups, *Vinson* and *Ranger*. The *Ranger* battle group successfully transited undetected in radio silence from southern California to Hawaii, where they joined *Vinson*, then headed to Japan for the Annualex exercise with the Japanese Maritime Self-Defense Force (JMSDF), then they went on to operations in the Bering Sea. Ed Clexton, now a rear admiral, participated in the exercise as a battle group commander. He recalled that the JMSDF

> participated heavily, sent a powerful antisubmarine force, including a submarine for the first time, as well as eight P-3C sub-hunters and a squadron of eight surface combatants. The scenario for the exercise was the defense of Pearl Harbor from air attack. Admiral Lyons wanted to make sure I made the Japanese actually in charge of some specific operations since they had been reticent to do so in previous fleet exercises, so I *put them in charge of defending Pearl Harbor from air attack!!* . . .
>
> The JMSDF weren't authorized to operate with the Brits, so I made the JMSDF destroyers "screen" the Brit carrier from air attack. *Ranger* operated as the enemy so they provided the airplanes used to attack the *Carl Vinson* and Pearl Harbor. The JMSDF had not operated this far east of Japan since World War II so they felt somewhat "out of sight" of their homeland and (I hoped) enjoyed all the irony at play. We held a "hot wash-up" in Hawaii after the exercise where all involved enjoyed the "lessons learned" to include the Japanese and the Brits.

Rear Adm. I. W. Knox of the Royal Australian Navy recently stated that during the Rimpac '86 allied naval exercises held in the Pacific in July 1986, the U.S. aircraft carrier *Ranger* successfully evaded Orange (i.e., "enemy") forces searching for it for a period of two weeks. The Orange forces, the admiral said,

> consisted of significant air, surface and sub-surface systems and had access to U.S. satellite surveillance and HF/

DF [high-frequency/direction-finding] systems, [and] were tasked with defending the Hawaiian Islands. The [attacking] Blue forces had two carrier groups tasked with striking the Hawaiian Islands. . . . I guess that the submarines and the aircraft were under the impression that it's easy to find each other out there because we know roughly where the opposing forces are going to be and we can draw the wrong conclusions. But the exercise out there was totally free play and one of the carriers, using deception and a very tight emission control policy, was not positively identified and targeted from the time it departed southern California exercise areas until it steamed into Pearl Harbor some 14 days later. And during that period the carrier contributed 2500 [aircraft-] hours of air effort, from land strike against the Hawaiian Islands to maritime strike, to ASW and air defense of the force.

On June 27, Admiral Lyons added some extra entertainment for the closely watching Soviets. The nuclear-powered cruiser *Long Beach* fired a Tomahawk cruise missile five hundred miles west to east along the Aleutian chain from just west of Attu Island. Had it been fired to the west, it would have reached Soviet targets.

While we were attempting to "speak softly," the Soviets decided to give these exercises major press coverage as an example of the new, global, offensive allied Maritime Strategy aimed at the Soviet Union. Moscow radio reported, "The attempt to give Rimpac a global flavor is nothing but the result of the new U.S. maritime strategy, a global and regional one for direct confrontations." Military newspaper *Red Star* characterized it as "anti-Soviet and a premier of a new U.S. maritime strategy, whereby Soviet forces must be destroyed in forward areas away from the United States."

Another serious challenge to the White House wish that we "speak softly" came on Independence Day 1986, when the president was the star of an event that we had been planning since 1981. From

The cruiser *Shiloh* launching a Tomahawk cruise missile. *(U.S. Navy photograph.)*

July 2 to 6, we hosted the spectacular International Naval Review '86, in New York Harbor. It was planned around the rededication and hundredth anniversary of the Statue of Liberty, which had just completed a five-year rebuilding and modernization. It was the fifth international naval review in U.S. history. Twenty-one foreign warships from fourteen allied countries joined twelve U.S. Navy warships, including *Iowa* and *Kennedy*. Reagan presided, breaking his flag on *Kennedy*. I broke mine on *Iowa* and held the biggest party ever on a battleship with the Beach Boys entertaining from a soundstage on the number-three turret. *Iowa*'s new skipper was Capt. Larry Seaquist, one of our team's leading strategists and a former member of the Strategic Studies Group. Eighty-six thousand small craft were in the harbor to watch the ships pass in review, followed, after dark, by the greatest fireworks show in history. This world-televised naval and patriotic display sent a strong message to the Soviets and others.

Continuing to increase our capability to operate in the frozen conditions of the Soviets' precious Kola Peninsula, a full SEAL platoon skied across Danish Greenland, arriving right after Independence Day, to great acclaim in Denmark. (The current Danish crown prince, Frederik, is a fully qualified Danish Navy SEAL, complete with requisite tattoo, much to his mother the queen's horror.)

NORPAC AND NORTHERN WEDDING '86

Now began the deliberate, coordinated, simultaneous global forward exercise program running from August through October 1986, churning the Norwegian, Mediterranean, Baltic, and Bering Seas, the North Pacific, and the Sea of Japan, as we had never done before. We would simulate and demonstrate to the Soviets that if they ever considered attacking NATO with their ground superiority, they would instantly be involved in a global conventional war that they were sure to lose.

In August, Admiral Lyons, having got Soviet attention with Rimpac, began using some of Admiral Hayward's proven moves in Norpac '86, with a "battle group surge" to the North Pacific, Gulf of Alaska, Sea of Japan, Sea of Okhotsk, and Bering Sea, including Lyons's trademark EMCON transits by *Vinson*, then *Ranger*, *Constellation*, and *New Jersey* battle groups.

As something of a decoy, the Aegis cruiser *Vincennes* and other surface combatants deployed into the Sea of Okhotsk. In an interview after he retired, Lyons said,

> The Soviets didn't know where we were for twelve days. They lost us. How do we know that? They were sending out all the reconnaissance aircraft *south* of the Aleutians. We were intercepting them in excess of two hundred miles away. The *Vinson* was up in the Bering Sea conducting its exercises—a full battle group—and [it was undetected until] it came down parallel with the Kamchatka Peninsula.

By this time, Lyons had achieved a semilegendary status with the Soviet Navy, as Edwin Rommel had with Second World War Allied

192 | J O H N L E H M A N

armies, and George Patton with the German Army. As described by an authoritative contemporary, "The early 1980s was a pretty busy time for the [Incidents at Sea] guys in [navy headquarters]. Ace was masterful in dealing with [the Soviets] after he took over [as deputy CNO], and they really respected him. [Much later Kevin Healey told me that when Kevin was at the Naval War College, the Soviets told him that Ace was the USN commander they most admired and feared from a war fighting standpoint.]"

Another recalled:

> I don't know if you ever heard the story the president of the Center of Naval Analyses tells about the meeting of retired admirals in Moscow. "Mickey"—Adm. (ret.) Maurice Wiesner, USN—called me after they returned and told me a story about the arrival of the U.S. admirals at the meeting site. Apparently the Soviets picked up each admiral in a separate car and delivered them to the site. Mickey was one of the first to arrive, but noticed that each time another car arrived, all the Soviet admirals ran to the windows to look. He finally asked a translator what was going on. The translator told him that the Soviet admirals had a contest to see who would be the first one to identify Ace Lyons!

In what was thought to be the first carrier deployment there since World War II, *Vinson* deployed into the Bering Sea under complete radio and radar silence (EMCON) conditions—undetected by the Soviets, accompanied by the U.S. destroyer *Paul F. Foster.* The skipper of *Foster* was Cmdr. Raymond P. Conrad, one of our original Maritime Strategy drafting team (now walking the walk, having talked the talk). From the *Vinson* log:

> *Vinson* steamed in the Bering Sea for the first time. [The air wing] observed that Soviet surveillance and harsh weather including high winds, low clouds and fog "tasked

every aspect of carrier operations to the limit." The ship's Supply Department noted that the "environment required imagination to overcome both the elements and the scarcity of logistics support in the area." *Vinson*'s aircraft flew low-level missions over the Aleutian Islands.

The ship had just completed an underway replenishment during the afternoon watch (16 August) when a huge wave slammed into Elevator No. 1, positioned at the Hangar Bay level about 25 feet above the sea, and swept seven men overboard at 1243. The sailors were in the midst of moving aircraft up to the flight deck when they went over the side. Shipmates too far away to reach them watched helplessly as the men disappeared into the frothing maelstrom, though as soon as they recovered their own footing they threw smoke flares and life rings into the water. Six of the men overboard formed a compact group to assist their rescuers in the high seas; the sea pushed the seventh away from the others.

Foster (on planeguard) could not directly recover the men in that weather and lowered her motor whaleboat. "We provided life rings to the men," noted Commander Conrad, the frigate's skipper, "but the wind and seas prevented a shipboard recovery. I then decided to send the boat." Despite the appalling conditions the craft's crew saved the first six men and returned them to the destroyer within the hour. The survivors later returned to the carrier via helicopter. A helo from *Vinson*, rescued the seventh man. The wave injured an eighth sailor when it smashed him against an aircraft, but thinking quickly, Third Class Petty Officer Joseph Bartosz, working nearby, ran onto the elevator and clung to his injured shipmate with one hand and an aircraft tie-down fitting with the other and grimly rode out a second swell as it rolled across the elevator. Bartosz and his fellows then pulled the sailor out of harm's way into the skin of the ship, where he successfully underwent surgery.

The U.S. frigate *Paul F. Foster* in the Bering Sea.
(Official U.S. Navy photograph, National Archives.)

Then, simultaneously with the launch in the Atlantic of Northern Wedding '86, Lyons shifted gears in the Pacific Fleet and kicked off Fleetex '86 operations in the Bering Sea with *Ranger, Constellation,* and *New Jersey*. The *Ranger* and *New Jersey* battle groups returned from Sea of Okhotsk operations to join *Constellation* in the Gulf of Alaska. It was the first time since World War II that two carriers and a battleship had worked together.

Northern Wedding '86
Vice Adm. Hank Mustin, a Lyons protégé, was now the NATO Striking Fleet commander and had boiled down the Maritime Strategy to four principles in his fighting instructions: (1) Defend far for-

ward in the Norwegian Sea. (2) Arrive early, prior to hostilities. (3) Operate in Norwegian leads and fjords to counter the threat. (4) Use the combined might of Striking Fleet carriers, antisubmarine forces, amphibious forces, and marines to win the battle of the Norwegian Sea and make the difference between winning and losing in northern Norway."

The operation began in the North Atlantic and the Norwegian and North Seas with eighty ships from eight NATO navies. For the first time, Supreme Allied Commander Gen. Bernie Rogers kicked off the operation with a visit to Norway. It was going to be the largest NATO naval exercise in its history. It soon swelled to ten nations and 150 warships including, in addition to the three carrier battle groups, Vice Admiral Mustin's command ship *Mount Whitney*, the nuclear-powered cruiser *South Carolina*, the Royal Navy carrier HMS *Ark Royal*, and many other front line combatants from eight different NATO navies. All available Soviet submarine and surface combatants and naval and air force fighters and bombers also came out to play.

After the success of the strategy the year before in Ocean Safari '85 with *America*, this would be a second and more ambitious testing of Norwegian fjords as "havens" and "radar shadowing" concepts. The *Nimitz* battle group would conduct antisurface, antiair, and antisubmarine attack fjord operations in Vestfjord. Northern Wedding '86 included a much more ambitious focus on amphibious operations with eight thousand U.S. Marines, and 3,500 British and Dutch marines. There were multiple amphibious landings in northern Norway, southern Norway, and Denmark. Eleven thousand U.S., UK, and Dutch Marines assaulted southern Norway, some close to Tromsø, followed by landings in Denmark and participation in a joint exercise in West Germany.

The Amphibious Strike Force was led by Rear Adm. Bill Fogarty, another Maritime Strategy planner and former skipper of *New Jersey*. Now he was back at sea walking the walk. His force included the battleship *Iowa*, commanded by Capt. Larry Seaquist, another one of our Maritime Strategy planners practicing what he had written. Seaquist remembers the exercise well:

> I began Northern Wedding as an Orange force strike group accompanied by real Soviet ships tailing me—we added up to a pretty good task force. On my own, since I was Orange and could do what I want, I went all the way north to the twelve-mile limit just south of Svaalbard. Partly this was for Bill Studeman (then chief of naval intelligence) who always believed the S. Islands were more important to the Soviets and therefore to us than normally credited. But I also wanted to show the Soviets just how far north we could push the left arm of the Maritime Strategy concepts. At the time, our onboard amateur historians thought we'd taken a battleship farther north than anyone ever had including the Germans. We finished this phase by attacking the Blue fleet as they were at anchor in a Norwegian fjord for Hank Mustin's change of command. I always relished that little gesture of "welcome aboard" to my new strike fleet commander.
>
> We then ran a port visit to Hamburg, repeating *Iowa*'s '85 visit under Gerry Gneckow—another signal of capital ships gluing the NATO alliance together.
>
> With me back on the Blue side, we ran a very interesting day/night quite close in to the western Danish coast (in water so shallow I occasionally had only a couple of feet under the keel). I pushed the envelope because I wanted to see what it would be like to fire [naval gunfire support] in that area in support of the marine invasion I considered a credible option. Probably this "signal" registered only in my own mind.
>
> I recall that I had "orders" from Lehman himself to prove that Battleship 16-inch gunnery was accurate and that my tycom, Vice Admiral McCauley, gave me carte

blanche to shoot all I wanted. ("You do the shooting. I'll do the counting"—best orders a gunnery guy ever had.) So that day (maybe two days running), as part of my constant exploration of gunnery practices, and since we were in the area, we fired both sides of the [World War 1] Battle of Jutland. In one series, we fired the German gunnery plan, the British method in the next. Just a little insider fun among us major-caliber-gun guys. We ended up, as I recall, liking the Brit method better but also seeing how they screwed up their attack. So while this may have been registering with the Soviets on one level, onboard the crew and I were back from May 31 to June 1, 1916. We left thinking that with our guns and fire control systems we could have wiped out both fleets and still been able to have lunch on time.

The Striking Fleet change of command took place during the exercise on *Nimitz* in the Vestfjord. Mustin turned over the Second Fleet to Vice Adm. Chuck Larson, an aggressive submariner who had been skipper of the submarine *Halibut* conducting sensitive far forward intelligence operations against the Soviet Union from 1973 to 1976, and who had commanded U.S. Navy and allied submarines forward in the Mediterranean in 1982–83. I happened to be aboard *Nimitz* flying with the air wing, so I presided at the change of command ceremony in the hangar deck.

Cmdr. William J. "Fox" Fallon was the deputy wing commander on *Nimitz* during the exercise. He was an A6 bombardier and outstanding leader who later rose to become four-star commander in chief of both the U.S. Pacific and Central Commands: "I was Deputy wing Commander (CAG) on *Nimitz* during Northern Wedding '86," he recalls.

Weather was terrible. Really bad. We worked up off Halifax and practiced as we went across. The Soviets came out in force to meet us. We practiced gunnery and bombing strikes at the Royal Navy gunnery and bombing range at Cape Wrath, at the northwest tip of Scotland. Excellent practice.

Then we decided to play with the Soviets. We went into EMCON (no emissions), doubled back to Iceland on our track, and put deception gear on a destroyer to simulate a carrier. The Russians lost us. Then we turned back, popped out in the Norwegian Sea, and started to emit again. The Russians were mad. And the weather was still terrible. We went into the Vestfjord to conduct "submarine seal" ops to seal us off from undersea attack. (This procedure, which we had proven to be very effective in '85, involves sending a nuclear attack submarine into the deep fjord to make sure there were no Soviet subs in the fjord and then dropping a string of Captor mines across the fjord entrance to seal it free of enemy subs. The Captors contain Mark 46 torpedoes that are programed to home in only on the unique sonar signature of Soviet submarines.) We did several days of ops in the fjord, with the Russians going crazy. Lots of excellent practice on both old and new tactics. Navy Secretary Lehman came out and flew with live ordnance on one of the Vestfjord missions.

Operating in these northern waters was always perilous. The air wing lost an A-7E fighter-bomber that crashed into the Norwegian Sea. Despite an intensive search, the pilot was not recovered. A marine helo and eight marines were also lost on the exercise—and thirteen other marines were rescued—when a CH 46 *Sea Knight* crashed into another helicopter on USS *Saipan*, then slammed into the sea.

Fallon summed up his experience: "Terrible weather with tragic losses, but invaluable experience. Certainly agitated the Russians. We learned the territory. We learned the terrain. We learned how to work with the Germans, the Norwegians, and the Brits."

LEFT: Vice-Adm. Hank Mustin.
RIGHT: Adm. Fox Fallon. *(Official U.S. Navy photographs.)*

The Striking Fleet commander Hank Mustin concluded: "You've got to come up here and do it. You can talk about it all you want. You can sit around the table and plan it. You can war-game it. But until you put it all together, until you go to Norway and combine . . . the carrier, the ASW, the amphibious and marine strike forces—and coordinate with the other NATO commanders, you really don't know if it will work. I think we showed it will work."

Later a Soviet Navy participant, Lt. Cmdr. (ret.) Maksim Tokarev, summed up his experience: "Look, [Soviet Navy commanders examined] the Northern Wedding's logs hard, every minute of evolutions, every launch and landing, every word on radio and so on. They understood that when the carriers came in the Norway fjords, it [would be] just too late to try to hit them [with] air assets."

A little later the Soviets responded heavily to U.S. Pacific Fleet Tomahawk-equipped battleship and carrier transits in the Sea of Okhotsk—the first such Cold War battleship operations.

After the Cold War was over, one of the most senior Soviet gen-

An A-6 Intruder fighter-bomber emerges from the Arctic snows
to land on the USS *Enterprise*, shadowed by a Soviet *Kashin*-class
destroyer. *(Painted by R. G. Smith. Reproduced with permission.)*

erals, Gen. Vladimir Dvorkin, described to me at the Bodø conference in Norway: "The longest that we were ever able to keep our Northern Fleet from destruction in our own analysis and our own war-gaming, starting with your Ocean Venture '81 through Northern Wedding '86, was only one week into the exercise. After the 1986 exercise, the general staff formally notified the president [of the Soviet Union] that to successfully defend the homeland on the Northern Theater, we must treble the budget for naval and air forces in the Northern sector."

When that demarche (notification by the Soviet General Staff) hit the Kremlin, it had a momentous impact. After decades of sacrificing the domestic economy to build the Soviet Navy and Air Force in the quest for superiority that would enable geopolitical dominance, the Russians had been falling behind since Reagan became president. And now there was simply no economic possibility to try to keep up.

In July, before the crescendo of the simultaneous successes of Northern Wedding '86, and of Fleetex '86 in the Atlantic and Pacific, the CIA Office of Soviet Analysis published a secret paper "Soviet Perceptions of U.S. Naval Strategy," using information available as of November 1, 1985, and recently declassified. The analysis described the Soviets as perceiving a marked U.S. increase in emphasis on sea power and an increased and rapidly developing threat to the Soviet Union from the sea. It said that the Soviets viewed U.S. aircraft carriers as increasingly capable and survivable systems in the Norwegian Sea and northwestern Pacific.

CHAPTER 7

The Soviets (and Others) Get the Message, 1986–1988

The Cold War Hurtles Toward Its End

THE SOVIETS' INITIAL response to the Reagan administration's Maritime Strategy had been their last hurrah. By 1986, they were starting to go dead in the water. Summerex '85 had been the last great Soviet Navy global exercise series. In 1986 the Soviets began to ratchet back their exercise activity considerably and to emphasize defensive operations closer to home. Their own system was beginning to totter, and the Americans and their allies refused to be intimidated—or sympathetic—and just kept on coming.

Soviet boss Leonid Brezhnev had died in November 1982 after almost two decades in power. He had built up an enormous military-industrial complex but otherwise had run most of his country's economy into the ground and alienated most of the world through his aggressive actions. He was succeeded by the hypersuspicious KGB boss Yuri Andropov, who was himself in ill health and who died of pneumonia only fifteen months later. Andropov was succeeded in turn by the Communist Party hack and propagandist Konstantin Chernenko, who passed away within thirteen months. Referring to the Soviets' bizarre succession practices, President Reagan is said to have remarked, "How am I supposed to get anyplace with the Russians if they keep dying on me?"

Before Andropov died, Chernenko, as his probable heir, had already abandoned his vow not to return to U.S.-USSR arms control talks as long as U.S. intermediate-range nuclear missiles remained in Europe. Accordingly, in January 1985, U.S. secretary of state George Shultz and the dour longtime (since 1957!) Soviet foreign minister Andrei Gromyko agreed to resume talks on strategic, intermediate-range, and space-based weapons. Ronald Reagan's landslide victory in the November 1984 presidential election showed Chernenko that he had no choice but to deal with the president. Progress over the next few years would be slow, however—not much different from the way it had been before the Soviets walked out on the talks in November 1983.

Chernenko replaced Marshal Nikolai Ogarkov, longtime chief of the Soviet General Staff, with Marshal Sergei Akhromeyev. Ogarkov, who had held the job since 1977, had become a firm advocate of the Soviet military exploitation of emerging new technologies and doctrines, which would, of course, require even greater expenditures from the increasingly strapped Soviet economy. He was also a strong advocate—like Admiral Gorshkov—of an offensive Soviet strategy, including amphibious assaults. Akhromeyev would become particularly appreciative—and fearful—of U.S. naval power and "would be briefed first of all on the location of U.S. naval forces when he came to his office each morning."

At the end of 1985, Admiral of the Fleet Sergei Gorshkov was piped over the side and relieved by Vladimir Chernavin as deputy minister of defense and commander in chief of the Soviet Navy. Admiral Gorshkov had headed the Soviet Navy since 1956—a month shy of thirty years. The Soviet Navy thus lost its master architect, its most highly influential and articulate spokesman, and a strong advocate for a powerful, globally deployed, offensively oriented blue-water Soviet fleet with vital missions beyond support of the ground forces.

Gorbachev would ultimately decide he had no choice but to suspend deployment of Soviet SS-20 intermediate-range nuclear ballistic missiles in Warsaw Pact states, and would begin to cut back on resources to the Soviet Armed Forces, including the navy. He tried to lower U.S. and global perceptions of the Soviet threat through unilateral force reductions, an aggressive campaign promoting a new Soviet "defensive" military doctrine, and a series of arms control propaganda and diplomatic initiatives. At the same time, however, the momentum of the Soviet naval modernization program continued, to the consternation and concern of many in the West, especially those in the U.S. Navy charged with deterring and defeating the ever-improving Soviet fleets.

In January 1986, Mikhail Gorbachev had been in power for ten months, assessing the political, economic, and social rot in his country. Finally, on the sixteenth of that month, he gave a shocking speech. The country was in trouble, he said, and to fix it, military spending had to be cut back. Strategic stockpiles needed to be reduced, conventional arms cut back, and military exercises scaled down. This speech coincided ironically with the U.S. Navy's published public version of its global forward strategy, outlining how it planned to use its command of the seas to defeat the Soviet Navy and project strategic and tactical power into Central Europe and the Soviet homeland itself if it tried to attack NATO. After watching each year the expanding U.S. and NATO forward naval exercises beginning with Ocean Venture '81—demonstrating at sea just how the U.S. Navy and its allies would go about doing this—it finally sank in to Kremlin leaders that their huge sacrifices to seek military dominance had left them worse off.

The Soviet Navy, of course, had a ready—and traditional—answer: even more sophisticated designs, even bigger exercises, even larger forces, and of course, even more money.

The 1985 Ocean Safari exercise had proved among other things that Soviet forces were simply not able to attack or interfere with American carriers operating in the sanctuaries of Norwegian fjords. A subsequent examination, by the Soviet General Staff, of the detailed operations analysis of the opposing fleets' performances made it clear that once again the Soviet Northern Fleet would have been effectively defeated seven days after the exercise began. It concluded that the budgets for the Northern Fleet and the Northern Air Forces must be immediately and substantially increased.

But Gorbachev wasn't buying it. He had learned that he couldn't. In February 1986, in a watershed address to the Twenty-seventh CPSU Party Congress, he unveiled a new policy: "Our country stands for . . . restricting military potential within the bounds of reasonable sufficiency." He and his supporters would hammer away on this theme from there on in. The moratoria that he had declared the previous year on intermediate-range nuclear missile deployments and nuclear testing now appeared as possible stalking horses for a major policy change, not just propaganda gestures. *Red Star* reported a straw in the wind that Soviet Naval Aviation Su-17 Fitter attack aircraft would henceforth concentrate on antiship and combat air patrol training instead of supporting amphibious assaults, as they previously had.

Only a few months later a Soviet civilian nuclear power plant at Chernobyl, in the Ukraine, melted down, spreading radioactivity in parts of Ukraine and Belarus. The Soviets at first denied there was much of a problem, then were slowly forced to admit that they had created an unprecedented international disaster. Gorbachev and his country were indeed in trouble.

In December 1986, Gorbachev threw down another glove before his country's military-industrial-technical complex: with the assistance of Marshal Akhromeyev, Gorbachev proposed—and the USSR Defense council formally ratified—a drastic new change in Soviet military doctrine. In the words of one well-placed American observer:

> Until 1986, Soviet strategy was "based on" active defense and, as soon as possible . . . striking deep into the West "to destroy the aggressor." From 1986 on, the new doctrine abandoned the concept of a prompt counteroffensive; in Akhromeyev's words, "We would repel aggression only

by defensive operations and simultaneously seek with the assistance of political measures to liquidate the conflict." Needless to say, this radical revision of military doctrine and strategy was a shock to most Soviet military men.

What this change would actually mean to the Soviet Navy was never really clear. The Soviet Navy had been active and aggressive in many of its peacetime and crisis operations, but since the 1970s it had been developing a wartime strategy to keep Western naval forces far from the USSR and its strategic missile submarines, and to prevent NATO ground and air attacks on the Eurasian littorals. As the navy increased, Soviet strategy began to include deployments off the American East and West Coasts, including land attack missiles in their armament. Of course, the Soviets' expansive view of "defense" meant that such naval operations—if successful—would sever all the links between the United States in North America and its forward forces and allies in Europe and Asia, and allow the Red Army undisturbed access to Western Europe and northeastern Asia—hardly a "defensive" outcome, in the view of the United States, NATO, Japan, and other allies.

January and February 1987 found Admiral Lyons's U.S. Pacific Fleet conducting exercises Kernel Potlatch '87-1 and Safe Haven. Ten thousand sailors and marines and fourteen ships participated in the exercise, which featured twin marine amphibious unit (MAU) assaults on both Adak and Shemya Islands in the Aleutians, supported by a carrier battle group. It was said to be the first-ever winter amphibious operation in the Aleutians since World War II and the first-ever winter carrier battle group deployment in the Bering Sea. It was a grueling exercise, with blinding snow, ice storms, high winds and seas, and below-freezing temperatures. The carrier was *Carl Vinson*, just returning from a deployment in the Arabian Sea. She had operated in the Bering Sea on the way out—the first carrier to do so in memory—back in the summer of 1986, but weather conditions now were much worse. Also participating were the helicopter carrier *Belleau Wood* amphibious ready group and 2000 marines. Said Admiral Lyons, in explaining the exercise, "No longer will we permit the Soviets to operate with impunity in this important area."

Regarding *Vinson*, the navy's official ship history noted:

> The ship conducted flight operations every day in a three-week operating period in the Northern Pacific and Bering Sea. The weather included snow showers, high winds and seas, air temperatures from 20 to 30 deg F and sea water temperatures around 32 deg F. To fight the continuing ice and driving snow, the Engineering Department rigged steam hoses and lances to keep the flight deck ready for flight operations. However, the most effective means of clearing snow and ice from the flight deck was the jet exhaust from Air Wing aircraft.

The *Vinson* battle group commander was again Rear Adm. Ed Clexton, who had served under Lyons as skipper of *Eisenhower* in Ocean Venture '81. Clexton recalls:

> The very interesting "cold war" operations we conducted in the Bering Sea, along the Aleutian Islands and across to the Kamchatka Peninsula, were much like the operations we did in the North Sea when I was CO, *Ike* in 1981, also under Admiral "Ace" Lyons. . . . The ships and Air Wing did well in these seldom experienced conditions. Just like what we had experienced in the Norwegian Sea off Norway in 1981 in *Ike*, the Russians became anxious to find out what we were doing so far north and, in their mind, infringing on their airspace. We used some of the same electronic "tricks" to "hide" the carrier from their long-range reconnaissance bombers as we closed in on their homeland, where many of their strategic submarines were based inside the Kamchatka Peninsula. Admiral Lyons

was very much attuned to what we were doing. He had been involved in the planning for these operations.

One "lesson learned" that surprised me when we were operating in the Bering Sea was counter to what we always thought about wind and fog, at least in the Atlantic and Mediterranean, we thought you couldn't have fog and wind at the same time because the wind wouldn't let the fog set, but this was not the case in the Bering Sea! It plagued us. This is important in carrier flying because while you can operate often with strong winds, you simply can't operate in fog because the pilot has to be able to see the ship to land! Well, in the Bering we had strong winds and fog at the same time, which caused some pretty dicey flying for the pilots and for the ship to find sea room that wasn't too foggy.

As Admiral Lyons explained to one researcher in June 2016: "During the Kernel Potlatch '87, the U.S. sailors used an antifreeze solution deployed on an aircraft carrier, but it made the carrier deck more slippery and exacerbated the situation. Unless you actually conduct exercises, you would never know this kind of thing."

A month after that exercise, Admiral Lyons sent a repair fly-away team from a submarine tender to Adak, in the Aleutians, to provide what was probably the first forward upkeep to a submarine in those islands since World War II.

Meanwhile in March, on the other side of the globe, the Fourth Marine Amphibious Brigade (MAB), commanded by Brig. Gen. Matthew B. Caulfield, was exercising in northern Norway in Cold Winter '87. A biannual winter field training exercise, Cold Winter '87 marked the first occasion on which a U.S. Marine general commanded an allied defensive force in Norway. Allied units under the command of Caulfield included the British First Parachute Battalion and the Norwegian Third Battalion of Brigade North. British and Dutch Marines acted as the opposing landing force. CNA analyzed

USS *Billfish*, USS *Sea Devil*, and HMS *Superb* surfaced together at the North Pole in the Ice Pack '87 exercise. (*U.S. Navy photograph. Combined Military Service Digital Photographic files, National Archives.*)

the exercise for the Marines: "The 4th MAB fought from defensive positions outnumbered 3–1 on the ground and 4–1 in the air, and contrary to recent criticism (May *Armed Forces Journal*), the brigade commander was able to bring his forces to bear with singular effect." After the exercise, General Caulfield said, "nobody underestimated the combat power of the MAB."

And on the top of the world, in that same month, March, the submarines *Billfish*, *Sea Devil*, and HMS *Superb* surfaced together at the North Pole in the exercise Ice Pack '87—the world's first multinational surfacing.

Gorbachev's December 1986 directive had a real impact on me. Unlike some of my cold warrior colleagues, I believed that this meant a profound change in Soviet policy. It set me thinking. We had worked hard to expand and improve the fleet and to brandish it in ways that would enhance its deterrent effect and also carry out the necessary day-to-day operational business of the republic. We were now only ten ships short of President Reagan's goal of six hundred, and those and more were being built. We had revived the forward, global, offensive Maritime Strategy philosophy and spirit of Alfred Thayer Mahan and reimbued the U.S. Navy's officer corps and sailors with Mahan's principles. In particular, we had used the fleet in a sophisticated program of coordinated, calculated, forward aggressive exercises—all around the world. The goal was to improve the fleet's capabilities; to demonstrate to our allies America's resolve and power; and to ensure that the Soviets clearly understood that if they sought to attack our country or its allies, the might of the U.S. Navy would be off their coasts in a heartbeat, assuring that they wouldn't get very far, wherever and however they tried.

After much discussion with my wife, Barbara, I decided that the mission assigned to me by the president had been accomplished, and it was time to move on. In January 1987 I informed the president that I planned to resign in April, giving him ample time to find a successor.

After I left office, some in the left-wing press and academia penned solemn predictions that with my departure, the Maritime Strategy and its exercise program would be a thing of the past. But I knew—and they soon learned—that that simply was not to be. Whatever policy differences might have existed between me and my successors, disputing the strategy was not one of them. The strategy endured. President Reagan published a National Security Strategy explicitly enunciating the principles of maritime superiority. The SSG continued to imaginatively attack operational problems posed by a Soviet fleet that continued to grow as ships and weapons, authorized well before Gorbachev's momentous policy change, continued to be delivered to the Soviet Navy. Global war games continued at Newport. And exercise after exercise continued to be conceptualized and implemented in the fjords of Norway, through the storms of the Bering Sea, among the islands of the Aegean, and under the polar ice. The strategy would eventually wind down, of course, but due—among other reasons—to its own success in frustrating Soviet belligerence and militarism, not to any falling off in support within the U.S. or allied governments and their navies.

An embarrassing event occurred on May 28, 1987: daredevil German teenager Mathias Rust landed an aircraft in Red Square, close to Gorbachev's office in the Kremlin. Young Rust, hoping to ease East-West tensions, had flown a small single-engine Cessna sports airplane undetected from Helsinki to Moscow, through Soviet airspace, incidentally exposing blatant weaknesses in Soviet air defense. General Secretary Gorbachev immediately fired his defense minister, Marshal of the Soviet Union Sergei Sokolov, who had been in that position since 1983. He also fired the head of Soviet air defense and other senior officers. Rust gave Gorbachev the pretext to eliminate many of the key military opponents of his December 1986 policy changes.

Very soon after on May 31, 1987, Gorbachev proclaimed a change in Warsaw Pact alliance military doctrine from offensive to "strictly defensive," aimed at "prevention of war," "defense," and "repelling aggression." This strengthened his orders of the previous December. In East Berlin, he directed Eastern European leaders to approve new military doctrine in which the Warsaw Pact was now to be considered a strictly defensive alliance. All Warsaw Pact leaders signed on. Andrei Kokoshin, then-deputy director of the Soviet USA and Canada Institute, in highly unusual 1989 testimony before the U.S. Congress, opined that "this was the biggest change in our strategic thinking since the late 1920s." Gorbachev aimed at demonstrating to the world—above all, to Western Europe—that the Soviet Union should no longer be considered threatening. To some, this represented the end of the Cold War.

Others—including the U.S. Navy—having to focus on the capabilities not the rhetoric, remained skeptical. "Strictly defensive" Soviet fleets and Warsaw Pact navies possessing modern long-range warships and aircraft could still launch land attack missiles into the

United States and target the vital Atlantic, Mediterranean, and Pacific sea lines of communications, all in the name of "repelling aggression."

Meanwhile, as Gorbachev was beginning to preach the virtues of "reasonable sufficiency," the U.S. Navy published the unclassified version of the Maritime Strategy in January 1986, which "obviously caught the Soviet party-military propaganda organs unprepared."

Izvestia lashed out immediately—and intemperately. Former Soviet diplomat, senior Communist party official, and Kremlin spokesman and propagandist Valentin Falin took *The Maritime Strategy* to task for being "remarkably odious." "It is hardly possible to imagine anything worse," he raged. His remarks were vituperative and over the top. The U.S. Navy had obviously got his attention. Back in the Pentagon, a triumphalist U.S. Navy staff officer, who had helped craft the special *Proceedings* issue, rose to the occasion. He created and plastered posters throughout the five-sided building, ballyhooing the "It is hardly possible to imagine anything worse" phrase and proudly noting its source as *Izvestia*.

In May, *Red Star* published an interview with longtime first deputy commander in chief of the Soviet Navy, Adm. Nikolai I. Smirnov, who in particular zeroed in on our exercises: "The U.S. Navy together with its allies, is intentionally rehearsing the provisions of this Maritime Strategy in exercises and maneuvers both in Europe and in the Atlantic, as well as the Far East, and has concentrated strike forces commensurate with wartime dispositions in close proximity to the Soviet Union's territory." The next month brought a barrage of Soviet criticism of our latest Rimpac exercise. Moscow radio reported "The attempt to give Rimpac a global flavor is nothing but the result of the new U.S. maritime strategy, a global and regional one for direct confrontations." *Red Star* characterized it as "anti-Soviet and a premiere of a new U.S. maritime strategy, whereby Soviet forces must be destroyed in forward areas away from the United States."

Finally, on July 27, 1986 (Soviet Navy Day), Commander in Chief Fleet Admiral Chernavin himself weighed in. In an interview on prime-time Soviet TV, he intoned, "The tense situation in sea and ocean theaters is further aggravated by the marked change in the nature of the day-to-day activity of the U.S. and NATO navies. I have in mind the numerous large-scale exercises held by U.S. and NATO naval forces. . . . They are offensive, aggressive in nature, and have a clearly pronounced anti-Soviet thrust." He also reviewed Soviet naval arms control proposals and deplored that "the United States and its NATO allies have not accepted those proposals and continue to build up their arms—including naval arms—and this is fraught with fatal consequences."

In May of the following year came the first official Soviet unclassified military pronouncement on *The Maritime Strategy* by Fleet Admiral Smirnov. Among his points was his view that the strategy would "considerably increase the offensive potential of the U.S. Navy." The next couple of months saw publication of the most comprehensive unclassified Soviet Navy commentary yet on the operational implications of the Maritime Strategy: a two-part series of articles by Soviet Navy Chief of Intelligence Vice Adm. Ivan Khurs in *Foreign Military Review*. Admiral Khurs emphasized to his readership that the United States and its allies planned to move very early and decisively to contain and destroy enemy naval forces in the event of war. He had clearly gotten the message.

In July, Capt. 1st Rank A. G. Rodin, in *Military Thought*, warned his compatriots of the increased threat posed by the U.S. Marine Corps's acquisition of over-the-horizon landing capabilities (LCAC air cushion landing vehicles and V-22 tilt-rotor aircraft) and forward prepositioned stocks (in Norway, Denmark, and on Diego Garcia). In November, a *Soviet Naval Digest* article—"Drawing the Nuclear Spear"—reacted to the new U.S. Navy strategy in the North Pacific. It pretty much got things right, including identifying its key elements: U.S. Navy objectives, the U.S. abandonment of the "swing strategy" that would move U.S. Pacific forces to the Atlantic, the importance of forward exercises, the new roles of the Third Fleet, and cooperation with the U.S. Air Force.

Continuing to drive home the point, in July 1987 Admiral Lyons conducted more forward submarine maintenance operations in Aleutians. This time a tender—*McKee*—deployed to Adak, the first U.S. Navy submarine tender since World War II. It was to provide submarine maintenance upkeep in the Aleutians, on attack submarines and the new *Ohio*-class Trident ballistic missile submarine *Alaska*, just to remind the Soviets that our newest strategic system was very close to them.

In September, Adm. James Busey kicked off NATO exercise Display Determination in the Mediterranean, from Gibraltar to the Black Sea, with participation by the French, Spanish, and German navies, as well as the carrier *Saratoga* and battleship *Iowa*. At the same time, the NATO armies were engaged in Certain Strike, the largest and most innovative ground exercise that NATO had ever held. Almost an entire U.S. Army corps moved forward from the United States to Germany. And in Ocean Safari '87, the Striking Fleet Atlantic operated a carrier farther north in Norwegian territorial waters than ever—north of Narvik in Andfjord. *Iowa* was present in that exercise, too, having deployed from the Mediterranean to the Norwegian Sea in complete silence, without the Soviets knowing where she was until she started emitting again off Trondheim.

At the end of the month, the Atlantic submarine force held another no-notice surprise "submarine flush" of most East Coast attack submarines. All submarines not involved in major maintenance were under way to their wartime patrol areas within seventy-two hours. They returned to port instead of deploying all the way forward, to attack as they would have done in war.

Finally in the Pacific, Adm. Dave Jeremiah—a future Vice-Chairman of the Joint Chiefs of Staff—who had relieved Lyons as Pacific Fleet commander, sent his Third Fleet in rotten weather off the Aleutians to practice disguising itself in "near land operating areas," much as the carriers in the Atlantic had been doing in the Norwegian fjords, and those forward in the eastern Mediterranean were so using the Aegean Islands. In this exercise, civilian CNA analysts were deployed forward in strength to reconstruct and analyze procedures, tactics, and operations for the fleet.

U.S. and allied naval exercises continued in that pattern in 1988 and 1989 as well. I may have left the Pentagon, but the exercise program we had built was carrying on as before, honing our skills, pressing the Soviets, and reassuring our allies. As 1987 ended, Soviet academic Vladimir Ivanov weighed in in the *Far Eastern Economic Review* with some accurate commentary:

> It has become routine for the U.S. Navy to carry out exercises of pre-emptive action, including the blocking and destroying of the Soviet surface fleet in the Seas of Okhotsk and Japan. The U.S. naval command has gradually shifted from ensuring the safety of the sea lanes to "sealing" the Soviet fleet in coastal waters, and to blocking such vital straits as the Korea, Tsugaru (between the Japanese islands of Honshu and Hokkaido) and La Perouse (between Hokkaido and the Soviet island of Sakhalin). This has resulted in a threat not only to the Soviet Pacific Fleet. most of which, as even U.S. intelligence data shows, is on permanent duty in coastal waters, but also to areas where Soviet strategic submarines are located.

Meanwhile Norwegian Vice Adm. Torolf Rein asserted in an article published the same month:

> A successful defense of NATO depends largely on the Soviet Northern Fleet being denied operations in the Norwegian Sea. To this end we need powerful NATO maritime forces in the area at the earliest possible time in a crisis to contain the Northern Fleet and prevent them from entering the Norwegian Sea. The NATO exercises comprising carrier battle groups in the Northern Areas in the recent years bring hope of a more tangible NATO

commitment to early forward operations. . . . I believe that
the majority in this country tacitly agrees that a Soviet
naval monopoly in the Norwegian Sea is unacceptable and
that the only way to thwart a Soviet free ride into all our
adjacent sea areas is through a credible forward maritime
strategy and a firm NATO commitment to go North if
the situation so dictates.

Nineteen eighty-eight saw mounting Soviet concern regarding
potential amphibious assaults on its territory. In a June article in *Military Thought*, Soviet Army General Anatoly V. Betekhtin proposed
new joint-service principles for antilanding defense, expressing army
worries about defending against seaborne assaults. Betekhtin was
first deputy chief of Soviet Ground Forces and had previously served
in the landing-prone Baltic and Odessa military districts.

The FBI finally arrested John Walker and his family in May 1985,
bringing to an end one of the most sordid chapters in Cold War naval
history. The damage he and his associates had wreaked on the U.S.
Navy was broad and deep. The navy pressed for the Justice Department to prosecute all of them for treason and seek the death penalty
since they were responsible for many navy and air force deaths in
Vietnam. I was infuriated when instead the Department of Justice
plea-bargained for a life sentence with eligibility for parole. Walker's
son is now free.

Then, in September 1985, the United Kingdom expelled thirty-one Soviet intelligence personnel for spying, whereupon the Soviets under Gorbachev expelled a similar number of Britons. This was
probably fallout from the defection to Britain of KGB double agent
Oleg Gordievsky earlier in the year.

A couple of months later the FBI arrested Ronald Pelton, who
in 1980 had compromised Operation Ivy Bells, an important U.S.
source of intelligence in the Pacific. But he had not known about all
of the navy's wire-tapping activities, which continued to yield valuable data and insights.

In August 1986, the FBI arrested UN employee and Soviet citizen Gennadi Zakharov for espionage. The arrest triggered a Soviet arrest for espionage of American *U.S. News and World Report* journalist Nicholas Daniloff in Moscow, heightening U.S.-Soviet tensions. After rapid and intense negotiations, Zakharov was allowed to leave the United States and Daniloff was allowed to leave the USSR in September. In October, the United States expelled fifty-five Soviet diplomats from their missions in Washington and New York for undiplomatic behavior, souring relations just before the Reagan-Gorbachev Reykjavik summit. The Soviets retaliated by expelling five U.S. diplomats from Moscow, including the senior U.S. naval attaché, a former submarine captain.

Then, just as 1986 drew to a close, U.S. Embassy Moscow marine security guard Sergeant Clayton Lonetree turned himself in as a spy. He had helped the Soviet KGB bug the U.S. embassy in Moscow since November 1985, through fraternization with a Russian woman—a KGB employee. This additional incident stressed U.S.-Soviet relations, just as Gorbachev was appearing to want to improve them. Moreover, in April 1987, the Reagan administration announced that the KGB had installed listening devices in the brand-new U.S. embassy in Moscow.

The Toshiba-Kongsberg sales to the Soviets of very sensitive classified submarine propeller manufacturing technology had ended in 1984, but this would not be announced publicly until April 1987. The announcement strained relations among the three countries, resulting in the arrest and prosecution of two Toshiba executives and the imposition of sanctions on Toshiba by the United States and Japan. The Norwegian authorities shut down the Kongsberg manufacturing company that had been part of the conspiracy and took other punitive actions. This loss of submarine propeller technology had been yet another serious setback to the U.S. Navy's ability to detect Soviet submarines at sea. Big Japanese companies learned a lesson from the scandal: stay well clear of the Soviets. A month after the announcement, four Japanese citizens were arrested for spying for the Soviet Union and China, specifically for selling information on U.S. military aircraft. Four Soviet diplomats were implicated in the case and slipped out of Japan to avoid being deported. (In August, the Soviets ordered the Japanese naval attaché and the Mitsubishi representative in Moscow out of the country. This was the first expulsion from the Soviet Union of Japanese citizens since World War II.)

Intimidation ops didn't seem to be working for the Soviets, and panic wasn't getting them anywhere either. The Americans and their allies refused to be intimidated and thought Soviet paranoia simply bizarre. But there was no way they were going to pander to the "Evil Empire," by pulling in their horns and allowing Soviet forays in the Third World and saber-rattling in Eurasia to resume with impunity. U.S. and allied forward exercises continued at sea, involving increasing numbers of carriers and submarines, new and innovative tactics, and obvious well-thought-out coordination on all fronts, especially the Barents and Norwegian Seas, the eastern Mediterranean, the northwestern Pacific, the Arctic, northern Norway, and the Aleutians. President Reagan's new National Security Decision Directive (NSDD 238) in September 1986, was explicit on that score: it was the national security policy of the nation

> To limit Soviet military capabilities by strengthening the U.S. military, by using both strategy and technology to force the Soviets to redirect assets for defensive rather than offensive purposes
>
> We must continue to build and modernize national forces sufficient to retain maritime superiority.
>
> In coalition with our allies we will continue to maintain in peacetime major forward deployments for land, naval and air forces in both Europe and the Pacific, and other deployments in the Western Hemisphere and the Indian Ocean.
>
> U.S. military systems which particularly stress Soviet defenses, or require a disproportionate expenditure of

Soviet resources to counter, represent an especially attrac-
tive investment

We will seek to prosecute the war as far forward and as
close as possible to the sources of greatest threat.

So we continued our full court press, and the increasingly weary
Soviets felt they had no choice but to continue to respond—wearing
out their forces and burning up their resources.

The pace was beginning to tell on the Red fleet. On October 6,
1986, just days before the Reykjavik Summit between President Reagan and Secretary Gorbachev, a fifteen-year-old, poorly maintained
Yankee I-class nuclear-powered ballistic missile submarine K-219
sank in the Atlantic northeast of Bermuda following an explosion in
one of its missile tubes. There was some press speculation and official Soviet comment that she had collided with the U.S. attack sub
Augusta, which was operating in the area and which subsequently
underwent significant repairs. The U.S. Navy later categorically
denied that such a trail operation or collision took place, or that the
U.S. Navy had anything to do with the explosion or sinking.

As 1986 gave way to 1987, heavy and continuous Soviet air reconnaissance reappeared over the U.S Pacific Fleet's Kernel Potlatch and
Safe Haven cold weather exercises off the Aleutians. Towards the
end of that year, the Soviets deployed large air and sea surveillance
forces—Tu-95 Bears, Tu-16 Badgers, and a *Balzam*-class spy ship—
to cover U.S. Pacific Fleet exercise Norpac '87 in Aleutian waters.

Nineteen eighty-eight wasn't much different. As a good example,
in its six-month deployment to the western Pacific and the Arabian
Gulf, the *Enterprise* carrier battle group faced incessant interceptions
by Soviet surveillance ships and aircraft: first in Westpac by Bear B
and D aircraft from the USSR and Cam Ranh Bay; then in the South
China Sea by Bear Ds and Fs and MiG-23 Floggers from Cam Ranh
Bay; then by a trailing Soviet AGI spy ship. In the North Arabian
Sea, *Enterprise* was overflown by Mays and Cubs from Aden, Helix
helos from an *Udaloy*-class destroyer tattletale, then back in West-

pac by Bear Ds and Badgers from Petropavlovsk, and Backfires from Alekseyevka, with "Soviet air activity . . . moderately heavy despite intermittent fog."

While *Enterprise* was on deployment, a Soviet Charlie-class nuclear cruise missile submarine arrived at Visakhapatnam, India, from Vladivostok. It had been leased by the Indian Navy from the Soviets and christened INS *Chakra*. Partially manned by the Soviet Navy, it served in the Indian Navy—ostensibly as a training vessel— for three years before being returned to the Soviet Union in 1991. The U.S. Navy (and some within the Soviet government) regarded this transfer of a nuclear submarine to a potential combatant in a volatile region of the Third World as a dangerous precedent.

As 1986 drew to a close, the U.S. Navy noticed something new: the Soviets had actually—and finally—scaled back. While they were still trailing our ships with AGIs and sending fleets of aircraft out to watch our exercises, they had not conducted any major exercise of their own far from their shores. Soviets had in fact reduced their own naval operations and exercise levels significantly. Major exercises were now conducted in waters close to the Soviet mainland—a departure from the ever-more-distant exercises of recent years. The 1986 building program, however, had remained robust. And the Soviet naval arms control propaganda offensive had ramped up.

Soviet bluster had begun to yield to hardheaded realism. If the Americans were going to press up against Soviet coasts, they had better draw back and circle their wagons. Worried by this new tiger that their own actions had unleashed, they pulled back their naval and air forces to defend their nuclear-powered ballistic missile submarine bastions, their ports, and their littorals. That, of course, eased the pressure they had been applying to vital Western sea-lanes and to exposed allies like Norway, Iceland, Turkey, and Japan, not to mention key neutrals like the People's Republic of China.

What we were seeing at sea was reflected in the data, said our analysts: Soviet worldwide ship deployments had peaked in 1984, after rising steadily for years. Then they began decreasing in 1985. Global deployments of Soviet Naval Aviation did not peak until 1987, however, before starting to fall off. Nevertheless a big change was appearing on the Communist side.

By 1987, the trend was unmistakable. Soviet exercise sea days dropped from 456 in 1985 to 207 in 1986 to 114 in 1987. (Soviet ship and submarine construction, however, was proceeding as before). Also, by 1987, Soviet "analogous response" nuclear-powered ballistic missile submarine operations had ended. As was described earlier, since January 1984, the Soviet Navy had deployed nuclear-powered missile submarines off the U.S. coasts, stationed closer to likely targets than before, as an "analogous response" to U.S. deployments of intermediate-range U.S. nuclear ballistic missiles and nuclear ground-launched cruise missiles (GLCMs) in Western Europe. These Soviets deployments were by Delta-class nuclear-powered ballistic missile submarines and Echo II-class cruise missile submarines, and they augmented the normal patrols of older Yankee-class nuclear-powered ballistic missile submarines—three off the U.S. East Coast and two off the West Coast.

Monitoring their own corners of the Atlantic, our Canadian, British, and other allies, especially their submariners, noticed the trend too. A Canadian submariner recollected that "in 1987 Soviet submarine activity in the Northwest Atlantic virtually ceased when incoming Premier Mikhail Gorbachev scaled back naval operations, including the forward deployment of nuclear-powered ballistic missile submarines off North America." Also, "1987 had seen the last major surge of Russian submarines into the Atlantic and this was not to be repeated."

As an exception—and a last gasp—the Soviets launched Operation Atrina in March 1987. Five Soviet Victor III nuclear-attack submarines sortied from their Kola bases to the Bermuda Triangle southwest of Bermuda, coordinating their operations with Tu-20 Bear D reconnaissance and missile guidance aircraft flying from bases on the Kola and from Cuba. As in earlier times, they were try-

An Su-27 Flanker fighter aircraft.
(U.S. Navy photograph, National Archives.)

ing to test U.S. Navy and allied surveillance and other reactions and ascertain relative capabilities.

Despite the new defensive emphasis by Gorbachev and declining defense budgets, Soviet exercises near their own coasts showed quite professional and effective naval power. During one Soviet naval exercise in the Norwegian Sea, Norwegian air surveillance for the first time spotted Su-27 Flanker fighter aircraft now escorting Badgers during simulated ship strikes. U.S. Navy fighter pilots realized that the hunting would become more challenging than before as the likelihood of finding and splashing unescorted Badgers, Bears, and Backfires was diminishing.

By 1988, the larger trend was unmistakable. The Soviet Navy operational tempo was clearly reduced. Major Soviet naval exercises continued to be conducted, but in waters close to the Soviet Union. In the spring, all four Soviet Navy fleets and their Mediterranean Squadron participated in joint force exercises, but in home waters. This reflected Soviet domestic economic constraints, a desire to appear "defensive" to Western publics, and the need to develop an improved close-in, combined arms counter to the U.S. Maritime Strategy of forward deployment at the start of hostilities. Most Soviet Navy exercises in 1988 were short, conducted in ocean areas contiguous to the Soviet landmass, and emphasized defense of the homeland and submarine bastions. As was also true of the United States and other nations, the Soviets temporarily increased their normal force posture in the Persian Gulf to two major and three minor combatants, primarily to escort merchant ships and tankers because of the ongoing Iran-Iraq "tanker war." But global deployments of Soviet Naval Aviation also began to fall, including in the Pacific.

In July 1988, *Red Star* reported that Soviet ground forces were now conducting defensive antilanding defense exercises. Motorized rifle battalions, reinforced by other arms, conducted the exercise, which was keyed specifically to the new Soviet defensive doctrine. A similar exercise would take place the following year. In a *Naval Review* article in February 1989, former Soviet Naval Infantry (SNI) commandant B. I. Sergeyenko expressed fear that future warning time for enemy amphibious landings would be reduced "from weeks or days to hours" because of new U.S. capabilities in amphibious assault from over-the-horizon, night operations, and *maskirovka* (cover, concealment, and deception). In October, also in *Naval Review*, SNI commandant Maj. Gen. Ivan Shuratov said the SNI would concentrate in the future on defensive missions. Nevertheless, he did not rule out the use of counteroffensive landings in a strategic defense.

In the fall of 1988, the Baltic Fleet held a large defensive exercise in Soviet territorial waters, with thirty-two warships and twenty-six naval aircraft. But Soviet overseas operations also continued. During the same season, the Soviet Mediterranean Squadron held a large exercise with Syrian armed forces, followed by a visit by all eleven ships in the exercise to their facility at Tartus, including the new carrier *Baku*. The Soviet Navy also visited Cuba, deploying an *Udaloy*-class destroyer, a frigate, a Tango-class submarine, and an oiler. The visit, however, lasted only thirty days (shorter than usual), included fewer Bear aircraft than previously, and did not include showing the Soviet flag in the Gulf of Mexico, as some previous squadrons had.

Rather than just wave goodbye to the Soviets, the U.S. Navy followed them back to their home waters. U.S. Navy freedom of navigation operations (FONOPs) continued. In June, the frigate *Hammond*

The nuclear-powered cruiser *Arkansas*.
(Courtesy of the Naval History and Heritage Command.)

legally transited Golovnin Strait in the Kuril Islands, eliciting another Soviet protest.

The next year *Arkansas*—the U.S. Navy's newest nuclear-powered cruiser—asserted U.S. Freedom of Navigation in Avacha Bay, where the port city of Petropavlovsk is situated. The Russians asserted that the bay was internal waters, drawing a line of more than 50 miles between two points at its mouth, but the United States disputed that claim. *Arkansas* penetrated the bay in May 1987 and was immediately surrounded by Soviet intelligence-gathering ships, cruisers, destroyers, submarines, and fighter aircraft. *Arkansas* was not rammed, however, and no shots were fired. The Soviets publicly protested mightily that this was a violation of their territory, but neither side published any details of the encounter.

When *Arkansas* finished her mission, she withdrew back across the North Pacific, followed much of the way by Soviet forces. The press on both sides was full of reports on the contretemps. UPI reported a number of interviews with *Arkansas* crewmen in August. Sample comments:

> "They weren't happy with us being there. They dogged us the whole time."
> "I was scared to death, man."
> "I would consider it a thrill. It got the adrenalin flowing. It was a hell of a carnival ride."
> "It was a very unique experience," said one man, who called it one of the highlights of his fifteen years in the navy.

In February 1988, the cruiser *Yorktown* and destroyer *Caron* were carrying out another freedom of navigation cruise in the Black Sea. This time they got a much more violent reaction from the Soviets. While "innocently passaging" nine miles off Crimea, they were both rammed by a Soviet frigate and destroyer. Previous Black Sea FONOPs in 1968, 1979, 1984, and 1986 had elicited hostile Soviet responses but nothing like this. Keeping his cool on the bridge of *Yorktown* while asserting his nation's rights was the cruiser's skipper, Capt. Philip Dur. Another Lyons protégé, Dur's career had encompassed planning strategy in the Pentagon and on the NSC staff and then implementing it at sea. This was a serious incident, with protests and counterprotests on both sides. What we did not know at the time, however, was that it would also be the last major incident at sea between Soviet and U.S. surface forces.

THE DIPLOMATIC FRONT

By the summer of 1985, Gorbachev was seriously worried about the direction his country was headed and decided to try some new gambits. He focused at first on issues of nuclear arms control. In August, endeavoring to cut U.S. weapons levels through example and negotiation, he announced an unconditional unilateral moratorium on the further deployment of Soviet intermediate-range nuclear missiles. He also announced a moratorium on nuclear weapons testing (on the fortieth anniversary of the Hiroshima bombing) and pledged to extend it indefinitely if the U.S. followed suit. In November, he met President Reagan in Geneva. This was Reagan's first meeting with any Soviet leader as president, and the first of five meetings between Reagan and Gorbachev, principally to discuss nuclear arms control. U.S.-Soviet relations began to thaw somewhat, although the meeting had no formal results. Reagan and Gorbachev agreed to resume talks on a treaty constraining intermediate-range nuclear missiles in Europe.

They met again in October 1986, in Reykjavik, Iceland, where they agreed in principle to remove intermediate-range nuclear missile systems from Europe. Vindicating Reagan's muscular defense policies over the preceding five and a half years, Gorbachev pro-

Reagan and Gorbachev in Geneva. *(National Archives and Records Administration; Ronald Reagan Presidential Library and Museum.)*

posed to destroy both countries' nuclear arsenals if only Reagan would pledge to abandon his SDI initiative and throttle back his U.S. defense budget increases. Reagan refused, but his policies had clearly had their desired effect on the Soviets. The diplomatic thaw in U.S.-Soviet relations accelerated. This was not yet reflected in relations at sea, however.

In September 1987, as relations between the two leaders and countries warmed somewhat, and as the result of an American initiative, an agreement was signed on the establishment of Nuclear Risk Reduction Centers, to be set up in Moscow and Washington to notify each other of upcoming strategic ballistic missile launches and other information. Naval launches were specifically included.

President Reagan was keenly interested in nuclear arms control and the reduction of the superpowers' bloated nuclear arsenals. He and Gorbachev slowly formed a partnership over the next three years or so to reduce the amount of nuclear weaponry on both sides. He was far less keen than Gorbachev, however, to constrain the U.S. Navy, which he regarded as an essential and unique pillar of U.S. military strength.

Gorbachev had a different idea. He noticed that he was popular in the West and that when he spoke, civilian pundits and some politicians on the far side of his Iron Curtain paid attention and even echoed his words. So he increased those words advocating naval arms control. Less than a year after taking power, in speeches and diplomatic demarches, Gorbachev began to call for reductions in naval armaments, the establishment of antisubmarine warfare-free zones, and other "mutual" arms control measures that would barely constrain the Soviets but hamstring us. Most tellingly, he called for fewer and smaller naval exercises, staged farther away from Soviet shores. What he couldn't accomplish at sea by intimidation or outbuilding the West—which would cost him money he realized that he didn't have—he sought to achieve through a major global propaganda offensive.

But that didn't seem to work either. Neither the United States, nor NATO, nor America's Pacific allies saw much benefit in hobbling the one American armed service that kept them all linked and united and enabled them to push back against Soviet threats and blandishments.

Responding to *The Maritime Strategy* and U.S. and allied forward naval exercises at sea, Gorbachev fired the first salvo of his naval arms control campaign in March 1986. This was just a month after he had unveiled his new policy of "reasonable sufficiency" to the party faithful and military establishment. To bring his potentially recalcitrant generals and admirals on board, he tried to accomplish through diplomatic and propaganda offensives what they wanted to do with more and more powerful ships in the water and aircraft overhead: push the Americans back across the oceans and reduce the size, scope, and effectiveness of their naval exercises. The March venue was a dinner in Moscow for the president of Algeria. Gorbachev condemned the ongoing U.S. Navy Attain Document III operations against the Libyan forces of his client, Muammar Gaddafi, remarking that "the imperial bandit face of neoglobalist policy has become visible in the past few days."

Gorbachev then proposed U.S.-USSR talks to withdraw Soviet and U.S. naval forces from the Mediterranean—the first of many such proposals from him and echoing earlier bids by his predecessor Leonid Brezhnev. Of course, withdrawal of the Soviet Mediterranean Squadron back to its Crimean bases would have only a slight effect on Soviet capabilities arrayed against NATO's southern region, while a withdrawal of the U.S. Sixth Fleet would leave all of southern Europe and the Middle East to the mercies of an invading Red Army and Air Force, not to mention Soviet long-range naval aviation.

Soviet naval arms control proposals would prove consistent for the remainder of the decade, portraying the U.S. Navy as an offensive force and proposing a series of measures that would seriously hinder or interfere with its operations and capabilities: antisubmarine warfare-free zones, nuclear-free zones, offers to trade reductions in the numbers of Soviet submarines for U.S. aircraft carriers, limitations on the numbers and ranges of land-attack sea-launched cruise missiles (SLCMs), prior notification of major naval exercises, closing of forward naval shore facilities, and a ban on naval activity in international shipping lanes, straits, and designated bodies of water such as the Baltic.

In May 1986, the USSR unsuccessfully proposed mutual naval arms control measures at the United Nations, continuing its major naval arms control diplomatic offensive. The next month Soviet arms control negotiators proposed allowing SLCMs, but only on submarines, a ploy the U.S. side rejected. And in July, in a major speech in Vladivostok that received worldwide publicity, Gorbachev called for a range of arms control measures in the Far East, and some two dozen major specific initiatives in the Pacific, including reduced naval activity, reductions in numbers of nuclear armed ships, and sea areas where all antisubmarine activity would be prohibited.

"If the United States gave up its military presence, say, in the Philippines," he said, "we would not leave this step unanswered," probably dangling a carrot that he would leave Cam Ranh Bay. Gorbachev also offered to withdraw troops from Mongolia, thus easing Soviet tensions with China and seeking to make the Chinese less likely to join the United States against them. The U.S. Navy noted, however, that just a couple of weeks after his speech, Gorbachev's Soviet Pacific Fleet conducted a large-scale exercise in and around the disputed Soviet-occupied Kuril Islands, involving sixteen submarines, fourteen to eighteen surface combatants, and two carriers.

In October 1986, as part of the arms control discussions at Reykjavik, the Soviets suggested a limit of four hundred nuclear-armed SLCMs, to be deployed only on submarines. The United States agreed to continue to discuss the question of limiting SLCMs but insisted they not be included in START treaty-agreed strategic force ceilings, and that only nuclear-armed SLCMs could be limited. A month later in Finland, Politburo and Central Committee member and Gorbachev supporter Yegor Ligachev called for elimination of

Reagan and Gorbachev at Reykjavik. *(National Archives and Records Administration; Ronald Reagan Presidential Library and Museum.)*

large-scale naval exercises from the North, Norwegian, Barents, and Baltic Seas, and a nuclear-free northern Europe, in exchange for Soviet removal of ballistic missile submarines from the Baltic—a pretty unequal trade. The Soviet effort to constrain U.S. Navy exercises through diplomacy and propaganda was escalating, as it became clear that using the Soviet Navy as a tool of intimidation had proven to be a dead end for them.

In November 1986, the ubiquitous Gorbachev was in New Delhi, again personally preaching the gospel of naval arms control. In his Delhi Declaration, he called for naval arms control measures in the Indian Ocean (to counter the Maritime Strategy), as well as counters to President Reagan's SDI program. Gorbachev proposed reduced sizes and levels of activities of naval forces in that ocean and prenotification of exercises. He and his client, Indian prime minister Rajiv Gandhi, called for dismantling of all foreign military bases in the Indian Ocean, specifically the U.S. base at Diego Garcia.

In early 1987, the Soviets announced plans to withdraw some

troops from Mongolia, seeking a rapprochement with the Chinese. They followed this up by actually making the withdrawals. And Sino-Soviet border negotiations reopened in Moscow after an interruption of eight years. This Soviet attempt at rapprochement between the two great Communist rivals was testimony to the geopolitical wisdom of the historic Nixon-Kissinger opening to China and the Reagan-Shultz opening of military-to-military cooperation agreements of 1984. The first of these were the naval cooperation agreements negotiated during my trip to Beijing in August 1984. This dimension of the Reagan Maritime Strategy was like fingernails on a blackboard to the Soviets.

NATO-Warsaw Pact talks on limiting armaments in Europe began in Vienna in 1987. In reaction to *The Maritime Strategy* and NATO's *Concept of Maritime Operations*, the Soviets continually pressed for inclusion of limitations on sea-based naval forces in the discussions, but the U.S. position throughout was to exclude them.

The Soviet drumbeat continued, both at home and abroad. In June 1987, Colonel General V. Lobov, first deputy chief of the Soviet General Staff, in a major *Red Star* article, emphasized the Soviet Union's "far-reaching proposals . . . aimed at limiting naval activity and naval arms," describing them in detail and citing Soviet proposals made the previous May, July, and November. Gorbachev himself, visiting Indonesia the next month, gave an interview in *Merdeka* repeating his naval mantra: reducing naval activity in the Pacific Ocean, restricting nuclear-armed ships, banning antisubmarine warfare activity in certain areas, limiting antisubmarine rivalry, limiting the scale and number of naval exercises, prenotifying about naval exercises, and banning such exercises in international straits and adjacent waters. At the end of the month, during ongoing strategic arms limitation talks, the Soviets again sought to constrain SLCM deployments, tabling a draft strategic arms limitation treaty text that would place a limit of four hundred nuclear SLCMs on each side—a limit unacceptable to the U.S. government, not just to the U.S. Navy.

In October, Gorbachev traveled to Murmansk, where his speech contained yet another set of proposals to restrain U.S. naval operations. He called for a whole set of northern European arms control measures, including an Arctic "zone of peace." These proposals would counter the Maritime Strategy and strengthen the Soviet Navy in antisubmarine warfare, an area where it was relatively weak. In summary, he declared that "the USSR proposes . . . reducing military activity and limiting the scale of activity of naval and air forces in the waters of the Baltic, Northern, Norwegian, and Greenland Seas . . . including an understanding on limiting competition in antisubmarine weapons."

A month later Soviet ally Vietnam pulled twenty thousand troops out of Cambodia, designed to ease tensions with China. But that same month North Korean agents used a planted bomb to blow up a South Korean passenger flight from Baghdad to Seoul, over the Andaman Sea, killing all 115 souls on board. Clearly the peace offensive had a few ingredients missing. Such incidents indicated to many, including in the U.S. Navy, that the Soviets and their allies still could not be trusted.

For over three years, U.S. and Soviet diplomats had been negotiating to reduce or eliminate intermediate-range nuclear missiles in Europe. Finally, in Washington in December 1987, at their third meeting, President Reagan and General Secretary Gorbachev signed the historic Intermediate-Range Nuclear Force (INF) Treaty, agreeing to eliminate completely all their nuclear and conventional ground-based ballistic and cruise missiles with ranges of 500 to 5,500 kilometers. This was a major milestone in the warming relations between the two superpowers. The two sides also stated that "the sides shall find a mutually acceptable solution to the question of limiting the deployment of long-range, nuclear-armed sea-launched cruise missiles. Such limitations will not involve counting long-range, nuclear-armed SLCMs within the 6000 warhead and 1600 strategic offensive delivery systems limits. The sides committed themselves to establish ceilings on such missiles, and to seek mutually acceptable and effective methods of verification of such limitations."

In discussing the issue of nuclear SLCMs on subs and surface ships with the secretary of defense and the White House, I made it clear that the navy would be willing to have them used as a bargaining chip. The truth was that we in the navy wanted to get rid of all of them because they took up too much room and personnel that measurably reduced conventional combat capability.

With the arms control action shifting from intermediate range to strategic weapons, the Soviet campaign to limit the U.S. Navy through controlling its operations and capabilities changed its context but not its goals. Reducing U.S. Navy SLCM numbers had emerged as a core Soviet objective, but limiting U.S. Navy exercises remained an important end as well. Memories of Ocean Venture, Northern Wedding, and Norpac—not to mention freedom of navigation operations—still haunted the Soviets.

In March 1988, General Secretary Gorbachev was at it again, this time in Belgrade, Yugoslavia. In a major speech there, he proposed a freeze on U.S. and Soviet naval forces in the Mediterranean, ceilings on naval forces in that critical sea, eventual withdrawal of U.S. naval forces from the Mediterranean entirely, and prenotification of naval exercises. Again, such moves would affect the Soviet military posture against NATO's southern region only slightly, while effectively gutting the U.S. Sixth Fleet's ability to protect America's other forces in the region, as well as its southern European and Middle Eastern allies. As newly appointed U.S. secretary of the navy Will Ball noted later that year, "The Navy's continuing forward posture has influenced Soviet perceptions as well: recent Soviet 'zone of peace' and arms control initiatives clearly suggest that NATO's naval strength is an important factor in the deterrence equation."

A month later, faced with an unwinnable war in Afghanistan that was draining his treasury and adversely affecting Soviet civilian as well as military morale, Gorbachev agreed to withdraw his troops from that unhappy and chaotic country. That long and grudging

234 | JOHN LEHMAN

retreat began in May, but it wasn't accompanied by any relaxation in the Soviet naval arms control offensive. A day after it began, a Soviet spokesman restated his country's naval arms control demands, this time at a symposium in Stockholm. Lt. Gen. Viktor Starodubov, a former Soviet naval aviator and disarmament director for the Central Committee's International Department, reiterated the now-familiar Soviet position.

As a Swedish reporter related, the general was particularly concerned with the size, scope, and—apparently—the effectiveness of U.S. and NATO forward naval exercises:

> I do not need to explain what modern exercises mean. It is impossible to know what will happen in 10 minutes, a continuation of the exercise or war. And this is the source of suspicions, of instability, of what worries us both. The Soviet Union understands very well that if we were to conduct similar exercises, NATO would probably react in the same way. We try to put ourselves in the situation of the opposite side, so to speak. And thinking of that, in 1986 and 1987 we conducted only one exercise in the Northern and in the Baltic Fleets.
>
> In October 1987, M. S. Gorbachev made several proposals, which if realized would stabilize the Nordic situation. And they were further concretised and developed during Nikolai Ivanovich Ryzhkov's visit in Sweden and Norway. It was suggested to begin consultations between NATO and the WTO aiming at reducing the activities of naval and air forces and to delimit their operations in the Baltic, the Sea of Greenland and in the Norwegian Sea, and to introduce CSBMs also in the Barents Sea. Such concrete measures would be limits on ASW activities, notification of large air and naval exercises, invitation of observers from all CSCE participants. We also proposed to invite observers unilaterally, we were willing to

show our manoeuvres and exercises. . . . We must strive to increase security by reducing the activity of naval forces and of military forces on the whole in this region, General Starodubov concluded.

While the Soviets continued to press their arguments to constrain our navy, they were slowly yielding on issues that they saw as less important. President Reagan took notice. In a widely reported incident during a summit meeting visit to Moscow in May 1988, the president signaled a major change of attitude toward the Soviet Union: while walking through Red Square, he was asked by reporters if he still considered the Soviet Union an "evil empire." He had supported this characterization as recently as the previous year. This time, however, Reagan answered no. Surprised, the reporters asked why. The president responded, "I was talking about another time and another era." Many interpreted this public statement as signaling a major—and much less confrontational—U.S. policy shift vis-à-vis the Soviet Union. That began to be the case in some areas, but the president and the administration still hung tough and resisted Soviet attempts to constrain America's navy, whose freedom to operate forward and globally they rightly saw as fundamental to U.S. and allied security.

A month later General Secretary Gorbachev beat yet another retreat from the aggressive legacy of his predecessors: he seemed to renounce the Brezhnev Doctrine of 1968, which asserted a right to intervene militarily in the domestic affairs of Warsaw Pact allies. At the Nineteenth Congress of the Communist Party of the Soviet Union, he declared that "the external imposition of a social system, of a way of life, or of policies by any means, let alone military, is a dangerous trapping of the past." It remained to be seen, however, if he really meant the renunciation—or could enforce it in a skeptical Soviet Army and Navy.

In July 1988, the chief of the Soviet General Staff, Marshal Sergei Akhromeyev, again visited the United States, this time with the Soviet service vice chiefs, as guests of the chairman of the U.S. Joint Chiefs of Staff (JCS), Adm. Bill Crowe, and all the joint chiefs. Marshal Akhromeyev had earlier accompanied General Secretary Gorbachev to Washington in December 1987 and had visited the Pentagon and the JCS then as well.

During the visit, Akhromeyev presented Admiral Crowe with a map, showing the Soviet Union at the center, surrounded by global U.S. forward forces and bases, in which U.S. forward naval forces—especially submarines and carriers—figured prominently, as did Tomahawk SLCM-range arcs. The map more or less replicated—and conveyed the same message as—many of the graphics in *The Maritime Strategy*. At a reception, the marshal looked the American chief of naval operations, Adm. Carlisle Trost, in the eye and declared, "You, you the United States Navy, are the problem." Trost later told an interviewer that he responded, "I'm very pleased to hear that we're being effective . . . that our strategy is working." According to the interviewer, "It made Trost feel very, very proud and very, very effective." Later, in October 1989, Trost told a Soviet audience at the Marshal Grechko Naval Academy in Leningrad that Akhromeyev had added, "Your Navy and bases surround my country and threaten the security of the Soviet Union."

Admiral Crowe's experience was similar:

> Akhromeyev . . . talked at length about America's offensive orientation and in particular about the United States Navy, whose strength seemed almost to mesmerize him. He described how the U.S. Navy had surrounded the Soviet Union with its carrier forces, how his country had been encircled since the end of World War Two. To bolster his contention he gave me a carefully prepared chart that supposedly pinpointed our global system of military facilities. The map was thick with flags—a sobering visual presentation of the Soviet view of American naval deployment worldwide. . . . That was Akhromeyev's view of

America's ability to roam the world and control the seas, all of it designed to surround the U.S.S.R. and intimidate the Kremlin.

From the Pentagon, the marshal was whisked out to sea, where he watched an air show aboard the brand-new carrier *Theodore Roosevelt*, as the personal guest of Admiral Crowe. Atlantic Fleet commander Adm. Frank Kelso and others accompanied Admiral Crowe, while deputy commander in chief of the Soviet Navy Adm. K.V. Makarov and others accompanied the marshal. The event included an air wing firepower demonstration and marked the first carrier landing for the Soviets. Shaken, Marshal Akhromeyev would later counter Admiral Crowe's arguments on the defensive nature of the U.S. defense pos-

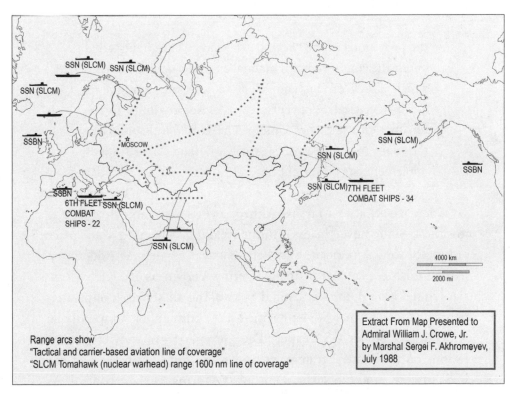

Range arcs show
"Tactical and carrier-based aviation line of coverage"
"SLCM Tomahawk (nuclear warhead) range 1600 nm line of coverage"

Extract From Map Presented to
Admiral William J. Crowe, Jr.
by Marshal Sergei F. Akhromeyev,
July 1988

The Akhromeyev Map. (© *John Lehman*)

ture by emphasizing the "threat" that carriers posed to the Warsaw Pact, citing his carrier visit. *Theodore Roosevelt* would deploy the following month for the Norwegian Sea, to participate in NATO exercise Teamwork '88, pointedly directed at Soviet forces threatening the alliance's northern flank. In Admiral Chernavin's view, "There is no way that such an operation can be called defensive. According to the new Maritime Strategy . . . U.S. Navy objectives are to achieve advantages . . . to seize the initiative with the beginning of conflict and to deliver strikes against targets situated deep in Soviet territory."

Soon after he returned home, Marshal Akhromeyev summarized his conclusions on U.S. naval power in an article in *Pravda* titled "Naval Forces and Universal Security." The article proved to be yet another major blast at the United States for not entering into naval arms control agreements with the Soviets. His visits to the United States had confirmed his view that:

> the provisions of the "new naval strategy" are being tried out in the course of naval maneuvers and exercises, during which attack groups equivalent to wartime contingents are systematically concentrated in close proximity to the territory of the Soviet Union. The U.S. naval forces are the main instrument of pressure whereby United States implements its power politics.

A few weeks after Marshal Akhromeyev's visit, an informal and unofficial—but nevertheless groundbreaking—meeting took place among Soviet, American, and British naval experts at Adderbury, in Oxfordshire. In this historic meeting known as RUKUS (Russia, United Kingdom, and United States), the all-star cast of participants included former Soviet Pacific Fleet commander Adm. Nikolai Amelko and Soviet USA expert Dr. Alexei Arbatov. Soviet presentations on their own strategy proved to be harsh criticisms of the U.S. strategy, and (no surprise) proposals for naval arms control. As participant Eric Grove related:

Marshal Akhromeyev and staff watch
flight operations aboard *Theodore
Roosevelt. (Official U.S. Navy photograph
by Gary J. Ross, National Archives.)*

Soviet participants expressed general concern with the
"aggressive" nature of United States naval doctrine as perceived by them, the growth of the cruise missile threat,
the large size of the United States Marine Corps and the
growth planned for amphibious forces. Particular concern
was expressed with the major NATO maritime maneuvers
that take place close to Soviet territory, within range of
NATO strike systems. These exercises seem provocative
to the Soviet Union, for example, three carriers operating
simultaneously in the Sea of Japan.

In November 1988, the American people went to the polls again
and elected Reagan's vice president—George H. W. Bush—as their
president. It was a stunning endorsement of President Reagan and his
policies, especially toward the Soviet Union. Not in four decades had
an American political party won more than two presidential elections in a row. President Bush, after a careful review of the nation's
international situation, embarked on a similar policy to his predecessor's of "peace through strength." He would ease up on some of the
more provocative U.S. forward naval operations at sea and reduce the
aggressiveness of American naval rhetoric. But he supported a strong
role for the navy in the nation's policy quiver, hung tough on issues
of naval arms control, and cut back the fleet and its six-hundred-ship
force goal only marginally.

On December 7, 1988, at the United Nations in New York, Soviet president Gorbachev dramatically announced significant unilateral Soviet troop withdrawals from Eastern Europe. Among other moves, six Soviet armored divisions stationed there were to be disbanded. This clearly would weaken if not cancel entirely the Brezhnev Doctrine of Soviet intervention in the Communist Eastern Europe satellite countries—a move foreshadowed earlier by Gorbachev. It heralded a sea change in Soviet military policy and in the Western response to it. Gorbachev also trumpeted the changes made in Soviet military doctrine from offense to defense and announced planned unilateral cuts in Soviet forces by half a million troops.

The reaction throughout America—and indeed the world—was overwhelmingly favorable. For many, it represented the end of the Cold War and the vindication of the bipartisan naval strategy first urged by Senators John Tower and Scoop Jackson, planned out in Sea Plan 2000 and aggressively executed by President Reagan and his team.

Later on the day of the speech, Presidents Reagan and Gorbachev met for the fifth and last time, at the Governor's Island Coast Guard base in New York Harbor. President-elect Bush was also present. Navy SLCM limitations were inevitably a topic of discussion, but no commitments were made nor agreements reached.

A week later Gen. Mikhail Moiseyev replaced an increasingly unhappy Marshal Akhromeyev as chief of the Soviet General Staff. Akhromeyev would return to Gorbachev's side over a year later, however, as a presidential adviser.

In another sign of the times, a few days before Christmas, Communist Cuba, Angola, and South Africa signed a peace accord at the United Nations, guaranteeing independence to the former South African United Nations trust territory of Namibia and agreeing to a phased removal of the fifty thousand Cuban troops then in Angola by 1991. Both the United States and Soviet Union backed the agreement.

And on New Year's Eve, the Soviet Union declared a cease-fire in Afghanistan.

Whatever changes might be occurring in Soviet policy and

strategy, they certainly weren't apparent yet at Soviet shipyards and outfitting bases. All through the last half of the 1980s, Soviet naval building and deployment programs continued apace—living off the momentum achieved in the previous two decades. In 1986, Admiral Chernavin deployed his first quiet Akula-class nuclear attack submarine, commissioned in 1984. Seven more would follow through 1991. He also began commissioning quiet Oscar II-class antiship cruise missile submarines, as well as the second *Slava*-class antiship cruiser. And he launched the third *Kirov*-class nuclear-powered battle cruiser and laid the keel for the fourth and last of the class, and the first of seven intended *Neustrashimyy*-class antisubmarine frigates. Only two were finally commissioned. Soviet Naval Aviation continued to modernize and upgrade, introducing new Backfire C models of the Soviets' already fearsome long-range supersonic antiship strike aircraft; new Su-24 Fencer-E maritime reconnaissance/strike aircraft; and Helix B amphibious assault helicopters on board Ivan Rogov-class amphibious warfare ships.

In 1987, during the same month that the Soviets' Vietnamese allies were pulling out of Cambodia, the first Soviet missile-carrying nuclear-powered 85,000-ton conventional takeoff and landing (CTOL) supercarrier was laid down. The ship—the *Ulyanovsk*—was to be the first fourth-generation of Soviet "aviation ships," following two *Moskva*-class, four *Kiev*-class, and one *Tbilisi*-class ships. A month later, with the ink on the INF Treaty still wet, the Soviet Navy commissioned *Baku*, its fourth and last *Kiev*-class vertical and short takeoff and landing (V/STOL) carrier. And continuing the momentum of their building program, the Soviets laid down the last of seven Delta IV-class nuclear-powered strategic ballistic missile submarines (SSBNs).

These continuing building programs were evidence of both the reluctance of the Soviet defense establishment to support Gorbachev's reversal of long standing offensive doctrine, and the run-out momentum of the massive program of Admiral Gorshkov to achieve naval supremacy that was adopted by Brezhnev in the 1970s.

Meanwhile the Soviets continued to respond to the revelations of U.S. Navy antisubmarine prowess that had been brought to them by their willing American moles dug deep in U.S. national security agencies, especially the navy itself. They deployed more and more successive copies of the new, quieter submarine class leaders that they had begun to put into service in the early 1980s. By December 1988, a U.S. National Intelligence Estimate (NIE) on Soviet strategic nuclear capabilities judged:

> The Soviets currently lack an effective means of locating U.S. SSBNs in the open ocean. We judge that they will not deploy such a capability in the 1990s, and we see no Soviet solution to the problem on the horizon. On the other hand, the Soviets will increase the threat to U.S. attack submarines attempting to operate in areas close to the Soviet Union.

It was that continued—and increasing—Soviet naval threat to American forward submarine operations that most concerned the U.S. naval leadership, whatever reductions now-President Gorbachev might make in his missile forces and troops deployed in landlocked Asian countries. The U.S. Navy also looked askance at the continued development of Soviet carrier aviation. On December 4, 1988, the second *Tbilisi*-class 65,000-ton carrier—laid down as the *Riga* in 1985—was launched and began to be outfitted. This was just days after Gorbachev's dramatic gesture at the United Nations. A few weeks later, just as the Soviets declared their cease-fire in Afghanistan, the Soviet Navy commissioned the *Kalinin*, third of its four 28,000-ton nuclear-powered *Kirov*-class battle cruisers, and another quiet Oscar II-class nuclear-powered cruise missile submarine, designed for long-range anticarrier operations.

December 1988 might have looked like a turning point in world history to many, but that was hard to swallow for many U.S. Navy officers, charged with keeping the Soviet Navy in its place and worried at the clear and continuing scope of Soviet naval modernization. The month was also marred by the heinous Libyan downing of a civilian airliner, Pan Am flight 103, over the town of Lockerbie, Scotland, killing all 259 persons on board—189 of them American. Given that Libyan dictator Muammar Gaddafi was a Soviet client—and one against whom President Reagan had often launched his navy—this event cast a pall on Gorbachev's peace overtures and militated against any ratcheting back in U.S. Navy capabilities, readiness, or strategy.

The U.S. Navy had other reasons to be wary. In 1988, retired admiral of the Soviet Union Sergei Gorshkov edited and wrote the introduction for yet another tome: *The Navy: Its Role, Prospects for Development, and Employment.* This major new book on the Soviet Navy was written as an advocacy piece for Soviet defense intellectuals and proponents of the navy, and it represented the final statement of Gorshkov's recommended Soviet naval policy, published in the wake of perestroika, glasnost, the U.S. Maritime Strategy, and Soviet naval cutbacks and arms control initiatives (which Gorshkov regarded as ineffective). As one knowledgeable U.S. Navy expert on the Soviet Navy concluded, "This was a nuclear war-fighting book with a focus on the role of the Soviet Navy if it should go to war tomorrow. Its goal would be to sink Western nuclear-powered ballistic missile submarines at the war's outset—so much for viewing strategic antisubmarine warfare as destabilizing." Gorshkov gave new increased emphasis to strategic antisubmarine warfare, mobile basing, and Soviet V/STOL carrier aircraft, and he projected a highly dynamic future undersea warfare environment—none of which would be possible without increasing already robust funding from the strapped Soviet treasury.

But the defensive military doctrine and stringent resource policy being imposed on the navy by the Soviet leadership did not support the offensive posture and enhanced capabilities that Admiral Gorshkov advocated. This book, for which he wrote the introduction, proved, in retrospect, to have been "a last-ditch attempt to argue that Gorshkovian-style sea power remained relevant in an era of tight budgets and perestroika."

It fell on deaf ears.

CHAPTER 8

The Cold War Ends, 1989

The East European Bloc Disintegrates

THE BIG STORY of 1989 was the collapse of the Soviet-imposed international system in Eastern and Central Europe, as well as elsewhere. This was the first fruit of Reagan's grand strategy of adding "rollback" to "containment" of the Soviet Empire. He had first encountered this strategic vision in 1975, upon reading *A Forward Strategy for America*, published in 1961 by Strausz-Hupé and Kintner. Their view was that shifting from the successful postwar American strategy of containment to a more activist increase of naval, military, and political pressure against the periphery of the Soviet land empire would bring about unsustainable internal contradictions and hasten the crumbling of Communism. This belief had been the foundation of President Reagan's defense buildup, counterinsurgency, the six-hundred-ship navy, and its aggressive use in operations like Ocean Venture '81 and successors. And now it was beginning to come to pass with the tumultuous events of that year in Eastern Europe and in Asia.

With a shattering Soviet empire as a backdrop, the Soviet Navy spent the year cutting back and retreating, while—seemingly on another planet—its huge defense bureaucracy continued its modernization plan. Meanwhile the U.S. Navy continued to look askance at that modernization and to resist the tenacious Soviet diplomatic and propaganda push for arms control agreements that would hamstring the U.S. Navy.

In January, East Germany, Poland, Czechoslovakia, Hungary, and Bulgaria all announced future reductions in their conventional forces and military budgets. Also, the first contingent of Cuban troops left Angola, as agreed the previous month. In midmonth, right before President Bush's inauguration, anti-Soviet demonstrators in Prague were beaten by Czech police, and the demonstrations' organizers—including playwright Václav Havel—were arrested.

In February, the last contingent of Soviet troops withdrew from Afghanistan, and the first contingent began to withdraw from Czechoslovakia. In April, Soviet forces began to leave Hungary. In March and April, the Soviet Union held the freest legislative elections in its seventy-five-year history. While the Communist Party still retained a majority of seats, many CPSU officials were defeated. Also in April, in Poland, independent trade unions—including Solidarity—were legalized, and more ominously, Soviet troops dispersed a Georgian anti-Soviet demonstration in Tbilisi with bullets, causing twenty deaths and hundreds of injuries.

In May, the Iron Curtain began to crack: Hungary started to dismantle its border fence with democratic but neutral Austria, allowing thousands of East Germans and others to cross into the West. June saw the Communist Chinese massacre of pro-democracy students in Beijing causing an abrupt halt in America's support for the People's Republic. But it also saw Solidarity sweeping the first genuinely democratic elections in Poland since 1928, making Poland the first Warsaw Pact state in which democratically elected representatives gained real power. In July, President Bush visited Warsaw and Budapest to encourage nonviolent change in the rapidly disintegrating East Bloc. In August, two million Balts formed a human chain linking Vilnius, Riga, and Tallinn to protest Soviet occupation.

On September 10, a dam broke: the government in Budapest announced the freedom of East Germans in Hungary to leave the country for the West. Within three days, more than thirteen thousand East Germans fled to the West through Hungary, the largest such exodus since the building of the Berlin Wall in 1961. Also the end of September, Vietnam had withdrawn the last of its troops from Cambodia, due in part to pressure from their Soviet longtime ally and benefactor. On October 9, seventy thousand East Germans demonstrated for peace, freedom, and nonviolence in Leipzig. Local Communist Party leaders refused German Communist leader Erich Honecker's order to attack the demonstrators. When the regime did not respond with violence, the populace lost its fear of the regime, and a week later Honecker was forced from office. Late in October, reflecting on recent and ongoing events, Soviet Foreign Ministry spokesman Gennadi Gerasimov used the catchy term "Sinatra Doctrine" to describe the Soviets' new policy of now allowing each satellite country to "do it my way."

By November, events were accelerating. On the fourth, some half a million people were in the streets demonstrating in East Berlin, and a week later the Berlin Wall itself was breached. As video of Germans dancing on top of the wall was broadcast all over the world, Gorbachev refused to use Soviet troops to bolster the Communist East German government, which toppled within a month. In December, it was Czechoslovakia's turn. In a "velvet revolution," longtime Communist leader and Czechoslovak president Gustav Husak resigned, having appointed the first largely non-Communist government in Czechoslovakia since 1948. Things didn't go as peacefully in Romania, however. Three days before Christmas, Communist leader Nicolae Ceausescu and his wife were executed by an army firing squad. This would prove to be the only violent removal of a Communist government in the course of the revolutions of 1989, a wave that resulted in the fall of Communism in Communist Central and Eastern Europe. Soviet-style socialism would also soon be abandoned in Cambodia, Ethiopia, Mongolia, and South Yemen. Communist institutions would remain in power, however, in China, Cuba, North Korea, Laos, and Vietnam.

With the vaunted Soviet Bloc collapsing, Soviet Navy overseas operations and some capabilities underwent a precipitous decline. During 1989, the Soviets sent three or four dozen obsolete 1950s-vintage submarines and surface combatants to overseas scrapyards. There was a big fall-off in U.S.-Soviet surface and air incidents at sea as well. Yankee-class nuclear-powered ballistic missile submarine patrols off the U.S. coasts were almost eliminated. Golf II-class diesel ballistic missile submarine patrols in the Baltic ceased.

No large-scale Soviet naval exercises were conducted in 1989, and out-of-area deployments were fewer: a Bear F visited Cuba, but no warships. Submarine and surface combatant presence in the Mediterranean and at Cam Ranh Bay was cut back, and by the end of the year, all Soviet naval aircraft had been withdrawn from the Mediterranean. The MiG-23 Flogger fighters at Cam Ranh Bay were shipped back to the Soviet Union, and the Badgers there were retired. Bear D and Bear F operations from Cam Ranh continued, however. Development of the facility at Tartus, Syria, trailed off. Soviet Naval Aviation deployments to Syria and Libya were cut by two-thirds, and those to Luanda, Angola, were markedly reduced. The Soviet presence in the Indian Ocean was also considerably lowered, as a direct result of the cease-fire between Iran and Iraq.

On the other hand, the momentum of Admiral Gorshkov's building program was imposing and unflagging. Soviet Navy ship and aircraft construction and modernization programs continued. Tonnage added to the fleet in 1989 actually *exceeded* tonnage lost to scrapping. In fact, 1989 was the most productive year, in terms of tonnage delivered to the Soviet Navy, in more than two decades. Submarine tonnage launched in 1989 was the highest since 1986, and the number of combatant submarines launched (nine) exceeded the total for each year since 1982.

Also the Soviets made their first arrested landings and ski-jump takeoff of an Su-27 Flanker, a MiG-29 Fulcrum, and an Su-25 Frogfoot on their new 65,000-ton carrier *Tbilisi*, which had its first flight operations and sea trials.

The Russian carrier *Admiral Kuznetsov* was launched in
1990. (*U.S. Navy photograph, National Archives.*)

Introduction of these aircraft into the Soviet Navy was for both
land-based and sea-based use. Su-17 Fitter and Su-24 Fencer fighter/
attack aircraft were also transferred from the Soviet Air Force to the
Soviet Navy. This was, however, probably just a shell game to escape
Conventional Armed Forces in Europe (CFE) Treaty arms control
constraints on land-based air force aircraft, but it certainly increased
the Soviet Navy's capabilities.

In February 1989, a recently declassified U.S. National Intelligence Estimate judged Soviet Navy missions and capabilities as little changed:

> Soviet naval general purpose forces continue to have the
> major missions of protecting the Soviet missile-launching
> submarine force and defending the USSR against NATO
> strategic and theater forces. Although the Navy can be
> expected to bear a share of spending reductions, major
> emphasis will be placed on improving anti-submarine and

anti-surface combatant operations, gradually modernizing Soviet naval aviation, and increasing the availability of
sea-based airpower as larger aircraft carriers enter service
during the 1990s. Support for land TMOs remains a primary wartime task of naval theater forces, and we project
a slow continuation of several organizational and weapon
trends that should provide land theater commanders with
more capable naval forces for combined arms operations.

Soviet safety practices at sea—always iffy—appeared to be dete-
riorating, however, as tragic submarine accidents followed one after
another. In April 1989, the Soviet Navy's lone Mike-class nuclear-
powered attack submarine, the *Komsomolets*, sank in the Norwegian
Sea after fire broke out on the surface. While the crew was rescued,
forty-two later died from the effect of smoke inhalation and other
causes. The submarine was six years old. The death toll due to the
sluggishness of the rescue attempts shocked the Soviet public. The
Norwegian Air Force offered helicopter rescue assistance from Bodø
airfield, but the Soviet Navy inexplicably refused the offer. This was
unfortunately only the first of three major Soviet submarine disasters
in 1989. In the second such incident, a fire was reported on a Soviet
Navy Echo II-class nuclear-powered cruise missile submarine in the
Norwegian Sea. And the following month another fire was reported
on an Alfa-class nuclear-powered attack submarine in the Barents Sea.

The Soviets continued to surveil U.S. Navy operations and exercises. For example, against the biggest U.S. Navy exercise of the year,
Pacex '89, they flew near-daily surveillance flights, except (as the carrier *Enterprise* command historian pointed out) they couldn't find the
U.S. battle groups as they transited under "emissions control" conditions. During the exercise's final phase, Valiant Blitz, Soviet inter-
ference increased, as *Enterprise* transited the Strait of Tsushima into
the Sea of Japan. In one instance, they sent a huge Soviet simulated
strike of at least thirty-four Badgers toward the carriers. During the

exercise, the Soviets conducted one of their own, launching seven missiles coordinated with a regimental attack by Soviet aircraft into the Arctic and Gulf of Alaska.

Late in the year, CNO Admiral Trost visited the Soviet Union as the guest of Soviet Navy commander in chief Admiral Chernavin. The two old submariners toured a Victor III-class attack submarine together. An interviewer later debriefed Admiral Trost, recording that

> during Admiral Trost's visit to the Soviet Union in October 1989 . . . he found their shipbuilding program for the nuclear cruiser stopped, but other shipbuilding and modernization programs continuing for both carriers and submarines. He also confirmed for the first time that the MIG 29 was being adapted for carrier launches, and that the Soviet Navy had been given continued priority for Russian conscripts, assuring the quality of manpower needed to achieve the Soviet goal of a fully modernized, but smaller, naval force by the mid-1990s. He left the Soviet Union with the clear impression that while the country was suffering major economic problems that would eventually affect their military capabilities, their naval forces would continue to modernize, presenting "massive capabilities" for the foreseeable future. They, the Soviet naval forces at least, had not yet "backed off" from the cold war.

In April, President and General Secretary Gorbachev traveled to the Guildhall in London to press his case yet again for naval arms control negotiations between the United States and the Soviet Union, and between NATO and the Warsaw Pact. That same month the U.S. intelligence community counseled American decision makers that "the Soviet approach to arms control also retains some propagandistic elements. Many Gorbachev proposals are obviously self-serving or quixotic (nuclear weapons-free zones, reductions in naval exercises, etc.)."

Some useful cooperative measures were adopted by both sides, however, which did not impinge on U.S. naval freedom of action. Visits among the two countries' military leaders continued. In June, the chairman of the U.S. Joint Chiefs of Staff, Adm. Bill Crowe, visited the Soviet Union as the guest of General Moiseyev, the chief of the Soviet General Staff. They cruised together on a Soviet guided-missile cruiser and boarded a nuclear submarine at Murmansk, among other military activities. They also signed an agreement on the Prevention of Dangerous Military Activities (PDMA) in Moscow, which reaffirmed the commitment by both sides to resolve peacefully any "unintentional" violations of national territory and prohibited the harmful use of lasers.

During the summer of 1989, the U.S. and Soviet navies conducted reciprocal diplomatic exchange port visits: three Soviet Navy surface combatants visited Norfolk and two U.S. Navy surface combatants visited Sevastopol—the first major military exchanges between the two nations and the first Soviet warship visit to a U.S. port since 1975. U.S. Navy ships at Sevastopol were the cruiser *Thomas S. Gates* and the frigate *Kauffman*. NATO Strike Fleet commander Vice Adm. Jerome Johnson hosted Vice Adm. Igor Vladimirovich Kasatonov, first deputy commander in chief of the Soviet Northern Fleet, and commanding officers of the three visiting Soviet Navy ships, for dinner in the carrier *John F. Kennedy* flag mess, in Norfolk. Vice Admiral Johnson was an A-7 attack pilot and a dynamic leader who had overseen refinement of the Maritime Strategy as a commodore in the Pentagon in the mid-1980s, and only a few months previously he had commanded NATO exercise Teamwork '88, featuring practice in offensive operations against the Soviet Northern Fleet and other Soviet forces. This port visit exchange inaugurated a series of reciprocal port visits over the next few years, at San Diego and Vladivostok, and later at Mayport and Severomorsk.

At about the same time, a joint civilian scientific party conducted a nuclear warhead verification experiment on a Soviet Navy SS-N-12 Sandbox medium-range cruise missile (SLCM), on board the Soviet cruiser *Slava* in the Black Sea at Sevastopol. The event was organized by Gorbachev adviser Yevgeni P. Velikhov, director of the Kurchatov Institute of Atomic Energy. The U.S. side was led by a private nongovernmental environmental organization, the Natural Resources Defense Council, comprised of American civilian scientist arms control experts concerned over the risk that nuclear war might start at sea.

The U.S. government had opposed the event, the navy arguing that it was impossible to verify nuclear warheads on nuclear SLCMs. Velikhov and the left-leaning U.S. scientists wanted to prove this false. The KGB was against the experiment too, but Gorbachev overruled them. The scientists spent four hours using various tools to determine whether they could ascertain if a SLCM had a nuclear warhead on it, and they concluded that they could. They published their findings and argued for their cause in the *Bulletin of the Atomic Scientists* in November 1989.

The Soviets noticed that the Americans weren't applauding their policy changes but focusing instead on their continued buildup and force modernizations. At the start of 1989, Admiral Chernavin bleated in *Morskoy Sbornik*:

> Representatives of the NATO countries could not fail to see changes that have taken place in the theory and practice of Soviet military development under the influence of perestroika and the new political thinking. However, NATO's leadership prefers to pretend that nothing important has happened, and an adequate response has not been forthcoming from their side. They continue to hold large-scale exercises in the spirit of offensive strategy, often near the frontiers of the Soviet Union. And lately the intensity and extent (of these exercises) have increased. . . . According to the 'New Maritime Strategy' adopted by the

Pentagon in 1986, gaining advantages through preventive measures, taking initiatives when a conflict begins, and inflicting strikes against objectives located deep within Soviet territory are the navy's missions.

Frustrated by the Americans' spurning of the Soviet naval arms control offensive, he complained, "Our proposals are being ignored. This reality has to be taken into consideration." He concluded correctly that "the American leadership is trying to violate the military-strategic parity between the USSR and the United States and ensure their military superiority."

In February, *U.S. Naval Institute Proceedings* published Admiral Chernavin's responses to its editors' questions. This event was seen as yet another "breakthrough in ongoing efforts to establish a dialogue between Soviet and western naval strategists." Theretofore "Soviet naval leaders have not spoken directly to readers through the Western media." Throughout the published interview, Chernavin reacted strongly against—and was clearly worried about—the aggressive nature of forward U.S. Navy presence and exercises at sea, most especially in the northwestern Pacific. Among his comments:

> The most important feature of Soviet military doctrine is its particularly defensive character.
>
> In building our armed forces, we are guided by the principle of defensive sufficiency.
>
> The U.S. naval strategy has the pure appearance of an active offensive—I will allow myself to say it more harshly—an aggressive bent. In addition, the U.S. Navy now has three divisions of marines fully prepared for operations, which, according to former Marine Corps Commandant General P. X. Kelley, can be landed at Nordkapp, in the eastern part of the Baltic sea, on the coast of the Black Sea, on the Kuril Islands, or on Sakhalin.

That same month the second tripartite RUKUS talks were held, this time in Moscow. A British organizer and participant noted that "operations by Western carrier task forces in the Vestfjord area caused concern on the Soviet side. Attack aircraft could reach from these areas into Soviet territory. . . . It was clear that the Soviet Union was worried about the threat posed by United States carrier battle groups and amphibious forces to the Soviet Union itself, for example, the Kola Peninsula."

In the fall, NATO's commander in chief Channel Command conducted the exercise Sharp Spear to improve NATO maritime shallow-seas and reinforcement capabilities in the Baltic, the Baltic approaches, the North Sea, the UK waters, and the English Channel. Some 270 ships and 320 aircraft from ten NATO nations (including the United States, France, and Spain) participated.

Once again the Soviets were "mirror-imaging" their own doctrine, fearing NATO at-sea exercises as launching pads for sneak attacks on the Soviet Union.

A third RUKUS meeting was held in November 1989, again at Adderbury in Oxfordshire. During the discussions, a Soviet speaker "emphasized the threat felt by the Soviet Union when three carrier battle groups exercised off Kamchatka, with weapons capable of reaching deeply into the Soviet Union." Admiral Lyons must have grinned.

On September 22, President Bush signed out National Security Directive (NSD) 23, "United States Relations with the Soviet Union." This authoritative policy statement superseded the Reagan administration's January 1983 National Security Decision Directive (NSDD) 75 "U.S. Relations with the USSR." Of central importance to the navy and its exercise program, it contained a major change in national guidance: "The purpose of our forces is not to put pressure on a weak Soviet economy or to seek military superiority."

The next day, meeting in Jackson Hole, Wyoming, U.S. secretary of state James Baker and Soviet foreign minister Eduard Shevardnadze agreed to a *U.S.-Soviet Agreement on Reciprocal Advance Notifi-*

cation of Major Strategic Exercises. Each agreed to notify the other no less than fourteen days prior to carrying out any major strategic exercise involving heavy bombers. Of far greater importance to ending the Cold War at sea, they also agreed to a U.S.-USSR *Joint Statement on Uniform Acceptance of Rules of International Law Governing Innocent Passage.* Through this agreement and a subsequent State Department notification, Secretary Baker declared that the United States no longer needed to conduct Freedom of Navigation Operations to assert the right of innocent passage through Soviet territorial waters—a right the Soviets now acknowledged. Henceforth there would be no further U.S. Navy warship incursions into Soviet territorial waters in the Black Sea, and incidents at sea between the two navies fell off markedly.

Shevardnadze also agreed to drop the Kremlin's long-standing insistence that sea-launched cruise missiles (SLCMs) be limited under the impending START Treaty limiting strategic nuclear weaponry. Instead, the Soviet foreign minister proposed that SLCMs be consigned to a separate negotiation. Aware of the U.S. Navy's protectiveness toward the SLCM program, Baker held firm against any limits, even outside the START framework.

Conforming to the NSD, the U.S. Navy had reformatted Pacex '89—its big and long-planned Pacific Fleet exercise of the Maritime Strategy—to steer clear of the Soviet littoral, keeping its ships and aircraft in the eastern Pacific, the Gulf of Alaska, off the Aleutians, and in the Sea of Japan—but no longer planning to deploy into the Sea of Okhotsk.

On December 2 and 3, 1989, U.S. president Bush and Soviet president Gorbachev met at sea in the Mediterranean, in what wags wound up terming the "seasick summit." The shipboard venue was reminiscent of momentous at-sea meetings between FDR and Winston Churchill to sign the Atlantic Charter at Placentia Bay, Newfoundland, in 1941, and between Napoleon and Czar Alexander on a raft on the Neman River almost a century and a half earlier, to sign the Treaty of Tilsit.

A couple of weeks before the meeting, the president's special adviser for arms control, Lt. Gen. (ret.) Edward Rowny urged continued U.S. opposition to naval arms control measures at the Malta talks. In an internal memorandum to the president and Secretary of State Baker, he advised that

> Gorbachev will certainly attempt to involve us in naval arms control. The mounting campaign which began with Akhromeyev's visit and was continued by Shevardnadze in Wyoming will be advanced by the media who will exploit the symbolism of a meeting at sea to advance the "reasonableness" of naval arms control. We must be prepared to combat this no-win situation, to include a statement by the president upon his arrival on the cruiser that the U.S. Navy is not on the bargaining table.

Their meetings were supposed to take place off Malta on board the Soviet guided-missile cruiser *Slava* and on the American cruiser *Belknap*—flagship of the U.S. Sixth Fleet and the NATO Striking and Support Force South. The venue had to be shifted at the last minute to the Soviet luxury civilian cruise liner *Maxim Gorky*, alongside a pier, due to high winds and heavy seas. Together the two leaders declared the Cold War to be over.

According to two leading historians of the event,

> Gorbachev handed Bush a blue and white map prepared by Marshal Akhromeyev, showing the Soviet Union's "encirclement" by American bases as well as U.S. aircraft carriers and battleships. The map's purpose was to underscore the Soviet General Staff's contention that U.S. vessels armed with SLCMs posed an especially lethal threat to the Soviet Union.
>
> For a moment, Bush was at a loss for words. Tartly, Gorbachev said, "I notice that you seem to have no response."

"That's because what you're saying gives me a lot of trouble," said Bush. "Naval arms control is going to be hard to get." He pointed out that the Soviet landmass was shown on the map as a giant white empty space, with no evidence of the imposing military complex that the U.S. forces were intended to deter. "Maybe you'd like me to fill in the blanks on this. I'll get the CIA to do a map of how things look to us. Then we'll compare and see whose is more accurate."

"We are encircled by your navy," said Gorbachev. "As we go to lower levels in these other weapons systems [land-based missiles and bombers], you need to reduce naval weapons as well. Geography is a special factor in all this."

Historically, Gorbachev continued, the Soviet Union had always been mainly a land power, while the United States had used its navy to protect its interests on the far side of two oceans. . . .

"We don't consider you an enemy any more," Gorbachev told Bush. "Things have changed. We want you in Europe . . . So don't think we want you to leave."

Baker considered this the most vital and hopeful statement that Gorbachev had made all weekend.

Veteran submariner Vice Adm. J. D. Williams, who commanded the U.S. Sixth Fleet and the NATO Striking and Support Force, was present at the meeting. He recalled that as Gorbachev presented a copy of the map to Bush, the Soviet leader remarked, "We have read every one of your submarine messages for ten years and have been unable to find or kill even one of them. We quit."

No agreements were signed at Malta. Gorbachev proposed eliminating all naval nuclear weapons except strategic missiles on submarines. Leading American Sovietologist and diplomat Raymond Garthoff later wrote that "Bush brusquely dismissed the idea." Later it would come to pass.

At the Malta Summit of December 1989, Presidents Bush and Gorbachev declared the Cold War to be over. *(Photograph by David Valdez. National Archives and Records Administration, George H. W. Bush Presidential Library.)*

In January 1990, in the journal *Voennaya Mysl* (Military Thought), two Soviet Navy captains laid out sober, lengthy, objective, and accurate descriptions and analyses of the tenets of the Maritime Strategy and its manifestations at sea. Gone was the semihysterical phraseology of earlier Soviet naval analyses of what the U.S. Navy was up to.

Capt. 1st Rank V. M. Mikhaylov correctly concluded that "the new strategy's content bears a more aggressive nature. While previously the primary idea was to await the enemy on organized lines, now the mission is assigned to anticipate the enemy in operational deployment and impose battle with his subsequent defeat." His article included Soviet-style maps illustrating the intended at-sea campaigns by both sides along the Warsaw Pact's European and East Asian littorals.

Capt. 1st Rank V.A. Galkovskiy's analysis grasped that:

The U.S. military-political leadership sets aside a leading role in implementing its plans for the naval forces as
a branch of the armed forces which meets to the greatest extent the fundamental principle of all U.S. strategic
concepts—waging war only on foreign territories without
allowing strikes against its own administrative and industrial centers and making maximum use of forces of the
countries allied with it.

He went on to tally up those allied forces in some detail and
explain their role in implementing western naval policies and strategy. He noticed in particular that "rehearsal of amphibious landing
operations under northern conditions has begun" and that "preparation of a new Arctic Ocean theater of operations also has begun."
Captain Galkovskiy further advised his audience:

Practical rehearsal of combat missions already has been
under way since 1986 by American-European coalition
force groupings in the Atlantic theater and by American-
Japanese-South Korean coalition force groupings in the
Pacific theater, above all for engaging ground targets and
landing assault forces in operations of the initial period
of war from areas immediately adjoining the borders of
the USSR and Warsaw Pact countries. For the first time
our coastal seas (Baltic, Black, Sea of Japan and Sea of
Okhotsk) have been included in the operations zone of
their forces and formations for this purpose.

The captains seemed resigned to achieving little progress on the
naval arms control front. Captain Mikhaylov finished his article by
observing that U.S. secretary of defense Dick Cheney "resolutely
spoke out in an interview with NBC against a reduction in the U.S.
Navy; in particular, he noted that 'naval forces are absolutely nec-

essary to the United States. We are not interested in limiting these forces.'" Captain Galkovskiy remarked that Cheney's predecessor, Frank Carlucci, had said that "for the United States to reduce the navy is the same as for the USSR to destroy railroads and highways. The navy is the main U.S. communications artery, so to speak, in trade, economics, and assurance of security." Both captains recognized that the feckless Soviet naval arms control offensive had run into a stone wall not just within the U.S. Navy but also within the American national security establishment writ large and among the American people.

The New Year didn't open auspiciously for the Soviet empire. Poland withdrew from the Communist alliance on New Year's Day. A few weeks later, came the "Baku massacre": Gorbachev sent Soviet Army troops to suppress Azerbaijani pogroms against Armenians and anti-Soviet protests, resulting in over one hundred dead and eight hundred injured. The next month, in elections in Nicaragua, Conservatives defeated the incumbent Marxist Sandinistas. This would lead to the withdrawal of Cuban military advisers from Nicaragua and a lessening of Cuban influence in Central America. And in March, Lithuania declared its independence from the Soviet Union, the first union republic to do so. Estonia, Latvia, and Armenia followed suit over the next few months. The Soviet Union was unraveling.

On August 2, 1990, Iraqi dictator Saddam Hussein marched his massive and well-equipped army into tiny but oil-rich Kuwait, his neighbor to the south. President Bush declared that "this will not stand," and began to form an international coalition to push Saddam and his army back to Baghdad. Iraq had long been a Soviet client state, and most of its military equipment had been made in the USSR. But on August 3, Soviet foreign minister Shevardnadze and U.S. secretary of state Baker, together in Moscow, jointly condemned the Iraqi invasion of Kuwait and called for an arms embargo on Iraq. In a remarkable policy change, the Soviet Union would now pose no threat to a Europe being denuded of U.S. and other NATO forces for service in Iraq and the Persian Gulf. Some date this as the true end of the Cold War.

In September, Gorbachev and Bush met again, in Helsinki, to discuss the Gulf crisis and agree to try to get Saddam Hussein to withdraw without more blood having to be shed. But while Bush was forging a new multinational coalition of the willing against Saddam, Gorbachev was losing his grip: that same month East Germany withdrew from the Warsaw Pact, and the next month it was absorbed into the West German federal republic. The Soviets and Germans signed a treaty on the maintenance and withdrawal of Soviet troops from the former East Germany, to be completed by 1994. Germany was to foot the bill for the withdrawal of the troops and their families (some 420,000 people) and their resettlement in the Soviet Union. Soviet forces had already withdrawn from Czechoslovakia and Hungary and would be out of Poland too by the end of 1991.

As had been the case the previous year as well, Soviet naval operations continued to decrease. Soviet global naval ship deployments continued to fall off, and Soviet Naval Aviation deployments plummeted precipitously, especially in the Pacific. As in 1989, there were no major Soviet fleet exercises. One brief ship visit to Cuba took place, but no exercise with the Cuban Navy. February saw the last Soviet Naval Aviation deployment to Cuba. Soviet presence at Cam Ranh Bay continued to decline until late in the year, when it showed a slight upward surge. The Soviet presence at Ethiopia's Dahalek Islands appeared to have diminished or ended, and the same was true in Angola, by November 1990. The Soviets also appear to have ceased maritime reconnaissance patrols from Aden.

The Soviet Navy continued to scrap older vessels instead of modernizing them: in 1990 they sent forty-four old combatant ships and submarines to be scrapped in foreign yards, but the Soviet naval shipbuilding program continued to produce record tonnages of submarines and significant numbers of surface ships.

Western intelligence estimated that the Soviet Navy now included 2,150 naval aircraft, up from 1,600 in 1985 and 1,400 in 1980. Su-

27 and MiG-29 fighters continued to work with the new 65,000-ton carrier *Admiral Kuznetsov.* The Soviet Navy also continued to receive numerous combat aircraft from the Soviet Air Force—probably to evade CFE arms limitation rules but in any event a significant addition to Soviet naval capabilities. The Soviet Navy also received three motorized rifle divisions complete with tanks, armored personnel carriers, and artillery, also probably to evade CFE restrictions.

The Soviet Navy also continued to seek to explain itself in the midst of the increasingly chaotic conditions surrounding it. In January and February 1990, *Morskoy Sbornik* published two authoritative extracts from a new book by Admiral Chernavin: *The Struggle for the Sea Lanes of Communication: Lessons of Wars and the Modern Era.* The articles—and book—touted the defensive nature of the Soviet Navy. They also stressed, however, the importance of interdicting sea lines of communication (SLOCs) in achieving past victories, and of the role of submarines and carrier aviation (but not surface combatants) in doing so. Chernavin clearly saw his navy as integrated into a joint military force, distancing himself from the previous Gorshkovian focus on the navy's unique missions.

In April, a recently declassified U.S. National Intelligence Community (NIC) memorandum concluded that, in light of scheduled Soviet withdrawals from pact states, "we now believe that the capability to conduct an unreinforced conventional Pact attack on NATO would be virtually eliminated." It also noted that

> although unilateral Navy reductions were not part of Gorbachev's speech, the Soviets have embarked on a program of naval measures. In 1989, 46 ships and submarines departed Soviet naval facilities to be scrapped in foreign yards. All but one were at least 30 years old; only one was operational. We have identified an additional 120 units that are candidates for scrapping in 1990. The Soviets have also reduced out-of-area deployments by both ships and Soviet naval aircraft. At the same time, the Soviets

continue with force modernization and construction of aircraft, submarines and surface combatants, including three conventional takeoff and landing (CTOL) aircraft carriers, although there is debate within the USSR over the need for carriers.

In interviews in May and again later in October, Admiral Chernavin asserted only defensive roles for his growing carrier fleet, which—he emphasized—carried only interceptors, not strike aircraft. He acknowledged, however, strike roles for the antiship cruise missiles on Soviet carriers, submarines, and surface ships.

As of midyear, the Soviet Navy was clearly sending mixed signals to its American rivals. When pressed by the Strategic Studies Group (SSG) at the Naval War College to acknowledge Soviet acceptance of their new defensive doctrine, U.S. CNO Admiral Trost reminded them that the head of the Soviet Navy, Admiral Chernavin, was still writing about offensive operations such as interdicting sea lines of communication. "Didn't Chernavin get the word?" he asked the SSG.

Later that summer, the U.S. and Soviet Navies implemented another set of reciprocal confidence-building port visits. A three-ship Soviet squadron called on San Diego, while the American missile cruiser *Princeton* and missile frigate *Reuben James* visited Vladivostok. By now the U.S. and other allied forces were building up in Saudi Arabia and the Persian Gulf to throw Saddam Hussein and his armies out of occupied Kuwait. While numerous navies joined the American-led international coalition at sea to enforce a United Nations–imposed trade embargo on Iraq, the Soviet Navy would play no role in that besides observing.

The Soviets continued to press for limitations on U.S. Navy sea-launched cruise missiles (SLCMs) but were usually rebuffed by the State Department, often under strong and effective internal U.S. government pressure from the U.S. Navy. On February 9, 1990, Secretary Baker met with President Gorbachev and Foreign Minister

The Soviets and some in the Bush administration and Congress continually pressured Secretary of State James Baker to accept reductions in the navy and naval weapons like the Tomahawk. He ignored them. *(U.S. Department of State photograph.)*

Shevardnadze in the Kremlin. The Soviets agreed to accept the U.S. approach on SLCMs. Instead of seeking verifiable limits, each side would simply declare to the other once a year the number of weapons it planned to deploy. In a follow-on meeting in Moscow in May, Baker and Shevardnadze agreed to limit nuclear SLCMs to 880 for each side, in an agreement separate from the START treaty. A limit of 880 was clearly no limit at all since neither side desired that many. The Soviets had lost the game and thrown in the towel.

From May 30 to June 3, Presidents Bush and Gorbachev held their second summit meeting, this time in Washington. They agreed that the START treaty would not constrain SLCM deployments, but that each side would make a unilateral declaration concerning nuclear SLCMs, and those declarations would be politically binding. In an extraordinary concession, Gorbachev also agreed with Bush that the "Germans should decide whether or not they're in NATO."

In October, U.S. secretary of defense Dick Cheney visited Moscow for the very first time. While he was conferring with the Soviet president, "Gorbachev castigated Bush for his use of the U.S. Navy in the Gulf. Said the Soviet leader, 'The president is a former navy man. Everyone in the U.S. government is obsessed with the navy.'"

Meanwhile U.S., Soviet, and European diplomats were finishing up work on a Conventional Armed Forces in Europe (CFE) Treaty and an agreement on Confidence and Security-Building Measures (CSBMs). Under the CFE Treaty, signed between twenty-two NATO and Warsaw Pact member nations, ground and air conventional forces in Europe would be reduced, but sea-based naval forces were not included. Under the Vienna Document on CSBMs, limited rules were to be applied to some naval activities, especially land-based naval aviation and amphibious forces, including naval gunfire support.

Nineteen ninety-one was a momentous year: the U.S.-led coalition drove Saddam Hussein out of Kuwait, the Warsaw Pact disbanded, and the Soviet Union finally wound up where President Reagan had predicted it would, on the "ash-heap of history."

The year didn't begin well for the Soviet Navy. The worm had finally turned, and the spigots maintaining its out-of-sync building program finally began to shut down. In January, continued construction of the 20 percent-complete 85,000-ton nuclear-powered supercarrier, the *Ulyanovsk*, was canceled. (She would be scrapped in 1992.) The Soviet Navy was, however, able to commission the 65,000-ton conventionally powered aircraft carrier *Admiral Kuznetsov*, the first full-deck carrier and the largest warship that would ever be completed by the Soviet Union.

During the same month, in what came to be known as Bloody Sunday and the Vilnius Massacre, Soviet Army troops seized government buildings and a TV station in Vilnius, Lithuania, suppressing anti-Soviet protests. Thirteen Lithuanian civilians were killed, and hundreds were injured. A week later, in Bloody Sunday II, Soviet Black Berets attacked demonstrators and seized Latvian Intelligence headquarters, killing four. Perhaps even more significantly, three hundred thousand demonstrated in Moscow in solidarity with the Balts.

Gorbachev denied that he had ordered the use of force. If he had, he was lying. If he had not, he was losing control of his country. He had already lost control of the Soviet satellites, however: in February the Warsaw Pact was formally declared disbanded, and in April, the Georgian republic declared its independence of the Soviet Union.

Also in April, former chief of the Soviet General Staff Marshal Sergei Akhromeyev, in *New Times* magazine, gave four reasons why the Soviet Union still needed whatever armed forces it could still muster, explicitly highlighting the U.S. Navy's capabilities and posture:

> The NATO bloc military organization has survived; the United States has multiple superiority over us in naval forces and does not want to reduce them. Having surrounded the Soviet Union 40 years ago with its military and naval bases, the United States still maintains those bases now. The USSR has state interests which do not coincide with the interests of other countries. . . . With regard to U.S. aircraft carrier strike groups, I can say: they are the most dangerous weapon for the Soviet Union that is in the hands of the United States. . . . Aircraft carriers are the U.S. military force that can arrive off the coast of the Soviet Union and create a military threat for us six to eight days after the order has been given.

In May 1991, in his office in the Kremlin, Marshal Akhromeyev received two American visitors—a commonplace now. One was Capt. Larry Seaquist, who as a member of the Strategic Studies Group (SSG) had been one of the seminal thinkers involved in the implementation of the Maritime Strategy. He had also skippered the battleship *Iowa* during her dash to Spitzbergen during the exercise Northern Wedding '86, confounding the Soviets. He was now assistant deputy undersecretary of defense for policy planning. Seaquist was accompanied by Rich Haver, who had been the navy's guiding hand behind the extraordinary intelligence-based appreciation of Soviet Navy capabilities and intentions that had underpinned the Maritime Strategy. Haver too had been pulled up to higher levels in the Pentagon and was now Secretary Cheney's assistant for intelligence policy.

The two Americans and the marshal met in a Soviet conference room absent any decoration except one: a small version of the "Akhromeyev map" showing U.S. forces—especially U.S. naval forces—ringing the Soviet Union. Seaquist and Haver were unable to ascertain if the map had been placed there especially for their meeting or if it was routinely displayed there, but there it was—a triumphant symbol of the effect of the Maritime Strategy—and its implementation through putting ships forward in the northern seas—on the wall in the highest levels of the Soviet government.

By July, in what was now becoming a routine program of engagement and confidence building, two Soviet Navy warships put in to the U.S. Navy base at Mayport, Florida. And on the twenty-ninth, the United States and Soviet Union signed the Strategic Arms Reduction Treaty (START) in Moscow, limiting strategic offensive nuclear weapons, including Trident and other submarine-launched ballistic missiles (SLBMs). The treaty resulted in the eventual removal of about 80 percent of all strategic nuclear weapons then in existence.

START itself did not constrain SLCMs, and they were not classified as strategic weapons. Shortly after the treaty was signed, both sides withdrew their nuclear SLCMs from service. The Soviet Union also declared that the Tu-22M Backfire naval bomber was just a medium bomber, not a strategic offensive arm, and committed to not giving that aircraft the capability of flying intercontinental distances in any manner, including in-flight refueling. It pledged that the number of naval Tu-22M airplanes would never exceed two hundred.

Despite its new carrier, the Soviet Navy by now was unmistakably in decline, posing an ever-decreasing threat to the interests and security of the United States and its allies. It still possessed, however, a formidable—if fragmenting—technical and knowledge base, especially in antisubmarine warfare—a continuing legacy, among others, of the Walker spy family's treason. According to a recently declassified August 1990 U.S. government National Intelligence Estimate:

The extensive Soviet anti-submarine warfare program has made some gains. The Soviets have an improved, although limited, ability to detect and engage enemy submarines in waters adjacent to the USSR. In the future, the combined effect of multiple layers of ASW systems may constitute a significant challenge to Western submarine operations in Soviet-controlled waters. We judge, however, that through at least the next 15 to 20 years the Soviets will remain incapable of threatening U.S. SSBNs and SSNs in the open ocean.

August was a pivotal month for the collapsing Soviet superpower. From the nineteenth to the twenty-first, desperate Soviet Communist reactionaries attempted an ultimately unsuccessful coup against President Gorbachev, striving to overthrow his government. In what may have been a related show of force planned by the defense minister, Marshal of the Soviet Union Dmitry Yazov, a Soviet Fleet SSBN, K-407 *Novomoskovsk*, on August 6, performed an unprecedented full-salvo underwater launch of all sixteen SS-N-23 strategic missiles on board. The first and the sixteenth missiles hit their targets at the Kura testing range on the Kamchatka Peninsula, while the rest were intentionally self-destructed in flight.

Russian Federation president—and Gorbachev opponent and rival—Boris Yeltsin successfully defied and defeated the coup. In the immediate aftermath of this near miss, Gorbachev dismissed many of his top military leaders, including Yazov, who had been one of the coup leaders. Admiral Chernavin, who did not actively support the coup attempt, remained as head of the navy—one of only two service chiefs to survive the postcoup purge.

August 24 was a momentous day: Gorbachev resigned from the Soviet Communist Party; Ukraine passed its independence act; and Marshal Akhromeyev committed suicide. Akhromeyev had sympathized with but not participated in the coup. He left a note explaining that he could not continue living when the institutions to which he had devoted his life were disintegrating. Less than a week later, the Soviet parliament banned Communist Party activities.

From August to December, ten Soviet republics declared their independence from the USSR. In September, the United States granted formal recognition to the three Baltic republics as independent states. Meanwhile, in honor of the fiftieth anniversary of the first British supply convoy's arrival in northern Russia during World War II (Operation Dervish), American, British, and Soviet veterans from that era celebrated in Murmansk and Arkhangelsk.

In September, it was the United States' turn to surprise with a grand gesture. On September 27, President Bush (with confidential navy support) announced on national television that all tactical nuclear weapons, including nuclear-armed Tomahawks, would be withdrawn from U.S. Navy ships, as part of his unilateral Presidential Nuclear Initiatives. Soviet leader Gorbachev promptly followed suit on October 5. (This did not constrain in any way, however, the U.S. Navy's continued deployment and use of the conventionally armed Tomahawk cruise missiles that had recently demonstrated their extraordinary military worth during the Gulf War against Saddam Hussein.)

In the fall, the Soviet-supported Vietnamese war in Cambodia came to a close, ending Vietnamese isolation from the United States, China, and ASEAN, and its total dependence on the Soviet Union.

China and Vietnam agreed to normalize relations after years of hostility. Presidents Bush and Gorbachev met yet again, at the Madrid Middle East peace conference. In another sign of the times, new Center for Naval Analyses (CNA) president Bob Murray, Ambassador Marshall Brement, and others traveled to the Soviet Union for the first in a series of bilateral discussions on naval cooperation with ISKRAN, a major Soviet think tank.

Also in the fall, Admiral Chernavin, commander of the Soviet Navy, visited the United States as the guest of CNO Admiral Kelso. He traveled to Washington, Norfolk, Newport, and Annapolis, reciprocating then-CNO Admiral Trost's visit to the Soviet Union in 1989. At Newport, he lectured at the U.S. Naval War College and answered questions.

Meanwhile that month he published an article on the Soviet Navy's future as he saw it, "The Navy: Problems of Reduction and Development," in *Morskoy Sbornik*. As one leading U.S. Navy analyst of Soviet thinking and behavior concluded:

> Chernavin's Soviet Navy of the future was cast in terms of a defensive military doctrine that did not accept the lack of an external threat from the U.S. It used mission terms like averting war, repelling aggression, safeguarding the maritime flanks, depriving the enemy of the opportunity of conducting offensive operations, and creating the conditions for the restoration of peace. . . . Chernavin's future general purpose forces were given the principal mission of ". . . ensuring the physical preservation and sound functioning of the naval strategic nuclear system under any condition." Secondary missions were to defend the maritime frontiers and to inflict "defeat on enemy naval strike groups and impeding the execution of broad-scale operations [and assist in] defensive operations in the continental theaters." Chernavin appeared to announce that the future building programs ruled out large surface or amphibious ships. Instead, primary attention was to be given to submarines and aircraft-carrying cruisers.

Another analyst noted that "concerning the navy, Chernavin espoused his oft repeated contention that the Soviet Navy existed as part of a unified strategy and as such had no separate agenda to pursue." He "identifie[d] the two-fold purpose of the Navy as that of deterrence and SLOC interdiction and protection." He made "a notable effort to emphasize the importance of increasing the number of aircraft carriers to the Soviet naval order of battle as a means to compensate for a simultaneous reduction (up to 60% total; 75%

strike units) in shore-based naval aviation units. . . . Specifically he called for a reduction in the frequency of naval exercises and the increase of on-scene observers on an exchange basis."

To many in the U.S. Navy, Chernavin's lecture and article didn't suggest that much had changed. The Soviet Navy had always been "defensive," to keep the U.S. Navy away from Soviet strategic submarines, Soviet forces operating on NATO's flanks, and the Soviet homeland itself. But its increasingly expansive "defensive" zones—if successfully defended—would have severed America's links to its own forces in Europe, and to our most important forward allies, ensuring their defeat and destruction.

December 1991 marked the end of the road for the Soviet Union and its once-mighty navy. Almost five years earlier the Soviet chief of staff, Gen. Vladimir Lobov, had pushed aggressively for constraints on the U.S. Navy through arms control measures. Now he was being shown around the Royal Navy nuclear-powered ballistic missile submarine HMS *Revenge* in Faslane, Scotland. The new Soviet carrier *Admiral Kuznetsov* was sailing from the Black Sea to her new home in the Northern Fleet (surveilled along the way by aircraft from the USS *Forrestal*). That fleet had meanwhile been reduced by eighteen ships and twenty-five submarines over the previous year. By the end of the month, all Soviet Navy combatants and most support ships had followed the *Admiral Kuznetsov* out of the Mediterranean. From 1985 to 1991, the number of major warships in the Soviet fleet had declined from almost 570 to under 429, with the retirement of numerous old submarines and surface combatants.

On December 20, a new organization met for the very first time: the North Atlantic Cooperation Council (NACC), attended by foreign ministers and representatives of sixteen NATO countries and nine Central and Eastern European countries, including the Soviet Union. As the final communiqué was being agreed, the Soviet ambassador announced that the Soviet Union had been dissolved during the meeting, and that he now represented only the Russian Federation. On Christmas Day, the then-twelve constituent republics of the Union of Soviet Socialist Republics declared themselves independent states, including the Russian Federation under President Boris Yeltsin. Soviet president Gorbachev called President Bush on the phone to tell him the news, and that he had resigned. Most of the Soviet Navy would be inherited by the Russian Navy, commanded by the last Soviet Navy commander in chief, Admiral Chernavin. As one observer wrote, "Thus, at the end of 1991, with the demise of the Soviet Union, the once powerful Soviet Navy faced being split into parts, had returned to home waters, reduced at-sea training, deteriorated in material condition, and declined in size."

Ronald Reagan came to the presidency with a vision that the West could end the Cold War without violence: "We win, they lose." From his study and exposure to the best geopolitical thinkers during the 1970s, he had come to believe that Western elites had become intimidated by Soviet bluster and aggression. He believed further that they had become myopic in viewing the East-West military balance as solely determined by the balance of armies in Central Europe. The 180 active and 100 reserve divisions of the Warsaw Pact could not be matched by NATO. That sole focus on the fearsome superiority enjoyed by the Communist armies had fostered an institutional pessimism in NATO. Reagan had come to believe the orthodoxy of Western elites ignored completely the huge advantage that geography and Western sea power granted NATO. The Warsaw Pact was essentially landlocked, and NATO had command of the seas within its grasp. If recognized and activated, this inherent maritime supremacy could more than compensate for the superiority of Warsaw Pact land forces.

Reagan believed it was time to venture forward from the successful but passive policy of containment to the more activist policy of rebuilding American naval forces to reassert maritime supremacy in all the seas surrounding the Soviet empire and convince them that if they attacked NATO, they would quickly lose the war at sea and expose themselves to attack from virtually all azimuths.

The president had spent much time with his advisers discussing implementation of the aggressive forward naval strategy, and he knew it had dangers and difficulties. First, the formal adoption of such a departure was a de facto challenge to the foreign policy establishment on both sides of the Atlantic, including not least, the Army–Air Force dominated Pentagon and NATO bureaucracies. He knew that he was likely to be derided as an inexperienced cowboy.

More important were the operational uncertainties. His naval advisers and his intelligence briefings gave him confidence, but he would not become privy to the most sensitive secrets until after inauguration. Once in the Oval Office, he gave the orders to execute the plan during his first year. Admiral Hayward, the CNO, and Gen. Bob Barrow, commandant of the U.S. Marine Corps, knew perhaps better than the president the risks and great difficulties of this bold new venture, and no one knew better than Ace Lyons, the man we had chosen to command this strike fleet, the challenges of an entire fleet venturing into the far north close to Soviet bases and exercising offensive operations.

That first thunderclap of Ocean Venture in the late summer of 1981 involved eighty-three ships from all the NATO navies and Spain. From it, the annual exercises expanded to the Pacific and ventured farther north and closer into Soviet targets. Every year they grew in frequency, numbers, and sophistication. The navy's appropriately educated and experienced cadre of midgrade and senior strategists supported the leadership well. When ashore, they inhabited the rabbit warrens and briefing theaters of the Pentagon and the gaming floors of Newport. Rotating to sea, they led the ships and squadrons that dared challenge the bear off North Cape, in the Aegean, in the Sea of Okhotsk, and under the ice. They helped conjure up the concepts we used, then went forth to implement them tactically and imaginatively at sea, themselves. Then they came back again to more responsible staff positions in D.C. and the fleets to drive the insights that they had gained in exercises and operations into refining the strategy that they had helped conceive. Many of the vignettes in this narrative have sought to capture their deeds, holding forth around conference tables as well as making split-second command decisions at battle stations on bridges and in cockpits throughout the fleet. They were the navy's Cold War warrior-intellectuals—another vital arrow in our quiver—and they were superb.

At first, the Soviets were aghast at the Maritime Strategy and then soon tried to react with increasing vigor. But as more and more ships, aircraft, and technology joined the fleet, it became clear to the Soviet Navy that it could not cope. After the Ocean Safari '86 confounded and humiliated the Soviet air and naval defenses with U.S. carriers now able to operate with impunity inside Norwegian fjords, the Soviet General Staff informed the Politburo that the budget of the Northern Fleet and the air force must be trebled if they were to be able to defend the homeland. Many have seen this as the point of collapse of Soviet will. After beggaring their economy to achieve the dream of military superiority, the Soviet Union now found itself worse off than ever.

The forward strategy and maritime supremacy that had been asserted and built since 1981, led by the president and supported by a bipartisan Congress, had been vindicated. Along with the modernization and increase in NATO land and air forces, ten years of aggressive forward naval operations had convinced the Soviet leadership that they could not defend their strategic assets and their homeland without impossibly large increases in spending. That fact had removed the political power of the Soviet military and created the political opportunity for strong leaders like Yeltsin and Gorbachev to pursue perestroika and glasnost and to seize the opportunity to negotiate an end to the Cold War.

We had won the Cold War at sea: the world's oceans had been ventured, and the world's oceans had been gained.

EPILOGUE

After winning the Cold War at sea, the United States cut its overall defense spending and reduced the size of its navy. This was reasonable: the six-hundred-ship navy had done its job and could afford to reduce. No power or combination of powers could now threaten American command of the seas.

This tranquil period could not be expected to last long, and it did not. Released from the disciplines of the bipolar Cold War, new powers moved to advance their interests. Islamist terrorism spread its multinational reach; Vladimir Putin and his fellow KGB alumni consolidated their power in Russia; and China, its economic strength unleashed by the adoption of capitalism and market economics, rapidly moved to develop its military and naval power. Enabled by the American removal of Saddam Hussein, Iran moved to establish its dominance in the Persian Gulf and Mesopotamia, while North Korea accelerated its drive to acquire nuclear weapons. But as the balance of power rapidly shifted, the distracted West continued to disarm. The U.S. Navy shrank from nearly six hundred ships to fewer than three hundred.

The history of deterrence is a lesson that schoolboys know: credible threats are respected, while weakness invites unwelcome outcomes. America's naval decline since the end of the Cold War has invited the challenges we face today. America's enemies, by increasing their forces at sea and gaining control of regional sea-lanes, exploit the void created by declining U.S. naval power. We are disarming while our potential enemies are arming. We have frozen budgets even as demands from combatant commands increase, with the result that we try to do more with less, cutting training, increasing social experimentation, and losing the basic skills even of seamanship, let alone war fighting. A decade of fading professionalism led to the disastrous collisions and groundings of 2017. Without a significant change in direction, our adversaries' ability to threaten or to use force will grow.

The unreadiness of our forces accelerates; Russian and Chinese pilots get far more flying time than their underfunded American counterparts, as but one example.

It is often said that while history does not repeat itself, it often rhymes. Such is the case today. Forgetting the lessons of history is a principal reason for such rhyming and has major consequences, particularly when it comes to sea power. States that wish to wield global influence maintain global navies, whereas states that abandon their focus on the seas, regardless of the reason, see their power decline and their hopes fade.

Three recent historical cases demonstrate the results of naval decline. The allied naval disarmament treaties of the 1920s and '30s emboldened Germany, Japan, and their allies and became a contributing cause of World War II. America's postwar naval disarmament increased Communist aggression and facilitated the Korean War. The post–Vietnam War U.S. naval disarmament had the same result, encouraging Soviet aggression and expansion globally. Like a law of nature, this fact holds true irrespective of time and place: a decline in sea power invites disaster.

In October 2016 the *Admiral Kuznetsov*, Russia's sole aircraft carrier, sortied from Kola Bay through the Barents Sea, around the North Cape, down the Norwegian Sea, the North Sea, the English

Channel, and the Bay of Biscay, past Gibraltar and through the Mediterranean, arriving off Syria in November. There it commenced flight operations against ISIS and American-supported rebels. After losing two jets to landing accidents, the air wing was transferred ashore, where it continued to operate against ISIS. After a month of flight operations, the air wing came back aboard, and the *Kuznetsov* headed back to Russia, stopping offshore of Libya along the way to host their Libyan friend, military leader Khalifa Hiftar. She then proceeded back to her homeport in the White Sea, arriving in early February. Vladimir Putin let it be known that he initiated and oversaw the mission. Western media was captivated and reported on the ship's progress and activities from start to finish.

From a public relations and diplomatic point of view, the initiative was a success for Putin. He demonstrated that his military rebuilding program, started a decade before, was having results. No more than four other powers in the world could have executed such a difficult mission. It was one more demonstration that Putin meant to play a major role in world politics and that he could be relied upon as an ally to provide sophisticated military support.

On the other hand, such close world attention brought unintended consequences. Naval analysts observed that the air wing carried about one-quarter as many aircraft as a U.S. carrier and that of them, only a dozen were frontline SU-33s and MiG-29s. Because the ship had no catapults, they noted, its fighter-bombers could not carry much armament or go very far. Its faulty arresting gear apparently caused the loss of two jets and required that the rest be put ashore in Syria. Moreover, the ship's engines failed several times during the voyage.

None of this was surprising to Western analysts, as the ship was the first of her class (the second and last, the *Liaoning*, now sails in the Chinese Navy) and was thirty years old. She had had very episodic maintenance during the long periods while she was tied up for lack of funds, and she went through several name changes, first *Riga*, then *Brezhnev*, *Tbilisi*, and *Admiral Kuznetsov*. This embarrassing performance was not the fault of the Russian Navy, which continues to maintain a high level of professionalism and training. Rather, it is the result of the much-reduced budgets of the post-Soviet era. Accepting its now-regional power and absorbing lessons learned from the U.S. Navy, the Russian Navy has realistically focused its efforts and budgets on submarine and antisubmarine warfare (ASW) in the unique environments of the northern Pacific, Arctic, and northern Atlantic.

The Russians have spent heavily to boost their navy's presence in adjacent regional seas, especially the Black Sea, where it illegally seized the great old czarist and Soviet naval base Sevastopol from Ukraine, then started rebuilding its fleet in that critical maritime theater. The Russians have also reinforced their naval bastion at Kaliningrad in the Baltic, and even farther afield, in the eastern Mediterranean, they are refurbishing their forward base at Tartus, in Syria. Submarine numbers will continue to shrink as Soviet-era subs are retired and not replaced, but the newest submarines are among the very best in the world. The Russians understand that the U.S. Navy has not kept up with many of the complex technologies necessary in the ASW world, and some analysts believe the Russian Navy will soon have the edge on the U.S. Navy in a local engagement. Nevertheless, Russian fleet activity is a small shadow of its Soviet heyday, and while the Russians are building fine ships, they cannot match the NATO fleet in numbers or quality.

Putin, however, unlike his navy, seems to suffer from delusions of grandeur. He clearly does not grasp the depth of industrial, seafaring, and aviation talent and infrastructure that is necessary to deploy naval aviation beyond regional waters. Not even Admiral Gorshkov's fleet, at the apogee of Soviet power, was able to do so. His hubris in the *Kuznetsov* episode illustrates the dangerous crumbling of American deterrence and disarmament. Today, as in the 1920s and '30s, Washington has forgotten Teddy Roosevelt's advice to speak softly and carry a big stick. Instead, the United States lashes out at adversaries with ultimatums, sanctions, and embargoes while disarming. Our adversaries will not be able to resist such opportunities.

Under Putin, Russia—which John McCain described as a gas station with an economy the size of Denmark—seized the Crimea and eastern Ukraine, then sent an aircraft carrier the length of the Eurasian landmass to displace American influence in the Middle East. It holds massive intimidating exercises close to the Baltic States, organizes joint naval exercises with China in the Baltic and the Pacific, and negotiates new defense agreements with Cuba and Nicaragua.

Putin has become the master of "hybrid warfare," using cyber-attacks, disinformation, "fake news," election meddling, paramilitary "little green men," intimidation, and occasionally assassination against adversaries.

There can be no doubt that Putin is committed to reestablishing the defensive buffer of client states echoing the Warsaw Pact and perhaps integrating them into a new Soviet-style economic zone. Russia's sole claim to superpower status is its tens of thousands of nuclear weapons. But Russia's economy is one-tenth that of the United States and one-twenty-second that of NATO. Hence Putin knows that revanchism is his only course to reestablish Russia as a global economic and military power. He knows too that he must do so while the United States is disarming and politically divided. But he lacks the economic strength to fulfill all that he has taken on, which increases the risk that he will take dramatic military action, say in the Baltic, before a perceived window closes.

China presents a very different kind of problem. Its leaders do not hide their intention to establish command of the western Pacific, and they are progressing rapidly toward achieving that regional goal. They have also clearly set out to become a global superpower, with their navy as a principal tool. For years China's navy has routinely maintained a forward presence in the Arabian Sea. Recently it opened its first forward naval base at Djibouti, in East Africa (it will not be the last), and it conducts exercises in the Mediterranean and even in the Baltic with its Russian counterpart.

The Chinese surface fleet includes more than one hundred combatants, a submarine force of around seventy boats, including six nuclear attack submarines and four SSBNs, and of course its single secondhand aircraft carrier. Half this force was constructed in the past fifteen years. But the Chinese GDP is still considerably smaller than that of the United States. China's illegal claim to sovereignty over the South China Sea and its building of military bases there must not be given recognition, although clearly that is not in itself reason to go to war, but it could become so if China interferes with free transit of international commerce.

So far China's cyber campaign has sought with great success to gain economic advantage and steal military and commercial technology, but it has also demonstrated the capability to become even more toxic and damaging. Perhaps its most dangerous activity is permitting and enabling North Korea's program to acquire nuclear attack capability. If the United States remains unable to deter, it will continue to be in China's interest to allow North Korea to dominate world attention and to keep American attention riveted there rather than on their Chinese provocations.

If one day it does in fact become necessary to use force against North Korea, the American president could be shocked, as Harry Truman was in 1950, to learn that the U.S. Navy is no longer large enough to execute a blockade of North Korea without stripping forces from the rest of the world.

As the 9/11 Commission predicted, the war against Islamist terror will be with us for decades. The West will be required to keep naval forces deployed and employed in the Middle East indefinitely, and they cannot be just token forces. The proliferation of precision missiles, drones, and sophisticated submarines means that projecting power and deterring and destroying terrorism will require the full range of air, surface, and submarine sea power.

Now that Iran has extended its power through the Persian Gulf and Mesopotamia to the shores of the Mediterranean and bids fair to become a full nuclear power within a decade, it is ever more important to reestablish the credibility of American deterrence and support for our Mideast allies. We must never again allow a territory to become a sanctuary for Islamist terror to train and organize to attack the United States. Nor should the United States be drawn into invasion, occupation, and nation building in the region. That means, for the foreseeable future, relying on special operations and precision strike from carriers and on land bases employing manned and unmanned aircraft, missiles, and inserted marines and special forces.

The velocity of technological advance is of course rapidly changing the nature of military and naval operations. Cyber; robotics; artificial intelligence; unmanned air, land, surface, and undersea weapons; and lethal swarms of micro-drones are just some of the applications now existing or operational that are rapidly changing the art and science of warfare and deterrence. But the necessity for sufficient deployable submarine-, surface-, and air-capable platforms to deploy the latest ever-changing technology does not change. The vital interests of the United States and its allies, and the threats to those interests, are regional and global. There is no security and no deterrence if there is no regional and global capable naval presence where our vital interests are present.

A more ominous development of the last few years is the emergence of an active military axis made up of China, Russia, and Iran. They are now exercising together, sharing intelligence and missile technology and hardware. Their cooperation is eerily similar to that of Germany, Japan, and Italy leading up to World War II. The three have completely different geopolitical objectives, sharing only the reality that the United States is the common obstacle to their success in achieving these objectives. They know that if they act in concert they can overstretch the too-small forces of the United States and its allies.

The world sees that in the near term the U.S. Navy cannot deal with all these urgent requirements with a fleet too small and with too many vital missions around the world. But as we have seen in this book, we can restore deterrence rapidly by establishing a strategy and leaving no doubt that it will be implemented.

By 1980, the consequences of the Vietnam War and a quarter-century of bipartisan neglect of our defenses had deeply eroded our ability to deter disturbers of the peace. During the 1980s, we reestablished the primacy of strategy. Carrying out the new global forward strategy, we rapidly expanded the navy and marine force structure to six hundred ships, including fifteen carrier battle groups with fourteen active and two reserve carrier air wings, four surface action groups built around four battleships, marine amphibious shipping sufficient for fifty thousand marines, one hundred attack submarines, one hundred frigates, 137 cruisers and destroyers, and more than thirty ballistic missile submarines. These platforms deployed our most fearsome new weaponry, including Tomahawk cruise missiles, Aegis antiair warfare systems, and under-ice submarine capabilities. Simultaneously we restored funding for training and maintenance.

Of equal importance, we carried out a massive program of global forward naval exercises to demonstrate our capabilities. In European waters, those exercises showed that NATO had the power to command the seas and to surround, attack, and defeat any Soviet offensive in central Europe and/or its flanks. In the Pacific, the exercises showed that the United States, Japan, South Korea, Australia, New Zealand, the Philippines, Thailand, Singapore, and China had the power to defeat any Soviet attack on our vital interests there.

At the time, we believed that we could achieve 90 percent of the deterrent power of this buildup in the first year, and that proved to be the case. We did it by publicly declaring and explaining the strategy, especially its naval component, and by taking actions that left no doubt in the minds of friend and foe alike that we would achieve it. Those actions included submitting a revised defense budget to Congress that fully funded the buildup; establishing a program to reactivate four battleships and modernize frigates and destroyers; commissioning into the U.S. Navy four ultramodern destroyers that had been built for the recently departed Shah of Iran; extending the lives of four carriers through a SLEP program; reopening two aircraft production lines; and increasing the output of others.

Lessons from the 1980s That Apply Today

Our situation today parallels that of 1980, and our adversaries are actively seeking to take advantage of our weakness. Notably North Korea, one of the poorest nations on earth, is currently holding us at bay. The president's diplomatic power is diminished by a navy that is stretched too thin and woefully underfunded. But he should have the option to prevent North Korea from launching any ballistic missiles that don't return to earth on its territory. He should also have the option to maintain carrier battle groups in the Yellow Sea and the Sea of Japan with a suitable number of Aegis ships, nuclear attack submarines, destroyers, and frigates that could prevent North Korean ballistic missile launches in the boost/ascent phase, or artillery and missile attacks against South Korea. Korea is a long peninsula; such a naval group could enforce UN sanctions or a full blockade.

The experience of the 1980s demonstrates that a restoration of American command of the seas could reap 90 percent of the deterrent benefits of naval supremacy almost immediately. It would force our adversaries to trim their sails. Russia knows that it cannot challenge a rebuilt U.S. fleet with its professional but very small one-carrier navy. The Chinese are at least a decade away from matching restored American naval and air capabilities, and more likely they will never be able to do so. Backed with naval and military superiority, American diplomacy would instantly regain credibility.

The U.S. and NATO navies retain many strengths, starting with the massive advantage of geography. Five NATO countries currently meet the objective of spending 2 percent of GDP on defense, and a growing number of others have announced such plans. The importance of exercises, also demonstrated in the 1980s, has not been lost, and while they are now fewer in number and size, they continue, including amphibious landings in Norway and the Baltic, followed by the old scripted Cold War protests from the Kremlin. After a thirty-year slumber, awareness of the central importance of strategy has reemerged as the U.S. Navy has tried to revive a strategy career path for its line officers and is developing new strategy statements. NATO navies are convening strategy courses and seminars. But much more needs to be done to reconstitute the navy's operator-strategist cadre that proved so vital in helping win the Cold War at sea.

The lesson of this book is that we must restore the capability of our naval forces and sailors not because we might have to go to war with North Korea, Russia, Iran, or some other adversary but because we must prevent having to go to war at all. We must be able to deter our adversaries from attacking our vital interests by leaving no doubt that if they do so, they will suffer more than they can hope to gain. Our capacity for deterrence has decayed and in some cases disappeared, but restoring it is well within our economic and political capability before the peace is lost either through miscalculation or intention.

Something Winston Churchill said in 1935 speaks to us today: "Want of foresight, unwillingness to act when action would be simple and effective, lack of clear thinking, confusion of counsel until the emergency comes, until self-preservation strikes its jarring gong—these are the features which constitute the endless repetition of history."

The choice we face is not between maintaining the balance of deterrence and following some other conceptual system, but between maintaining that balance and failing to do so.

ACKNOWLEDGMENTS

This book is dedicated to my sea-daddies, those naval leaders who inspired and mentored my naval service, and some of whom encouraged me to write this book. But I also want to express my gratitude to those great men and women who do incredible things every day, the young seamen, the chief bosun's mates, the marines and hospital corpsmen, the submariners, the aviators, the ship-drivers, the engineering duty officers, and all the sailors and marines who go down to the sea in ships. What inspiration, what a joy, what honor to be counted a shipmate among them. To paraphrase James Michener, where indeed do we get such men and women?! This book is their story.

I want to thank in special measure Dick Allen and Ace Lyons, both major subjects in this history, who encouraged me to tell this story and who read and corrected early drafts. I am especially grateful to Capt. (ret.) Peter Swartz, USN, who was a major strategic thinker and adviser to me and to three CNOs. He undertook and oversaw the difficult efforts of interviewing those many players who were still vertical and of researching among the oral histories and archives of those who have passed on. He was a strict disciplinarian chastising me and forbidding me to write anything that could not be backed by hard evidence. Without him, this book could not have been written.

The chiefs who helped build this strategy and then carry it out remain good friends and valuable counselors: Adm. Jim Holloway, Adm. Tom Hayward, Adm. Jay Johnson, and Marine Cmdts. P. X. Kelley, Al Gray, and the late Bob Barrow.

Paul Miller was my executive assistant and alter ego for the first four years of my tour, then went off to execute the strategy as commander of the Seventh Fleet. Later, as commander in chief of the Atlantic Command, he helped lead the successful end of the Cold War

Former marine Bing West was a major strategist and executor of the Maritime Strategy from its inception in Sea Plan 2000 to its victorious conclusion. He continues to move and shake with his best-selling books and his wise counsel to those in power.

Former marine Bud McFarlane, my accomplice on Kissinger's staff and later President Reagan's national security adviser, helped to develop, execute, and protect the forward strategy through to its successful endgame.

My friendships and continuing dialogue on the issues in this book with those mentioned above, and with Seth Cropsey, Joe Prueher, Hank Mustin, Mac Williams, Ed Clexton, Fox Fallon, Jim Patton, Bob Murray, Tom Lynch, George Fedoroff, Jim Service, Ned Hogan, Norman Friedman, Randy Papadopoulos, Bruce Powers, Ev Pyatt, Marty Simon, Chris Lehman, and Steve Lehman, have enriched this book in many, many ways. Sam Cox and his crew at Naval History and Heritage Command, and Charlie Niemeyer and his staff at Marine Corps History, were invaluable in finding crucial records and facts.

The many navy and marine operators who provided me with vignettes from their often harrowing experiences at sea are too numerous to mention here, but I hope I did them justice in recounting their tales and identifying them in the notes. I owe them all a vote of thanks, as does the nation.

This book has an unusually large number of action photographs.

Tracking them down and obtaining rights to use them was a real challenge. Arthur Davidson Baker III, my former special assistant, Robert Hanshew, photograph curator for the National Museum of the U.S. Navy, and Janis Jorgensen of the U.S. Naval Institute did incredible work in tracking down and providing most of the rare action photos. Norman Polmar generously lent rare photos from his collection, along with very helpful advice, especially on Azorian.

Mike Markowitz did a superb job in drawing all of the excellent maps, showing a real grasp of what the strategy was all about.

I was privileged to have as my editor at Norton, Starling Lawrence, dean of maritime publishers, with whom I had worked when he edited the 9/11 report book. His advice in structuring and restructuring the narrative was invaluable.

My wife, Barbara, did her own stylistic editing and added a touch of elegant improvements.

Responsibility for the nearly impossible job of supervising, tracking, and managing the many drafts of the manuscript fell on the marine-developed shoulders of Tyrone Horton, first sergeant, USMC (ret.). His performance was flawless.

Mark Geier undertook the dizzying responsibility of tracking down the maps and photographs and securing rights and credits. He also edited the key phrases for the endnotes and ensured the proper citations, while tracking their positions in the ever-changing draft chapters. Though not a marine, he emerged victorious.

Despite the help of these consummate professionals, it is possible that a few errors and omissions may have survived. Needless to say, they are all mine, as are those apostasies from received wisdom that are certainly present.

NOTES

PREFACE

xv **"Outlaw One, Joker"**: This account is based on Adm. James A. Lyons, interview by author, August 8, 2014, and others.

INTRODUCTION

xix **a highly classified program**: Richard Allen, interviews by author, August
25, 2014, and July 9, 2017.

xxi **"forty-two years ago"**: Jan Lodal, "Brezhnev's Secret Pledge to 'Do Everything We Can' to Re-elect Gerald Ford," *Atlantic*, July 26, 2017.

xxii **forward operations and offense**: Alfred Thayer Mahan, *The Influence of Sea
Power upon History* (Boston: Little, Brown, 1918), p. 268.

CHAPTER I: AMERICAN NAVAL STRATEGY
AND OPERATIONS IN THE COLD WAR

11 **"fleet problems"**: On the U.S. Navy's massive fleet exercises between the
world wars, see Alfred A. Nofi, *To Train the Fleet for War: The U.S. Navy Fleet
Problems, 1923–1940* (Newport, R.I.: Naval War College Press, 2010).

15 **more than seven thousand ships**: Naval History and Heritage Command,
http://history.navy.mil.

21 **titanic struggle**: Jeffrey Barlow, *Revolt of the Admirals: The Fight for Naval
Aviation, 1945–1950* (Washington, D.C.: Naval Historical Center, Department of the Navy, 1994).

22 **"There's no reason"**: Charles C. Krulak, "Expeditionary Operations,"
Marine Corps Doctrinal Publication 3, PCN 14200000900 (Headquarters
Marine Corps, April 16, 1998), p. 61.

23 **rowing a boat on a lake**: E. B. Potter, *Admiral Arleigh Burke* (Annapolis,
Md.: Naval Institute Press, 2005), p. 320.

24 **full naval blockade**: "Memorandum of Information for the Secretary—
Blockade of Korea," Truman Presidential Library Archives, July 6, 1950.

30 **nuclear weapons delivery capability**: Vice Adm. (ret.) Jerry Miller, *Nuclear Weapons and Aircraft Carriers: How the Bomb Saved Naval Aviation* (Washington, D.C.: Smithsonian Institution Press, 2001), p. 109.
30 **Single Integrated Operational Plan (SIOP)**: Ibid., pp. 222–23.
35 **Operation Azorian**: Norman Polmar and Michael White, *Project Azorian* (Annapolis, Md.: Naval Institute Press, 2010).
38 **Project SIXTY**: See Declassified "Project SIXTY" in John B. Hattendorf, ed., *U.S. Naval Strategy in the 1970s: Selected Documents*, Newport Paper no. 30 (Newport, R.I.: Naval War College Press, 2007).
38 **revised and adjusted**: Adm. James L. Holloway III, *Aircraft Carriers at War: A Personal Retrospective of Korea, Vietnam, and the Soviet Confrontation* (Annapolis, Md.: Naval Institute Press, 2007); and his "NWP Document 1" in Hattendorf, *U.S. Naval Strategy in the 1970s*.
39 **support to European commanders**: Miller, *Nuclear Weapons and Aircraft Carriers*, p. 152.
39 **"During this tour, I attempted"**: Ibid., p. 153.
41 **Operation Ivy Bells**: Sherry Sontag, Christopher Drew, and Annette Lawrence Drew, *Blind Man's Bluff: The Untold Story of American Submarine Espionage* (New York: Public Affairs, 1998).
42 **Naval Intelligence breakthroughs**: For our exploitation of the new intelligence on the Soviet Navy, see Christopher Ford and David Rosenberg, *The Admirals' Advantage: U.S. Navy Operational Intelligence in World War II and the Cold War* (Annapolis, Md.: Naval Institute Press, 2005).
46 **Carrier aircraft were withdrawn**: Miller, *Nuclear Weapons and Aircraft Carriers*, pp. 226–27.
47 **"naval supremacy"**: Adm. James Holloway, interview by author, December 1977. The contemporary accounts of this bitter Washington drama in the *New York Times* and the *Washington Post* are worth reading in full. See William Safire, "The Battle of Whizkid Gulf," *New York Times*, February 9, 1978, http://www.nytimes.com/1978/02/09/archives/the-battle-of-whizkid-gulf-essay.html; and "Washington's Naval Battle," *Washington Post*, September 4, 1978, https://www.washingtonpost.com/archive/politics/1978/09/04/washingtons-naval-battle/7fc58400-782e-4d5f-80d2-58b931b873bc/
48 **a firm believer**: Adm. Frank Kelso, interview by Paul Stillwell, October 2001–May 2002 (Washington, D.C.: U.S. Naval Institute Oral History Program, 2008).
48 **Hayward intended to use it**: Capt. Bill Cockell and Cmdr. Jim Patton, head of the Pacific Fleet's staff War Plans Branch, with a Ph.D. from Fletcher and experience on Henry Kissinger's State Department Policy Planning Staff (1974–77), but also forward operational experience off the Soviet Union as a submariner.
49 **"reoriented the staff"**: Dr. Bruce Powers, interview by Peter Swartz, Arlington, Va., July 31, 2014. Dr. Powers was the civilian Operations Evaluation Group (OEG) representative on the Sixth Fleet staff. A keen and experienced observer of U.S. naval officers, he became an admirer and friend of Admiral Lyons. For an informed characterization of Admiral Lyons's operational prowess, see "The Reminiscences of Vice Adm. David Richardson, U.S. Navy (ret.)," interview by Paul Stillwell (Annapolis, Md.: U.S. Naval Institute Oral History Program, 1998).
53 **"1,500 nautical miles"**: Harold Brown, *Thinking About National Security: Defense and Foreign Policy in a Dangerous World* (Boulder, Colo.: Westview Press, 1983), p. 177.

53 resupply of forward allies: Ibid., p. 174.

53 "Offensive naval operations": Robert W. Komer, *Maritime Strategy or Coalition Defense?* (Boulder, Colo.: Westview Press, 1983), p. 68.

53 neutralizing Japan: Capt. (ret.) James M. Patton, "Dawn of the Maritime Strategy," *U.S. Naval Institute Proceedings* 135, no. 5 (May 2009): 56–60.

54 Sea Plan 2000: The Sea Plan 2000 executive summary is reprinted in John B. Hattendorf, ed., *U.S. Naval Strategy in the 1970s: Selected Documents*, Newport Paper no. 30 (Newport, R.I.: Naval War College Press, 2007).

55 "As dean of research": Bing West to Everett Pyatt, July 20, 2016, notes attachment.

56 a drastic transformation: Patton, "Dawn of the Maritime Strategy."

59 the funding to buy them: That stream of funding began with a supplemental funding bill sent to Congress shortly after Reagan's inauguration and continued into the Bush administration. But even with that substantial funding stream, it was necessary to take draconian measures to stop the "gold plating," the constant design changes by the Pentagon bureaucracy that drive the costs of weapons so unnecessarily high. We immediately froze design changes on all production programs unless they were a matter of life or death. We established at least two qualified production sources for each weapon to compete annually in fixed-price competition. The vast defense bureaucracy fought these measures relentlessly, but as a result, the prices of these systems came down each year of the Reagan administration. The Reagan procurement wave included four *Nimitz*-class nuclear carriers, dozens of Aegis cruisers and destroyers, *Perry*-class frigates, Trident nuclear missiles and strategic missile submarines, *Los Angeles*–class attack submarines, A-6, F-14, and F-18 fighter-bombers, Tomahawk nuclear and conventional cruise missiles, Harpoon antiship missiles, SH-2 and SH-60 antisubmarine helicopters, MK 46 and MK 48 torpedoes, the SM-2, the NATO Sea Sparrow missile system, the AIM-9L Sidewinder missile, the RIM-116 Rolling Airframe missile, AMRAAM antiaircraft missiles, the Phalanx CIWS Gatling gun close-in antimissile system, the SLQ-32 radar jamming and chaff system, and many others.

59 some of the crown jewels: Carter, *Keeping the Faith*, pp. 251–53.

60 Gulf of Sidra: Joseph T. Stanik, *El Dorado Canyon: Reagan's Undeclared War with Qaddafi* (Annapolis, Md.: Naval Institute Press, 2003).

61 unrealistic requirement: Komer, *Maritime Strategy*, p. 54.

63 two Libyan MiG aircraft: Stanik, *El Dorado Canyon*, pp. 29–31.

63 "cut President Ford's": 1980 Republican National Committee Platform Detroit, Michigan. The American Presidency Project. July 15, 1980. http://www.presidency.ucsb.edu/ws/?pid=25844.

64 "Peace through Strength": Ronald Reagan address accepting the presidential nomination at the Republican National Committee, July 17, 1980, Detroit, Michigan. The American Presidency Project. http://www.presidency.ucsb.ws/?pid=25970.

CHAPTER 2: OCEAN VENTURE '81:
A BOLD NEW STRATEGIC OPERATION

71 "Let me say that": Unless otherwise indicated, the quotations in this chapter are from Adm. James A. Lyons, interview by author, August 8, 2014.

77 "The four helos": Edward Clexton to author, February 17, 2016.

80 "With the heavy seas": Rear Admiral (Ret) Clarence "Skip" Armstrong e-mail to Dr. John Hanley, December 13, 2014.

86 **"Between August and November"**: Rear Adm. Boris D. Yashin, "The Navy in US Military-Political Strategy," *International Affairs* 2 (1982): 80.

CHAPTER 3: TAKING A NEW NATIONAL STRATEGY
TO SEA: SENDING A MESSAGE

90 **"Following the movie's release"**: James L. Holloway III, *Aircraft Carriers at War: A Personal Retrospective of Korea, Vietnam, and the Soviet Confrontation* (Annapolis, Md.: Naval Institute Press, 2007), pp. 422–23.

93 **an air strike against Syria**: For a complete account, see John F. Lehman, Jr., *Command of the Seas* (New York: Charles Scribner's Sons, 1988), p. 299, and Adm. James A. Lyons's letter to the author dated August 4, 2017, at www .johnflehman.com.

99 **"In the event of war"**: Hearings on Military Posture and H. R. 2970 Department of Defense Authorization for Appropriations for fiscal year 1982 and H. R. 2614 Department of Defense Supplemental Authorization for Appropriations for Fiscal Year 1981 before the Committee on Armed Services. Status of U. S. Naval Forces, Research and Development Subcommittee, Norfolk, VA. 97th Congress, 1st Session. March 30, 1981. U. S. Government Printing Office, Washington, DC 1981.

100 **aggressive forward naval maritime strategy**: Peter Schweizer, *Reagan's War: The Epic Story of His Forty-Year Struggle and Final Triumph Over Communism* (New York: Doubleday, 2002).

102 **"The U.S. Navy of the near"**: John F. Lehman, Jr., "Rebirth of a U.S. Naval Strategy," *Strategic Review* (Summer 1981): 9–15.

102 **a special supplement**: "The Maritime Strategy," a special supplement to *US Naval Institute Proceedings* 112, no. 1 (January 1986), comprised the following articles: Adm. James D. Watkins, USN, "The Maritime Strategy," pp. 2-17; Adm. James D. Watkins, USN, "The Real Reformers," pp. 15–17; General P. X. Kelley, USMC, and Major Hugh K. O'Donnell, Jr. USMC, "The Amphibious Warfare Strategy," pp. 18-29; John F. Lehman, Jr., "The 600-ship Navy," pp. 30–40; and Captain Peter M. Swartz, USN, "Contemporary U.S. Naval Strategy: A Bibliography," pp. 41–47.

102 **"The President said we would"**: Michael E. Reagan, "A Tale of Two Presidents," MichaelEReagan.com, November 1, 2012, https://michaelereagan. com/a-tale-of-two-presidents.

103 **"I also wanted to send"**: Ronald Reagan, *An American Life* (New York: Simon and Schuster, 1990), p. 201.

104 **"We need to focus"**: John B. Hattendorf, *The Evolution of the U.S. Navy's Maritime Strategy, 1977–1986*, Newport Paper no. 19 (Newport, R.I.: Naval War College Press, 2004), pp. 50–51.

105 **"We made the transit"**: Vice Adm. (ret.) Dennis V. McGinn, USN, to Capt. (ret.) Peter Swartz, September 14, 2015.

105 **"The annual joint U.S.-South Korea"**: Capt. (ret.) Vance Morrison, USN, to Captain (ret.) Peter Swartz, November 6, 2015, attachment.

107 **quietly but significantly supported**: John F. Lehman, Jr., "Reflections on the Special Relationship," *Naval History Magazine* 26, no. 5 (October 2012).

108 **joint naval drills in the Sea of Japan**: *Commander in Chief Pacific Command History*, vol. 1, *1982*, prepared by the Command History Division Office of the Joint Secretary Headquarters CINCPAC, 1983, p. 725, http://nautilus.org /wp-content/uploads/2012/01/c_eightytwo.pdf.

109 **"lunched with Joint Chiefs"**: Douglas Brinkley, *The Reagan Diaries* (New York: HarperCollins, 2007).

110 **Sea of Japan to the Bonins**: *Commander in Chief Pacific Command History, 1982*, p. 1:729.

110 **"the apparent surprise appearance"**: *Commander in Chief Pacific Command History, 1983*, vol. 1, prepared by the Command History Division Office of the Joint Secretary Headquarters, 1984, at http://nautilus.org/wp-content /uploads/2012/01/c_eightythree.pdf; and *1984 CICPAC Command History*, http://nautilus.org/foia-document/uscincpac-command-history-1984.

110 **"Norpac '82 was right"**: Paul Giarra e-mail, Donald Chipman, "The Trans-formation of Soviet Air Operations: Implications for U.S. Maritime Strat egy," *Airpower Journal* 4, no. 2 (Summer 1990): 66–74.

111 **"four Backfires approached"**: Donald Chipman, "The Transformation of Soviet Air Operations: Implications for U.S. Maritime Strategy," *Airpower Journal* 4, no. 2 (Summer 1990): 66–74.

111 **"I think that everyone"**: Commander (Ret) Paul Giarra e-mail to Captain (Ret) Peter Swartz, March 21, 2015.

114 **"The world has also witnessed"**: This is an excerpt from the president's November 22, 1982, address to the nation. The citation is attributed to a Master Tape R-1180BR at the Ronald Reagan presidential library and museum. (There is another citation available from the presidency project at UC Santa Barbara online.)

116 **"Maritime superiority"**: President Reagan's remarks at the commissioning of USS New Jersey. December 28, 1982. The American Presidency Project. http://www.presidency.ucsb.edu/ws/?pid=42153.

CHAPTER 4: SOVIET PANIC; MISREADING THE MESSAGE: THE MOBILIZATION OF 1983

118 **"During the American presidential"**: Christopher Andrew and Oleg Gor-dievsky, *KGB: The Inside Story of Its Foreign Operations from Lenin to Gorbachev* (New York: HarperCollins, 1990), pp. 582–83.

119 **Soviets were particularly fearful**: This Soviet strategy in the air and on the ground is laid out in Gordon S. Barrass, *The Great Cold War: A Journey through the Hall of Mirrors* (Stanford, Calif.: Stanford University Press, 2009); and Gordon S. Barrass, "The Renaissance in American Strategy and the End-ing of the Great Cold War," *Military Review* (January–February 2010): 101–10.

120 **raid against a U.S. Navy carrier**: For a long and detailed vignette and *Vinson's* intercepts, see the *Carl Vinson* entry in *Supercarriers of the U.S. Navy: The Com-plete History* (Loschberg, Germany: Jazzybee Verlag, 2012). See also the USS *Carl Vinson* entry in *Dictionary of American Naval Fighting Ships*, Naval History Heritage and Command, http://www.history.navy.mil/dans/c3/carl_vinson.htm.

120 **"I was on Kennel Freelance"**: Captain (Ret) Kenneth McGruther email to Captain (Ret) Peter Swartz, 2014.

121 **"From the time she neared"**: *Supercarriers of the U.S. Navy: The Complete History* (Loschberg, Germany: Jazzybee Verlag, 2012), n. p.

122 **"Recently there were four"**: Remarks by Honorable John F. Lehman, Jr., Secretary of the Navy, Current Strategy Forum, Naval War College, New-port RI, June 21, 1983, "Nine Principles of American Maritime Power for the Future," 14.

122 **"These exercises are extremely"**: Testimony of Admiral James Watkins, Chief of Naval Operations, Before the Subcommittee on Sea Power and Force Projection, US Senate Armed Services Committee, March 14, 1984.

122 ***Kiev's* crew behaved**: *Dwight D. Eisenhower* (CVN-69), entry in *Dictionary of American Naval Fighting Ships*, Naval History Heritage and Command, at

https://www.history.navy.mil/research/histories/ship-histories/danfs/d
/dwight-d-eisenhower-cvn-69.html.

123 **Soviet submarine intrusions in Swedish waters**: Some believe the U.S.
Navy and the Royal Navy were involved in some of these intrusions. For the
various claims and charges, see Capt. (ret.) Peter A. Huchthausen and Alex-
andre Sheldon-Duplaix, *Hide and Seek: The Untold Story of Cold War Naval
Espionage* (New York: Wiley, 2009), chap. 14.

124 **"during the course"**: "Soviet Sub Collides with USS Kitty Hawk, 21 March
1984" Naval History and Heritage Command post on Naval History Blog,
U.S. Naval Institute, March, 11, 2011.

125 **John Walker, a U.S. Navy warrant officer**: Capt. (ret.) Edmond D. Pope
and Tom Schachtman, *Torpedoed: An American Businessman's True Story of
Secrets, Betrayal, Imprisonment in Russia, and the Battle to Set Him Free* (Boston:
Little, Brown, 2001), p. 27.

126 **"overt Soviet reaction"**: *Commander in Chief Pacific Command History 1983*,
vol. 1, prepared by the Command History Division Office of the Joint Secretary Headquarters, 1984, at http://nautilus.org/wp-content/uploads/2012
/01/c_eightythree.pdf; and *CICPAC Command History 1984*, pp. 396–97, at
http://nautilus.org/foia-document/uscincpac-command-history-1984.

126 **"When the navy studied"**: David E. Hoffman, *The Dead Hand: The Untold
Story of the Cold War Arms Race and Its Dangerous Legacy* (New York: Doubleday, 2009), p. 66.

127 **"When the three-carrier operation"**: Pete Earley, *Family of Spies: Inside the
John Walker Spy Ring* (New York: Bantam, 1988), p. 250.

128 **CIA officer Aldrich Ames**: Rear Adm. (ret.) Tom Brooks and Capt. (ret.)
Bill Manthorpe, "Setting the Record Straight: A Critical Review of Fall from
Glory," *Naval Intelligence Professionals Quarterly* 12, no. 2 (April 1996): 1–2.

129 **"A stranger with a Russian accent"**: Raymond L. Garthoff, *The Great
Transition: American Soviet Relations and the End of the Cold War* (Washington,
D.C.: Brookings Institution Press, 2000), p. 166.

130 **Adolf Tolkachev began selling**: David E. Hoffman, *The Billion Dollar Spy: A
True Story of Cold War Espionage and Betrayal* (New York: Doubleday, 2015).

130 **"this agent handed over"**: "Soviet Politburo Discussed Billion Dollar Spy"
(includes 1986 transcript), National Security Archive, February 5, 2016, at
http://nsarchive.gwu.edu/NSAEBB/NSAEBB540-Soviet-Politburo
-Discussed-CIA-Billion-Dollar-Spy-Adolf-Tolkachev.

131 **distant-area power projection**: Jay Winik, *On the Brink: The Dramatic
Behind the Scenes Saga of the Reagan Era and the Men and Women Who Won the
Cold War* (New York: Simon and Schuster, 1996), p. 211.

132 **Soviet Baltic Fleet carried out**: Barrass, *Great Cold War*; Barrass, "Renaissance
in American Strategy"; Diego A. Ruiz-Palmer, "The NATO-Warsaw Pact Competition in the 1970s and 1980s: A Revolution in Military Affairs in the Making
or the End of a Strategic Age?" *Cold War History* 14, no. 4 (2014): 533–73.

133 **Soviets began Springex '84**: President's Foreign Intelligence Advisory
Board (PFIAB), "The Soviet 'War Scare,'" February 15, 1990, pp. 83–84,
National Security Archive, at https://nsarchive.gwu.edu/nukevault/ebb533-
The-Able
-Archer-War-Scare-Declassified-PFIAB-Report-Released/2012-0238-MR.pdf.
PFIAB saw it as a reaction to *Able Archer*.

133 **In the Caribbean**: Norman Polmar, *The Naval Institute Guide to the Soviet
Navy*, 5th ed. (Annapolis, Md.: Naval Institute Press, 1991).

134 **another large naval exercise**: Office of Naval Intelligence, *Understanding*

Soviet Naval Developments, 6th ed. (Washington, D.C.: Office of the Chief of Naval Operations, Department of the Navy, 1991), p. 42.

136 **extending their sea control**: All this was laid out in detail in National Intelligence Estimate (NIE) 11-15-82/D, "Soviet Naval Strategy and Programs Through the 1990s," published at the secret classification level in November 1982 (a year after the Ocean Venture '81 exercise). It has since been declassified and published in John B. Hattendorf, *The Evolution of the U.S. Navy's Maritime Strategy, 1977–1986*, Newport Paper no. 19 (Newport, R.I.: Naval War College Press, 2004).

137 **"all of these 'risky unprincipled plans'"**: CAPT First Rank V. Strelkov, "Naval Forces in U.S. 'Direct Confrontation' Strategy." *Morskoy sbornik* no. 5 (1983), 78–82.

138 **"In his sometimes simplistic"**: Andrew and Gordievsky, *KGB: Inside Story*, pp. 582–83.

139 **"In May 1981, Soviet KGB"**: Stephen Cimbala. "Year of Maximum Danger? The 1983 'War Scare' and US-Soviet Deterrence," *Journal of Military Studies* 13, no. 2 (June 2000): 1–24.

140 **redeployment of Soviet submarines**: Christopher Ford and David Rosenberg, *The Admirals' Advantage: U.S. Navy Operational Intelligence in World War II and the Cold War* (Annapolis, Md.: Naval Institute Press, 2005), pp. 106-7.

141 **"The message to the Soviets"**: Hal Brands, *What Good Is Grand Strategy? Power and Purpose in American Statecraft from Harry S. Truman to George W. Bush* (Ithaca, N.Y.: Cornell University Press, 2015), p. 117.

143 **well over five hundred**: Figures are from Office of Naval Intelligence, *Understanding Soviet Naval Developments*, 4th ed. (Washington, D.C.: Office of the Chief of Naval Operations, Department of the Navy, 1980).

144 **number of major Soviet combatants**: Office of Naval Intelligence, *Understanding Soviet Naval Developments*, 4th and 5th eds. (Washington, D.C.: Office of the Chief of Naval Operations, Department of the Navy, 1980, 1985).

145 **the Soviets had perceived**: CIA, Office of Soviet Analysis, *Soviet Perceptions of U.S. Naval Strategy* (July 1986).

146 **"In Moscow"**: Kjell Inge Bjerga, "Politico-Military Assessments on the Northern Flank 1975–1990: Report from the IFS/PHP Bodo Conference of 20–21 August 2007." Norwegian Institute for Defense Studies, undated report, page 5.

147 **"However, the Reagan"**: Kjell Inge Bjerga, *Politico-Military Assessments on the Northern Flank, 1975–1990: Report from the IFS/PHP Bodø Conference of 20-21 August 2007* (Oslo: Norwegian Institute for Defense Studies, 2007), p. 5.

147 **to be named *Riga***: The ship was launched in 1985 and underwent sea trials in 1989 but did not deploy until 1995, after the breakup of the Soviet Union. Reporting on her progress was a staple of Western intelligence, press, and naval leaders throughout the 1980s.

149 **"a unique Soviet naval"**: PFIAB, "Soviet 'War Scare,'" p. 65.

CHAPTER 5: GAINING GLOBAL VELOCITY, 1983–1985

155 **"Quickly establishing"**: Admiral Wesley L. McDonald, "Our Atlantic Strategy: Strengths and Weaknesses," *Defense '83* (August 1983): 5, 8.

157 **"On April 12, 1982, Yuri Andropov"**: Evan Osnos, David Remnick, and Joshua Yaffa, "Annals of Diplomacy: Trump, Putin, and the New Cold War," *New Yorker*, March 6, 2017.

158 **"[We] had a Soviet minesweeper"**: Cmdr (ret.) David Winkler to Capt. (ret.) Peter Swartz, USN, March 7, 2016.

160 **His log**: "Kennel Freelance Highlights: 9 Nov–2 Dec 1984," attachment to Capt (Ret) Kenneth McGruther e-mail to Capt (Ret) Peter Swartz, December 9, 2014.

162 **"in fact the aim"**: Ken Weiss, "The New Strategic Outlook in the Pacific," Center for Naval Analyses (October 1985), p. 23.

163 **"For years I had chafed"**: Rear Adm. Burnham (Mike) C. McCaffree, Jr., interview by John Grady (Washington, D.C.: Naval Historical Foundation Oral History Program, 2014), p. 119.

163 **"Moscow appeared to view"**: Library of Congress, *North Korean, Chinese, and Soviet Reactions to Exercise Team Spirit, 1983–1985* (Washington, D.C.: Library of Congress Federal Research Division, 1985), pp. 6–7, 9.

165 **"Marine elements were airlifted"**: Lt. Col. William H. Schopfel, "The MAB in Norway," *U.S. Naval Institute Proceedings* 112, no. 1 (November 1986).

165 **"This exercise . . . demonstrated"**: Maj. Richard F. Natonski "Cold Weather Combat: What is the Marine Corps Doing About It?" (paper), Command and Staff College, USMC, Quantico, Va. (1988). See also Maj. Jerry Durrant, "In Every Clime and Place: USMC Cold Weather Doctrine" (monograph), School of Advanced Military Studies, Ft. Leavenworth, Kan. (1991).

165 **"submarine flush"**: Capt. (ret.) William H. J. Manthorpe, "The Soviet View," *U.S. Naval Institute Proceedings* 112, no. 2 (February 1986).

166 **"in the first five"**: Melissa Healy, "Lehman: We'll Sink Their Subs," *Defense Week* (May 13, 1985), p. 18.

169 **"I got a hold of the best"**: Vice Adm. Henry C. Mustin, speech to Navy Warfare Development Command's Navy Center for Innovation, Norfolk, Va., August 8, 2013; Vice Admiral Mustin, interview by Capt. (ret.) Peter Swartz, April 28, 2015.

170 ***Ticonderoga* used and built**: Mustin interview; Vice Adm. Henry C. Mustin, "Maritime Strategy from the Deckplates," *U.S. Naval Institute Proceedings* 112, no. 9 (September 1986).

173 **"Soviets could not locate"**: Mustin, "Maritime Strategy from the Deckplates."

173 **"The task dictated"**: Capt. (ret.) William H. J. Manthorpe, "The Soviet View," *U.S. Naval Institute Proceedings* 112, no. 2 (February 1986).

175 **"provocative"**: Ibid.

CHAPTER 6: THE BEGINNING OF THE END:
NORTHERN WEDDING, 1986

177 **authoritative unclassified version**: "The Maritime Strategy," a special supplement to *US Naval Institute Proceedings* 112, no. 1 (January 1986), comprised the following articles: Adm. James D. Watkins, USN, "The Maritime Strategy," pp. 2-17; Adm. James D. Watkins, USN, "The Real Reformers," pp. 15–17; General P. X. Kelley, USMC, and Major Hugh K. O'Donnell, Jr. USMC, "The Amphibious Warfare Strategy," pp. 18-29; John F. Lehman, Jr., "The 600-ship Navy," pp. 30–40; and Captain Peter M. Swartz, USN, "Contemporary U.S. Naval Strategy: A Bibliography," pp. 41–47.

178 **"We also train"**: John F. Lehman, "The 600-ship Navy," in *The Maritime Strategy* white paper insert, *U.S. Naval Institute Proceedings* (January 1986): 33.

180 **Operation Anchor Express**: Harry J. Stephan, "USMC to Bolster Nor-

wegian Flank, 4th MAB Ready to Deploy in a Crisis," *Armed Forces Journal International* (August 1987), p. 34.

181 **Navy Arctic Service Ribbon**: Capt. (ret.) Merrill Dorman, "Fifty Years Under the Ice: A Historical Look at the Scientific, Strategic and Operational Aspects of Submarine Arctic Operations," Naval Submarine League and the Naval Historical Foundation Submarine History Seminar, April 2008.

181 **"Either our [secrecy]"**: Dr. John Hanley notes from SSG files; Dr. John Hanley, interview by Peter Swartz, September 2016. Hanley had been deputy director of the CNO's Strategic Studies Group (SSG) in 1990.

181 **Operation Shooting Star and Operation Coyote**: Edward J. Marolda, *Ready Seapower: A History of the U.S. Seventh Fleet* (CreateSpace, 2012); Adm. James A. Lyons, interview by Edward J. Marolda.

182 **Lyons scrambled F-14s**: Lyons interview.

182 **Icex '86-1 was conducted**: Capt. Dorman, "Fifty Years Under."

183 **freedom of navigation operation in the Black Sea**: David E. Hoffman, *The Dead Hand: The Untold Story of the Cold War Arms Race and Its Dangerous Legacy* (New York: Doubleday, 2009); Raymond L. Garthoff, *The Great Transition: American-Soviet Relations and the End of the Cold War* (Washington, D.C.: Brookings Institution Press, 2000); William J. Aceves, "Diplomacy at Sea: U.S. Freedom of Navigation Operations in the Black Sea," *Naval War College Review* 46, no. 2 (Spring 1993): 59–79.

185 **"You have sent a message"**: Joseph T. Stanik, *El Dorado Canyon: Reagan's Undeclared War with Qaddafi* (Annapolis, Md.: Naval Institute Press, 2003), 139.

186 **attempting to get French permission**: Joseph T. Stanik, *El Dorado Canyon: Reagan's Undeclared War with Qaddafi* (Annapolis, Md.: Naval Institute Press, 2003), p. 173.

186 **"The U.S. Navy, together"**: Captain William H.J. Manthorpe, Jr., "The Soviet View," US Naval Institute *Proceedings* (November 1987): 145.

188 **"participated heavily"**: Ed Clexton, "My Life: A Life of Stories" (unpublished manuscript, 2016).

188 **"consisted of significant air"**: Ronald O'Rourke, *Nuclear Escalation, Strategic Anti-submarine Warfare, and the Navy's Forward Maritime Strategy*, report no. 87-138F (Washington, D.C.: Congressional Research Service, 1987), pp. 30–31.

189 **"The attempt to give Rimpac"**: Capt. William H. J. Manthorpe, "The Soviet View," *U.S. Naval Institute Proceedings* 112, no. 10 (October 1986).

190 **a full SEAL platoon**: Cmdr. Daniel Steward, USN, "Ski Across Greenland!" *U.S. Naval Institute Proceedings* 112, no. 12 (December 1986), pp. 33–38.

191 **"The Soviets didn't know"**: Frederick H. Hartmann, *Naval Renaissance: The U.S. Navy in the 1980s* (Annapolis, Md.: Naval Institute Press, 1990), p. 246.

192 **"The early 1980s was"**: Capt. (ret.) Patrick Roth, USN, to Peter Swartz, June 24, 2017.

192 **"I don't know if you"**: Philip DePoy (Center for Naval Analyses) to John Lehman, August 9, 2016.

192 **"*Vinson* steamed"**: "Carl Vinson (CVN-70)" entry in *Dictionary of American Naval Fighting Ships*, Navy History and Heritage Command website, https://www.history.navy.mil/research/histories/ship-histories/danfs/c/carl-vinson--cvn-70-.html.

194 **four principles**: Vice Adm. Henry C. Mustin, "Personal Experiences, Surface Warfare, and USN Strategy During the Cold War," interview by David

Winkler (Washington, D.C.: Naval Historical Foundation Oral History Program, 2001).

194 **"(1) Defend"**: David A. Perin, *SECONDFLT/STRIKFLTLANT Concept of Ops: Working Paper* (Alexandria, Va.: Center for Naval Analyses, February 25, 1988).

196 **"I began Northern Wedding"**: Capt. (ret.) Larry Seaquist to Capt. (ret.) Peter Swartz, March 12, 2016.

197 **Mustin turned over the Second Fleet**: John Fass Morton, *Mustin: A Naval Family of the Twentieth Century* (Annapolis, Md.: Naval Institute Press, 2003), p. 383.

197 **"I was Deputy"**: Cmdr. William J. Fallon, interview by John Lehman, April 29, 2016.

199 **"You've got to come up"**: Mustin, "Personal Experiences."

199 **"Look, [Soviet Navy commanders examined]"**: Maksim Tokarev quoted in John Solomon, "Soviet Oceanic Reconnaissance-Strike: New Observations from Maksim Tokarev (Part 1 of 2)," *Information Dissemination*, December 4, 2014, http://www.informationdissemination.net/2014/12/soviet-oceanic-reconnaissance-strike_4.html.

200 **"The longest that we"**: Lehman discussion with Gen. Dvorkin, August 19, 2007.

201 **a secret paper**: Office of Soviet Analysis, "Soviet Perceptions of US Naval Strategy" (Washington, D.C.: Directorate of Intelligence, Central Intelligence Agency, July 1986), at https://www.cia.gov/library/readingroom/docs/DOC_0000500708.pdf.

CHAPTER 7: THE SOVIETS (AND OTHERS)
GET THE MESSAGE, 1986–1988

203 **"would be briefed"**: Rear Adm. Tom Brooks testimony, February 22, 1989, cited in Norman Cigar, "The Navy's Battle of the Budget: Soviet Style," *Naval War College Review* 43, no. 2 (Spring 1990).

205 **"Our country stands for"**: Scott Michael Stanley, "Assessing the Impact of 'Reasonable Sufficiency' on the Structure and Missions of the Former Soviet Navy," master's thesis, Naval Postgraduate School, June 1992.

205 **"Until 1986, Soviet strategy"**: Raymond L. Garthoff, *Soviet Leaders and Intelligence: Assessing the American Adversary During the Cold War* (Washington, D.C.: Georgetown University Press, 2015), pp. 79–80.

207 **"No longer will we"**: David F. Winkler, *Cold War at Sea: High Seas Confrontation between the United States and the Soviet Union* (Annapolis Md.: Naval Institute Press, 2000), 157.

207 **"The ship conducted"**: Commanding Officer, USS *Carl Vinson* (CVN 70), 1987 *Command History* (December 6, 1988) https://www.history.navy.mil/content/dam/nhhc/research/archives/command-operation-reports/ship-command-operation-reports/c/carl-vinson-cvn-70-i/pdf/1987.pdf.

207 **"The very interesting"**: Ed Clexton to author, February 17, 2016.

208 **"One 'lesson learned'"**: Clexton, "My Life."

209 **"The 4th MAB"**: Harry J. Stephan, "USMC to Bolster Norwegian Flank, 4th MAB Ready to Deploy in a Crisis," *Armed Forces Journal International* (August 1987), p. 36.

211 **"this was the biggest change"**: James J. Tritten, *Military Doctrine and Strategy in the Former Soviet Union: Implications for the Navy*, Office of Naval Intelligence, Naval Postgraduate School, Monterey, Calif. (August 1993), p. 2.

211 **Gorbachev aimed**: James Mann, *The Rebellion of Ronald Reagan: A History of the End of the Cold War* (New York: Penguin, 2010), p. 174.

212 **"obviously caught"**: Capt. (ret.) William H. J. Manthorpe analyzed Soviet press reporting on the Maritime Strategy in "The Soviet View," *U.S. Naval Institute Proceedings* 113, no. 11 (November 1987).

212 **"It is hardly possible"**: On Soviet reactions to the special issue, see Capt. (ret.) William H. J. Manthorpe, "The Soviet View," *U.S. Naval Institute Proceedings* 112, no. 4 (April 1986); and David Alan Rosenberg, " 'It Is Hardly Possible to Imagine Anything Worse': Soviet Thoughts on the Maritime Strategy," *National War College Review* 41 (Summer 1988): 69–105.

212 **"The attempt to give Rimpac"**: Capt. (ret.) William H. J. Manthorpe, "The Soviet View," *U.S. Naval Institute Proceedings* 112, no. 10 (October 1986).

213 **"The tense situation"**: Capt. (ret.) William H. J. Manthorpe, "The Soviet View," *U.S. Naval Institute Proceedings* 113, no. 11 (November 1987).

213 **"considerably increase"**: Rosenberg, " 'It is Hardly Possible to Imagine,' " p. 79.

213 **a two-part series of articles**: Ibid., pp. 85–87.

213 **over-the-horizon landing**: "Soviets Expand Coastal and Anti-Landing Defense," *International Defense Review*, July 1990, pp. 731–34.

213 **"Drawing the Nuclear Spear"**: For details and verbatim text, see Capt. (ret.) William H. J. Manthorpe, "The Soviet View," *U.S. Naval Institute Proceedings* 114, no. 3 (March 1988).

215 **"It has become routine"**: Vladimir Ivanov, "Soviet Suggestions on Nuclear Negotiations," *Far Eastern Economic Review*, December 31, 1987, p. 28.

215 **"A successful defense"**: Vice Admiral Torolf Rein, Royal Norwegian Navy, "The Situation in the Norwegian Sea and the Norwegian Naval Interests," in Ellmann Ellingsen, ed., *NATO and U.S. Maritime Strategy: Diverging Interests or Cooperative Effort* (Oslo: Norwegian Atlantic Committee, 1987): 53–54, 58.

216 **new joint-service principles**: Betekhtin's operational concept is laid out in detail in "Soviets Expand Coastal and Anti-Landing Defense," *International Defense Review*, July 1990, pp. 731–34.

217 **four Japanese citizens were arrested**: Sergey Radchenko, *Unwanted Visionaries: The Soviet Failure in Asia at the End of the Cold War* (New York: Oxford University Press, 2014), p. 84.

218 **"To limit Soviet"**: National Security Decision Directive 238, September 2, 1986, Ronald Reagan Foundation and Institute, Simi, Calif., Federation of American Scientists. https://fas.org/irp/offdocs/nsdd-238.pdf.

219 **submarine K-219**: Capt. Peter Huchthausen, former U.S. Navy attaché in Moscow, collaborated with Igor Kurdin and R. Alan White on a book about the incident, *Hostile Waters* (New York: St. Martin's Press, 1997). It was made into an HBO movie under the same name. Rear Adm. (ret.) Tom Brooks issued a scathing denial in a review of the book in *U.S. Naval Institute Proceedings* 123, no. 10 (October 1997). According to James Jinks and Peter Hennessy, in *The Silent Deep: The Royal Navy Submarine Service Since 1945* (New York: Penguin, 2015), the sub that sank was not a Yankee but a more modern Delta I Soviet ballistic missile sub (p. 564).

220 **"Soviet air activity"**: "USS Enterprise (CVAN-65)" in *Dictionary of American Naval Fighting Ships* (DANFS), Naval History and Heritage Command, at www.history.navy.military/research/histories/ship-histories/danfs/e /enterprise-cvan-65-viii-1986-1990.html.

220 **arrived at Visakhapatnam**: Radchenko, *Unwanted Visionaries*, p. 119.

220 **Soviet worldwide ship deployments**: Office of Naval Intelligence, *Understanding Soviet Naval Developments*, 6th ed. (Washington, D.C.: Office of the Chief of Naval Operations, Department of the Navy, 1991), pp. 31–32; hereafter *USND6*.

221 **Global deployments**: Ibid., pp. 32–33.

221 **Soviet "analogous response"**: A U.S. Navy source says Soviet Navy "analogous response" to Delta strategic submarine deployments ended in 1986. Ibid., p. 33. A U.S. intelligence community source says that Soviet forward ballistic missile submarine deployments ended in 1987. See President's Foreign Intelligence Advisory Board (PFIAB), "The Soviet 'War Scare,'" February 15, 1990, p. 92, National Security Archive, at https://nsarchive.gwu.edu/nukevault/ebb533-The-Able-Archer-War-Scare-Declassified-PFIAB-Report-Released/2012-0238-MR.pdf.

221 **"in 1987 Soviet submarine activity"**: Michael Whitby, "'Doin' the Biz': Canadian Submarine Patrol Operations Against Soviet SSBNs, 1983–87," in Bernd Horn, ed., *Fortune Favours the Brave: Tales of Courage and Tenacity in Canadian Military History* (Toronto: Dundurn, 2009).

221 **"1987 had seen the last"**: Capt. (ret.) Dan Conley, RN, and Capt. (ret.) Richard Woodman, *Cold War Command: The Dramatic Story of a Nuclear Submariner* (Barnsley, UK: Seaforth, 2014), p. 232.

221 **Operation Atrina**: Norman Polmar and Kenneth J. Moore, *Cold War Submarines: The Design and Construction of U.S. and Soviet Submarines, 1945–2001* (Washington, D.C.: Potomac Books, 2005), pp. 171–72. Weir and Boyne say there were five quiet Victor III nuclear-powered attack submarines and don't mention nuclear-powered ballistic missile submarines. See Gary E. Weir and Walter J. Boyne, *Rising Tide: The Untold Story of The Russian Submarines That Fought the Cold War* (New York: Basic Books, 2003). According to a former Soviet admiral, the Soviets believed the U.S. Navy couldn't track them; that Soviet submarines were able to hide successfully in the boundary layers of the ocean; and that the U.S. Navy didn't have enough forces to confront large-scale Soviet submarine operations in the Atlantic or Pacific Oceans. See Huchthausen, *Hostile Waters*, pp. 262–63. For more details, see Jinks and Hennessy, *Silent Deep*, pp. 564–67.

222 **the hunting would become**: Lt. Gen. Tonne Huitfeldt, Norwegian Army, chairman of NATO Military Committee, "Soviet TU-16 Badgers in Norwegian Sea Exercise," in *Jane's Defence Weekly*, June 27, 1987, p. 1345, cited in Donald Chipman, "The Transformation of Soviet Air Operations: Implications for U.S. Maritime Strategy," *Airpower Journal* 4, no. 2 (Summer 1990): 66–74.

223 **"tanker war"**: Rear Adm. Thomas A. Brooks, "Gorshkov's Final Words: What Do They Mean? A Nuclear War-Fighting Treatise," *U.S. Naval Institute Proceedings* 115, no. 5 (May 1989).

223 **also began to fall**: *USND6*, 32–33.

223 **"from weeks or days to hours"**: B. I. Sergeyenko, former CMAT (Coastal Missile Artillery Troops)-SNI (Soviet Naval Infantry) commandant, cited in C. G. Pritchard, "Soviets Expand Coastal and Anti-Landing Defense," *International Defense Review*, July 1990, pp. 731–34.

225 **"They weren't happy"**: Capt. (ret.) William H. J. Manthorpe, "The Soviet Navy, 1987: The Soviets on the Soviets," *U.S. Naval Institute Proceedings* 114, no. 5 (May 1988).

226 **an unconditional unilateral moratorium**: The United States did not, citing

the need to ensure nuclear weapons safety, reliability, and effectiveness. The United States conducted an underground nuclear test in March 1986. Gorbachev resumed nuclear testing in February 1987.

226 **Reykjavik, Iceland**: Michael Beschloss, "The Thawing of the Cold War," *Newsweek*, June 14, 2004.

228 **"the imperial bandit face"**: "Gorbachev Hits Firing on Libya," *Los Angeles Times*, March 26, 1986.

228 **Soviet naval arms control proposals**: *USND6*, p. 119.

229 **the USSR unsuccessfully proposed**: For an in-depth explanation of that offensive, see Capt. (ret.) William H. J. Manthorpe, "Why Is Gorbachev Pushing Naval Arms Control?" *U.S. Naval Institute Proceedings* 115, no. 1 (January 1989).

229 **"If the United States"**: On failed Gorbachev policies in Asia, see Radchenko, *Unwanted Visionaries*.

229 **four hundred nuclear-armed SLCMs**: Raymond L. Garthoff, *The Great Transition: American-Soviet Relations and the End of the Cold War* (Washington, D.C.: Brookings Institution Press, 2000), p. 328.

231 **"far-reaching proposals"**: Capt. (ret.) William H. J. Manthorpe, "The Soviet View," *U.S. Naval Institute Proceedings* 113, no. 11 (November 1987).

232 **"the USSR proposes"**: Scott M. Stanley, *Assessing the Impact of Reasonable Sufficiency on the Structure and Missions of the Former Soviet Navy*, master's thesis, Naval Postgraduate School (1992), p. 1.

232 **"The sides shall find"**: President Ronald Reagan, *Public Papers of the Presidents of the United States: Ronald Reagan: 1987* (Washington, D.C.: Government Printing Office, 1989), 2:1493.

233 **"The Navy's continuing forward"**: "Pivotal in Sustaining Adequate Deterrence," an interview with U.S. Navy Secretary William. L. Ball III, *Naval Forces* 5 (1988), p. 24.

234 **"I do not need"**: Lars B. Wallin, ed., *The Soviet View on the Military-Political Situation* (Stockholm: Swedish National Defence Research Establishment, 1990), 31–32.

235 **"I was talking about"**: Reagan quoted in James G. Wilson, *The Triumph of Improvisation: Gorbachev's Adaptability, Reagan's Engagement and the End of the Cold War* (Ithaca, N.Y.: Cornell University Press, 2014), p. 129.

235 **"The external imposition"**: Mark Kramer, "The Demise of the Soviet Bloc," in Terry Cox, *Reflections on 1989 in Eastern Europe* (Abingdon, UK: Routledge, 2013), 20.

236 **The map more or less**: These graphics have since been declassified and reproduced in John B. Hattendorf and Capt. Peter M. Swartz, eds., *U.S. Naval Strategy in the 1980s*, Newport Paper no. 33 (Newport, R.I.: Naval War College Press, 2008).

236 **"I'm very pleased"**: Carlisle Trost, speech to Naval Submarine League, n.d.; Edgar F. Puryer, Jr., "Readiness: Carlisle Albert Herman Trost (1930–)," in John B. Hattendorf and Bruce A. Elleman, eds., *Nineteen-Gun Salute: Case Studies of Operational, Strategic, and Diplomatic Naval Leadership During the 20th and Early 21st* (Washington, D.C.: U.S. Government Printing Office, 2010).

236 **"It made Trost"**: Ibid.

236 **"Your Navy and bases"**: Carlisle A. H. Trost, USN, "Officer to Officer," *U.S. Naval Institute Proceedings* (December 1989), p. 51.

236 **"Akhromeyev . . . talked at length"**: Adm. William J. Crowe, Jr., and David

Chanoff, *The Line of Fire: From Washington to the Gulf, the Politics and Battles of the New Military* (New York: Simon and Schuster, 1993), p. 286.

238 **emphasizing the "threat"**: "*Theodore Roosevelt III* (CNV-71)," entry in *Dictionary of American Naval Fighting Ships (DANFS)*, Naval History and Heritage Command, https://www.history.navy.mil/research/histories/ship -histories/danfs/t/theodore-roosevelt-iii-cvn-71.html.

238 **"There is no way"**: Adm. Vladimir N. Chernavin, "Prepare Yourself for Modern Warfare," *Morskoy Sbornik*, January 1989, quoted in Capt. (ret.) William H. J. Manthorpe, "The Soviet Navy 1989: A Soviet View," *U.S. Naval Institute Proceedings* 11 no. 5 (May 1990).

238 **"the provisions of"**: Capt. (ret.) William H. J. Manthorpe, "The Soviet View," *U.S. Naval Institute Proceedings* 114, no. 11 (November 1988).

239 **"Soviet participants expressed"**: Eric Grove, *Maritime Security and European Security* (London: Brassey's, 1990), p. 95. Appendix I is a detailed report on the conference from Dr. Grove's point of view. For an American viewpoint, see Capt. (ret.) Roger W. Barnett, USN, *Memorandum for the Record* (Fairfax, Va.: National Security Research, August 2, 1988). Capt. Barnett had been one of the principal original conceptualizers and architects of the Maritime Strategy.

242 **"The Soviets currently"**: For more details, see Benjamin B. Fischer, *At Cold War's End: U.S. Intelligence on the Soviet Union and Eastern Europe, 1989–1991* (Center for the Study of Intelligence, 2000), no. 22.

242 **now-President Gorbachev**: Communist Party general secretary Gorbachev was also elected president of the Presidium of the USSR Supreme Soviet on November 1, 1988. Thenceforward he would combine the functions of head of state and of party.

242 **the second *Tbilisi*-class**: The first ship in the class, launched in 1985, had been named *Riga*. It was later renamed *Leonid Brezhnev* and then *Tbilisi*. Commissioned in the Russian Navy, she would be renamed *Admiral Kuznetsov*. As for the second *Riga*, launched in 1988, work would continue on her, but—unknown to anyone at the time—she would never be commissioned in the Soviet (or the Russian) Navy. Renamed *Varyag* in 1990, she was transferred unfinished to newly independent Ukraine. In 1998 she was sold still unfinished to China, which modernized her and in 2012 commissioned her in the People's Liberation Army Navy as the *Liaoning*.

243 **"This was a nuclear"**: Theodore A. Neely, Jr., "Book Reviews," *U.S. Naval Institute Proceedings* 115, no. 1 (January 1989).

243 **defensive military doctrine**: Capt. (ret.) William H. J. Manthorpe, "The Soviet View," *U.S. Naval Institute Proceedings* 116, no. 6 (June 1990).

243 **"a last-ditch attempt"**: Capt. Steve Kime, "Gorshkov's Final Words: What Do They Mean? Introduction," *U.S. Naval Institute Proceedings* 115, no. 5 (May 1989).

CHAPTER 8: THE COLD WAR ENDS

247 **withdrawn from the Mediterranean**: Office of Naval Intelligence, *Understanding Soviet Naval Developments*, 6th ed. (Washington, D.C.: Office of the Chief of Naval Operations, Department of the Navy, 1991), p. 41; hereafter *USND6*.

247 **the facility at Tartus**: The Soviets—and later the Russians—would continue to maintain a modest repair and replenishment facility at Tartus.

247 **Soviet Naval Aviation deployments**: Rear Adm. Tom Brooks, "The Soviet

Navy 1989: A U.S. View," *U.S. Naval Institute Proceedings* 116, no. 5 (May 1990).

247 **presence in the Indian Ocean**: *USND6*, p. 15.

248 **"Soviet naval general purpose"**: Benjamin B. Fischer, *At Cold War's End: U.S. Intelligence on the Soviet Union and Eastern Europe, 1989–1991* (Center for the Study of Intelligence, 2000), no. 16, p. viii.

249 **the *Komsomolets***: Capt. Peter Huchthausen, Igor Kurdin, and R. Alan White, *Hostile Waters* (New York: St. Martin's Press, 1997), p. 343.

250 **"during Admiral Trost's visit"**: Don M. Snider, "Strategy, Forces and Budgets: Dominant Influences in Executive Decision Making, Post-Cold War, 1989–91," paper presented at the U.S. Army War College Fourth Annual Strategy Conference held February 24–25, 1993, Carlisle Barracks, Pa.

250 **"the Soviet approach"**: Fischer, *At Cold War's End*, no. 13.

252 **scientists spent four hours**: David E. Hoffman, *The Dead Hand: The Untold Story of the Cold War Arms Race and Its Dangerous Legacy* (New York: Doubleday, 2009), pp. 319–20.

252 **"Representatives of the NATO"**: Quoted in Andrei A. Kokoshin, *Soviet Strategic Thought, 1917–91*, BCSIA Studies in International Security (Cambridge: MIT Press, 1998), p. 143.

253 **"Our proposals are"**: Ibid.

253 **"The most important feature"**: Fleet Adm. Vladimir Nikolayevich Chernavin, "Chernavin Responds," *U.S. Naval Institute Proceedings* 115, no. 2 (February 1989).

254 **"operations by Western"**: Eric Grove and Graham Thompson, *Battle for the Fiords: NATO's Forward Maritime Strategy in Action* (Annapolis, Md.: Naval Institute Press, 1991); Eric Grove, "The Challenge of East-West Naval Dialogue," *U.S. Naval Institute Proceedings* 115, no. 9 (September 1989).

254 **"emphasized the threat"**: Eric Grove, *Maritime Strategy and European Security* (London: Brassey's, 1990), 125–26.

255 **Kremlin's long-standing insistence**: Michael Beschloss and Strobe Talbot, *At the Highest Levels: The Inside Story of the End of the Cold War* (Boston: Little, Brown, 1993), p. 119.

256 **"Gorbachev will certainly"**: Edward Rowny to Secretary James Baker III, Information Memorandum, November 17, 1989, National Security Archive, http://nsarchive.gwu.edu/NSAEBB/NSAEBB298/Document%203.pdf.

256 **"Gorbachev handed Bush"**: Beschloss and Talbott, *At Highest Levels*, pp. 16–23.

257 **"We have read"**: Rear Adm. (ret.) Dave Oliver, *Against the Tide: Rickover's Leadership Principles and the Rise of the Nuclear Navy* (Annapolis, Md.: Naval Institute Press, 2014), p. 137.

257 **"Bush brusquely dismissed the idea"**: Capt 1st Rank V.A. Galkovskiy, "On the Role of Naval Forces in International Relations," *Voennaya Mysl* (January 1990): 66–78.

258 **"the new strategy's content"**: Capt. 1st Rank V. M. Mikhaylov, "U.S. Naval Strategy," *Voennaya Mysl* (January 1990): 59–65.

259 **"The U. S. military-political"**: Capt. 1st Rank V. A. Galkovskiy, "On the Role of Naval Forces in International Relations," *Voennaya Mysl* (January 1990): 66–78.

259 **"resolutely spoke out"**: Ibid.

261 **continued to decrease**: *USND6*, pp. 15, 32.

261 **record tonnages of submarines**: The Soviets launched ten submarines—six

nuclear-powered and four diesel-electric-powered—more than in any year since the early 1980s. This included their last Delta IV SSBN. Guided-missile destroyer production also continued apace, with the launch of the fourth *Slava*-class cruiser and the fifteenth *Sovremennyy* antiship destroyer. Also, the eleventh *Udaloy*-class guided-missile/antisubmarine warfare destroyer joined the Northern Fleet. Rear Adm. Tom Brooks, "The Soviet Navy in 1990: A U.S. View—Still Cautious," *U.S. Naval Institute Proceedings* 117, no. 5 (May 1991).

261 **2,150 naval aircraft**: Norman Polmar, "The Soviet Navy," *U.S. Naval Institute Proceedings* 116, no. 11 (November 1990).

262 **carrier *Admiral Kuznetsov***: Formerly named *Riga*, then *Leonid Brezhnev*, and then *Tbilisi*.

262 **numerous combat aircraft**: Brooks, "Soviet Navy in 1990."

262 **seek to explain itself**: Scott M. Stanley, *Assessing the Impact of Reasonable Sufficiency on the Structure and Missions of the Former Soviet Navy*, master's thesis, Naval Postgraduate School (1992), pp. 50–54.

262 **"although unilateral Navy"**: Fischer, *At Cold War's End*.

263 **only defensive roles**: Stanley, *Reasonable Sufficiency*, pp. 55–57.

263 **"Didn't Chernavin get"**: Dr. John Hanley notes from SSG files; Dr. John Hanley, interview by Peter Swartz, September 2016. Hanley had been deputy director of the CNO's Strategic Studies Group (SSG) in 1990.

263 **confidence-building port visits**: In October the fourth RUKUS talks were held, this time at Brown University. (Brown was Peter Swartz's alma mater. The NROTC unit that had commissioned him in the navy was kicked off campus soon after he left; he believes the former did not cause the latter.) U.S. delegates Capt. Dick Diamond, George Fedoroff, and John Hanley concluded that the Soviets were there to convey that their stance was now truly defensive and to lessen confrontation. They emphasized their unified military strategy, continuance of defensive naval doctrine, and lack of intent to interdict sea-lanes.

264 **Instead of seeking verifiable limits**: Beschloss and Talbot, *At the Highest Levels*, p. 183.

264 **"Germans should decide"**: Michel Beschloss and Strobe Talbot, *At the Highest Levels: The Inside Story of the End of the Cold War* (Boston: Little Brown, 1993).

264 **"Gorbachev castigated Bush"**: Ibid., p. 274.

265 **the CFE Treaty**: On the eve of signature in November, however, Soviet data were presented under the so-called "initial data exchange." This showed a rather sudden emergence of three so-called "coastal defense divisions" (including the third at Klaipėda in the Baltic Military District, the 126th in the Odessa Military District, and seemingly the 77th Guards Motor Rifle Division with the Northern Fleet), along with three artillery brigades/regiments, subordinate to the Soviet Navy. All had previously been unknown as such to NATO. Much of their equipment, which had been commonly understood to be treaty limited, was now declared to be part of this new "naval infantry."

266 **"The NATO bloc military"**: Capt. (ret.) William H. J. Manthorpe, "The Soviet View," *U.S. Naval Institute Proceedings* 117, no. 9 (September 1991).

267 **"Akhromeyev map"**: Capt. (ret.) Larry Seaquist, interview by Capt. (ret.) John Hanley USNR, October 2014; Capt. (ret.) Larry Seaquist to Capt. (ret.) Peter Swartz, January 31, 2016.

267 **a routine program**: To reciprocate, two American surface combatants and an oiler would deploy to Severomorsk—the Northern Fleet's headquarters

on the Kola Peninsula—for a port visit the following year. Senior U.S. naval officers present included Capt. Robby Harris, a principal drafter of the 1986 unclassified version of the Maritime Strategy that had aroused consternation in that same headquarters only a half-dozen years before.

267 **START itself did not**: A retired U.S. Navy captain, Ambassador Linton Brooks, had been the chief U.S. START negotiator.

268 **"The extensive Soviet"**: Fischer, *At Cold War's End*, no. 23. This NIE also has judgments on Soviet nuclear-powered ballistic missile submarines and nuclear-powered cruise missile submarines.

269 **celebrated in Murmansk**: As related a few months later by Fleet Admiral Chernavin in a speech at the U.S. Naval War College.

269 **all tactical nuclear weapons**: The nuclear-armed Tomahawks would be placed in storage until President Barack Obama directed their dismantlement two decades later.

269 **naval operations with ISKRAN**: Earlier in the decade, the CNA, the navy's federally funded research and development center, had conducted pathbreaking analyses of Soviet naval concepts and intentions, as well as some of the key tactical analyses supporting U.S. Navy forward operations in the Norwegian and Mediterranean Seas and the northwestern Pacific. Murray had initiated the Strategic Studies Group (SSG), which had aimed to "turn captains of ships into captains of war" against the Soviet Union since 1981. Brement had been one of Murray's successors at the helm of the SSG and was a former ambassador in Reykjavik, where he had garnered Icelandic support for the Maritime Strategy.

269 **visited the United States**: Fleet Adm. Vladimir Nikolaevich Chernavin, "Talk Followed by Questions and Answers: U.S. Naval War College, Newport, Rhode Island, 8 November 1991," *Naval War College Review* 45, no. 4 (Autumn 1992). Chernavin made the following by-now-familiar points (ending with shopworn proposals that were ostensibly even-handed but in fact would be far more detrimental to American than Soviet interests): "qualitative one" and "serious changes due to a significant reduction in the numerical strength and composition of fleet forces." The Soviet Union needed both nuclear deterrent forces and ready conventional forces, to "prevent regional conflicts and, in the case of aggression, to reliably repulse it and preclude escalation of the conflict:

> During the last two years we have removed from the order of battle of our navy over two hundred ships, among them submarines, cruisers, and destroyers. In the current year we plan to decommission over fifty ships. In order to implement the Treaty on the Reduction of Strategic Offensive Arms, we plan to decommission by the year 2000 over twenty strategic missile submarines and cut in half the number of formations of these submarines. We are also planning to decrease significantly the strength of the general-purpose forces. We are trying to create a navy smaller in size but more mobile, modern, of a better quality, and with better combat characteristics. . . .
> It is my firm belief that the question of starting negotiations on naval forces has been ripe for a long time. In our view it would be expedient to start without delay a concrete dialogue on the entire complex of issues relating to strengthening the security and stability of ocean and sea theaters of war, the elimination of sources of mili-

tary danger posed by naval activities, and the restriction and future
reduction of the offensive components of navies. . . .

At Cam Ranh it is a very limited composition of forces, which
has been greatly reduced. The base is not being used as a military
base but rather as a material-technical base for forces going to the
Indian Ocean or nearby areas. I repeat, the composition is very
limited. We proposed that the Soviet and U.S. navies in the area
withdraw from both Cam Ranh and the Philippines, in the interests
of a healthier atmosphere in the region. So far there has been no
positive resolution to our proposal.

The new Soviet military doctrine is "defensive." The Soviets need "less
numerous, and professional, armed forces . . . equipped with highly effective,
modern military hardware." He described the "replacement of a quantitative
approach to defense problems and to combat readiness of the Army and Navy
by an ostensibly even-handed, but in fact would be far more detrimental to
American than Soviet interests."

270 **"Chernavin's Soviet Navy"**: James John Tritten, *Military Doctrine and
Strategy in the Former Soviet Union: Implications for the Navy*, Office of Naval
Intelligence, Naval Postgraduate School, Monterey, Calif. (1993), pp. 101–2.
Tritten had been a leading U.S. Navy contributor to and proponent of the
Maritime Strategy. He was sent earlier by Secretary Lehman to the Naval
Postgraduate School as a professor to ensure that successive cohorts of stu-
dent officers understood its tenets.

270 **"concerning the navy"**: Stanley, *Reasonable Sufficiency*, pp. 90–92. Stanley
was one of Tritten's students.

271 **he was being shown around**: Jinks and Hennessy, *Silent Deep*, p. 590.

271 **From 1985 to 1991**: The numbers of carriers (from three to five), large
amphibious ships (from 33 to 35), and naval aircraft (from 1635 to 1875), however, had continued to swell. And the building program chugged on: in May
1991, the Soviets launched their second new *Neustrashimyy*-class antisubmarine frigate. In June, they commissioned their fifteenth *Sovremennyy*-class
frigate, and on December 19, they commissioned their twelfth *Udaloy*-class
destroyer. Office of Naval Intelligence, *Understanding Soviet Naval Developments*, 5th and 6th eds. (Washington, D.C.: Office of the Chief of Naval
Operations, Department of the Navy, 1985 and 1991).

272 **"Thus, at the end"**: Capt. (ret.) William H. J. Manthorpe, "The Final Soviet
View," *U.S. Naval Institute Proceedings* (February 1992), p. 103.

SELECTED BIBLIOGRAPHY

Allen, Richard V. *Peace or Peaceful Coexistence?* Chicago: American Bar Association, 1966.

Andrew, Christopher, and Oleg Gordievsky. *KGB: The Inside Story of Its Foreign Operations from Lenin to Gorbachev.* New York: HarperCollins, 1990.

Barlow, Jeffrey G. *Revolt of the Admirals: The Fight for Naval Aviation, 1945–1950.* Washington, D.C.: Naval Historical Center, Department of the Navy, 1994.

Beschloss, Michael, and Strobe Talbot. *At the Highest Levels: The Inside Story of the End of the Cold War.* Boston: Little, Brown, 1993.

Bjerga, Kjell Inge. *Politico-Military Assessments on the Northern Flank 1975–1990: Report from the IFS/PHP Bodø Conference of 20–21 August 2007.* Oslo: Norwegian Institute for Defense Studies, 2007.

Breivik, Vice Adm. Roy, Royal Norwegian Navy. "Fjord Operations." *NATO's Sixteen Nations* (February–March 1988): 32–36.

Brinkley, Douglas. *The Reagan Diaries.* New York: HarperCollins, 2007.

Broward, Jack G. "'Out There' in the Future." *Sea Power* (October 1988): 54–58.

Bruns, Sebastian. "U.S. Navy Strategy & American Sea Power from 'The Maritime Strategy' (1982–1986) to 'A Cooperative Strategy for 21st Century Seapower' (2007): Politics, Capstone Documents, and Major Naval Operations 1981–2011." *US Naval Strategy and National Security: The Evolution of American Naval Power.* Oxon, UK: Routledge, 2017.

Cabot, JO1 Lon. "Ocean Venture 81." *All Hands* 782 (March 1982): 20–29.

Chernavin, Fleet Adm. Vladimir Nikolayevich. "Chernavin Responds." *U.S. Naval Institute Proceedings* (February 1989).

Clexton, Vice Adm. (ret.) Edward. "My Life: A Life of Stories." Unpublished manuscript, c. 2016.

Connors, Cmdr. Tracy. "Further North: Ocean Safari '87." *Surface Warfare* (January–February 1988): 2–7.

———. "Northern Wedding '86," *All Hands* (January 1987): 18–26.

Cote, Owen. *The Third Battle: Innovation in the U.S. Navy's Silent Cold War Struggle with Soviet Submarines.* Newport Paper no. 16. Newport, R.I.: Naval War College Press, 2003.

Crist, David. "A New Cold War: U.S. Marines in Norway and the Search for a New Mission in NATO." In Randy Carol Balano and Craig L. Symonds, eds., *New Interpretations in Naval History: Selected Papers from the Fourteenth Naval History Symposium.* Annapolis, Md.: Naval Institute Press, 2001.

Cropsey, Seth. *Seablindness: How Political Neglect Is Choking American Seapower and What to Do about It.* New York: Encounter Books, 2017.

Curry, John, and Peter Perla. "Peter Perla's *The Art of Wargaming.*" Lulu .com, 2001.

"Dragon Hammer." *Surface Warfare* (November–December 1988).

Durrant, Maj. Jerry L. *In Every Clime and Place: USMC Cold Weather Doctrine.* Thesis. Ft. Leavenworth, Kans.: School of Advanced Military Studies, 1991.

Early, Pete. *Family of Spies: Inside the John Walker Spy Ring.* New York: Bantam Books, 1988.

Eliot, Christian, Manuel Ramirez Gabarrus, and Francisco Figeroa de la Vega. "Ocean Venture 81." *Naval Forces* 2, no. 6 (1981): 74–76.

Farrell, J. E. "Role Model: For Christine Fox, Top Gun Was More than Just a Movie." *Air and Space* (June–July 1987): 58–65.

Fetterman, Vice Adm. Jack. "COMNAVAIRPAC: PACEX 89." *Wings of Gold* (Winter 1989): 26–27, 57.

Ford, Christopher, and David Rosenberg. *The Admirals' Advantage: U.S. Navy Operational Intelligence in World War II and the Cold War.* Annapolis, Md.: Naval Institute Press, 2005.

Friedman, Norman. "Decoy, Deceive, Defeat." *U.S. Naval Institute Proceedings* (May 2015): 162–63.

Garthoff, Raymond L. *The Great Transition: American-Soviet Relations and the End of the Cold War.* Washington, D.C.: Brookings Institution Press, 2000.

Gile, Robert H. *Global War Game: Second Series: 1984–1988*. Newport Paper no. 20. Newport, R.I.: Naval War College Press, 2004.

Greeley, Brendan M, Jr. "Third Fleet Increases North Pacific Operations to Counter Soviet Activity." *Aviation Week and Space Technology* (December 22, 1986): 28–29.

Grimstvedt, Rear Adm. Bjarne, Royal Norwegian Navy. "Norwegian Maritime Operations." *U.S. Naval Institute Proceedings* (March 1986): 144–46.

Grove, Eric, with Graham Thompson. *Battle for the Fiords: NATO's Forward Maritime Strategy in Action*. Annapolis, Md.: Naval Institute Press, 1991.

Hall, Lt. David. "Arctic Maritime Patrol." *U.S. Naval Institute Proceedings* (September 1990): 109–11.

Hanley, John T., Jr. "Creating the 1980s Maritime Strategy and Implications for Today." *Naval War College Review* (Spring 2014): 11–29.

Hartmann, Frederick H. *Naval Renaissance: The U.S. Navy in the 1980s*. Annapolis, Md.: Naval Institute Press, 1990.

Hattendorf, John B. *The Evolution of the U.S. Navy's Maritime Strategy, 1977–1986*. Newport Paper no. 19. Newport, R.I.: Naval War College Press, 2004.

Hattendorf, John B , ed. *U.S. Naval Strategy in the 1970s*. Newport Paper no. 30. Newport, R.I.: Naval War College Press, 2007.

Hattendorf, John B., and Peter M. Swartz, eds. *U.S. Naval Strategy in the 1980s: Selected Documents*. Newport Paper no. 33. Newport, R.I.: Naval War College Press, 2008.

Hay, Bud, and Bob Gile. *Global War Game: The First Five Years*. Newport Paper no. 4. Newport, R.I.: Naval War College, 1993.

Hennessy, Peter, and James Jink. *The Silent Deep: The Royal Navy Submarine Services Since 1945*. London: Allen Lane, 2015.

Hernandez, Vice Adm. Diego E. "The New Third Fleet." *U.S. Naval Institute Proceedings* (July 1987): 73–76.

Hoffman, David E. *The Billion Dollar Spy: A True Story of Cold War Espionage and Betrayal*. New York: Doubleday, 2015.

———. *The Dead Hand: The Untold Story of the Cold War Arms Race and Its Dangerous Legacy*. New York: Doubleday, 2009.

Holland, Rear Adm. Jerry. "Reflections on the Cold War at Sea: Part One." *Submarine Review* (January 2010): 89–101.

Holloway, James L. III, *Aircraft Carriers at War: A Personal Retrospective of Korea, Vietnam, and the Soviet Confrontation*. Annapolis, Md.: U.S. Naval Institute Press, 2007.

Horseman, Martin. "Ocean Safari 83." *Armed Forces* (October 1983): 372–79.

Huntington, Samuel. "National Policy and the Transoceanic Navy." *U.S. Naval Institute Proceedings* (May 1954): 483–93.

Jones, Lt. Cmdr. Norris. "Pacex '89: Stress it Till it Breaks." *Surface Warfare* (November–December 1989): 10–12.

Lawrence, Vice Adm. (ret.) William P. "Reminiscences." Interviewed by Paul Stillwell. Annapolis, Md.: U.S. Naval Institute Oral History Program, 2011.

Lawrence, Vice Adm. (ret.) William P., and Rosario Rausa. *Tennessee Patriot.* Annapolis, Md.: Naval Institute Press, 2006.

Lehman, John F., Jr. *Command of the Seas.* New York: Charles Scribner's Sons, 1988.

———. *On Seas of Glory: Heroic Men, Great Ships, and Epic Battles of the American Navy.* New York: Free Press, 2001.

———. "The Rebirth of a U.S. Naval Strategy." *Strategic Review* 9, no. 3 (1981).

Lyons, Admiral James A., Jr. "Interview." *U.S. Naval Institute Proceedings* (July 1987): 9–15.

———. "A Peacetime Strategy for the Pacific." *Naval War College Review* (Winter 1987): 44–52.

Maeda, Tetsuo. *The Hidden Army: The Untold Story of Japan's Military Forces.* Chicago: Edition Q, 1994.

Mahan, Capt. Alfred Thayer. *The Influence of Sea Power upon History.* Boston: Little, Brown, 1890.

Manthorpe, Capt. (ret.) William. "The Soviet View" (series). *U.S. Naval Institute Proceedings* (February 1986–February 1992).

Marolda, Edward J. *Ready Seapower: A History of the U.S. Seventh Fleet.* Washington, D.C.: Naval History and Heritage Command, 2012.

McCaffree, Rear Adm. Burnham (Mike) C., Jr. "Oral History." Interviewed by John Grady. Washington, D.C.: Naval Historical Foundation Oral History Program, 2014.

Michishita, Narushige, Peter M. Swartz, and Davd F. Winkler. *Lessons of the Cold War in the Pacific: U.S. Maritime Strategy, Crisis Prevention, and Japan's Role.* Washington, D.C.: Woodrow Wilson International Center for Scholars Asia Program, 2016.

Miller, Vice Adm. (ret.) Jerry. *Nuclear Weapons and Aircraft Carriers: How the Bomb Saved Naval Aviation.* Washington, D.C.: Smithsonian Institution Press, 2001.

Morton, John Fass. *Mustin: A Naval Family of the Twentieth Century.* Annapolis, Md.: Naval Institute Press, 2003.

Murray, Robert J. "A Warfighting Perspective." *U.S. Naval Institute Proceedings* (October 1983): 66–81.

Mustin, Vice Adm. Henry C. "Maritime Strategy from the Deckplates." *U.S. Naval Institute Proceedings* (September 1986): 33–37.

———. "Personal Experiences, Surface Warfare, and USN Strategy During the Cold War." Interview by David Winkler. Washington, D.C.: Naval Historical Foundation Oral History Program, 2001.

———. "The Role of the Navy and the Marines in the Norwegian Sea." In Sverre Jervell and Kare Nyblom, eds., *The Military Buildup in the High North.* Cambridge, Mass.: Harvard University Center for International Affairs and University Press of America, 1986.

Nofi, Albert A. *To Train the Fleet for War: The U.S. Navy Fleet Problems, 1923–1940.* Newport, R.I.: Naval War College Press, 2010.

Office of Naval Intelligence. *Understanding Soviet Naval Developments*, 4th, 5th, and 6th eds. Washington, D.C.: Department of the Navy, 1981, 1985, and 1991.

Oliver, Rear Adm. (ret.) Dave. *Against the Tide: Rickover's Leadership Principles and the Rise of the Nuclear Navy.* Annapolis, Md.: Naval Institute Press, 2014.

O'Rourke, Capt. (ret.) Gerald G. "Great Operators, Good Administrators, Lousy Planners." *U.S. Naval Institute Proceedings* (August 1984): 75–78.

Patton, Capt. James M. (ret.). "Dawn of the Maritime Strategy." *U.S. Naval Institute Proceedings* (May 2009): 56–60.

Pendley, Rear Adm. William. "The U.S. Navy, Forward Defense, and the Air-Land Battle." In Robert Pfaltzgraff, Jr., et al., eds., *Emerging Doctrines and Technologies: Implications for Global and Regional Political-Military Balances.* Lexington, Mass.: Lexington Books, 1987.

Polmar, Norman. *The Naval Institute Guide to the Soviet Navy*, 5th ed. Annapolis, Md.: Naval Institute Press, 1991.

Polmar, Norman, and Michael White. *Project Azorian.* Annapolis, Md.: Naval Institute Press, 2010.

Prina, L. Edgar. "The Tripartite Ocean: The Air Force and Coast Guard Give the Navy a Helping Hand." *Sea Power* (October 1986): 32–45.

Radchenko, Sergey. *Unwanted Visionaries: The Soviet Failure in Asia at the End of the Cold War.* New York: Oxford University Press, 2014.

Reagan, Pres. Ronald. *National Security Strategy of the United States.* Washington, D.C.: White House, January 1987.

Rearden, Steven L., and Kenneth R. Foulks, Jr. *The Joint Chiefs of Staff and National Policy, 1977–1980.* Washington, D.C.: Office of Joint History, Office of the Chairman of the Joint Chiefs of Staff, 2015.

Rentfrow, James C. *Home Squadron: The U.S. Navy on the North Atlantic Station.* Annapolis, Md.: Naval Institute Press, 2014.

Research Guide to Submarine Arctic Operations: A List of Materials Available at the Submarine Force Library and Archives. Groton, Conn.: Submarine Force Library and Museum, c. 2008.

Robeson, Lt. Col. Edward J., IV. "Tactical Reflections on Norway." *U.S. Naval Institute Proceedings* (November 1989): 108–11.

Rosenberg, David Alan. "Process: The Realities of Formulating Modern Naval Strategy." In James Goldrick and John B. Hattendorf, eds., *Mahan Is Not Enough.* Newport, R.I.: Naval War College Press, 1993..

Schweizer, Peter. *Reagan's War: The Epic Story of His Forty-Year Struggle and Final Triumph Over Communism.* New York: Doubleday, 2002.

Smith, Michael W. *Antiair Warfare Defense of Ships at Sea.* Alexandria, Va.: Center for Naval Analyses, 1981.

Solomon, Jonathan F. *Defending the Fleet from China's Anti-Ship Ballistic Missile: Naval Deception's Roles in Sea-Based Missile Defense.* Thesis, Georgetown University, 2011.

Sontag, Sherry, Christopher Drew, and Annette Lawrence Drew. *Blind Man's Bluff: The Untold Story of American Submarine Espionage.* New York: PublicAffairs, 1998.

Soviet Navy: Intelligence and Analysis During the Cold War. Washington, D.C.: U.S. Central Intelligence Agency and U.S. Department of the Navy, 2017.

Stanik, Joseph T. *El Dorado Canyon: Reagan's Undeclared War with Qaddafi.* Annapolis, Md.: Naval Institute Press, 2003.

Strausz-Hupé, Robert, et al. *A Forward Strategy for America.* New York: Harper, 1961.

———. *Protracted Conflict: A Challenging Study of Communist Strategy.* New York: Harper, 1959.

Swartz, Peter. "Preventing the Bear's Last Swim: The NATO Concept of Maritime Operations (CONMAROPS) of the Last Cold War Decade." *NATO's Maritime Power 1949–1990.* Piraeus, Greece: European Institute of Maritime Studies and Research, 2003.

Swartz, Peter, with Karin Duggan. *U.S. Navy Capstone Strategies and Concepts (1981–1990): Strategy, Policy, Concept and Vision Documents.* Alexandria, Va.: Center for Naval Analyses, 2011.

———. *The U.S. Navy in the World (1981–1990): Context for U.S. Navy Capstone Strategies and Concepts.* Alexandria, Va.: Center for Naval Analyses, 2011.

Swift, Admiral Scott H. "'Fleet Problems' Offer Opportunities." *U.S. Naval Institute Proceedings* (March 2018): 22–26.

Tamnes, Rolf. *The United States and the Cold War in the High North.* Aldershot, U.K.: Dartmouth, 1991.

Thompson, Frederick. "Did We Learn Anything from That Exercise? Could We?" *Naval War College Review* (July–August 1982): 25–37.

Till, Geoffrey. "The Cold War at Sea." In Daniel Moran and James A. Russcll, cds., *Maritime Strategy and Global Order: Markets, Resources, Security.* Washington, D.C.: Georgetown University Press, 2016.

Tokarev, Maksim Y. "Kamikazes: The Soviet Legacy." *Naval War College Review* (Winter 2014): 61–84.

Turner, Andy. "Alaska." *All Hands* (January 1987): 28–31.

White, Rear Adm. Hugo M., Royal Navy. "'Teamwork '88 and the Striking Fleet Atlantic." *Army Quarterly and Defense Journal* (January 1989): 8–14.

Wieschhoff, Capt. Kenneth H. "Exercise Planners: War College Bound?" *U.S. Naval Institute Proceedings* (April 1987): 105–6.

Wills, Steven T. *Replacing the Maritime Strategy: The Change in U.S. Naval Strategy From 1989–1994.* Dissertation, Ohio University, 2017.

Winkler, David. *Cold War at Sea: High-Seas Confrontation Between the United States and the Soviet Union.* Annapolis, Md.: Naval Institute Press, 2000.

Youngquist, Dave. "Nimitz and Northern Wedding." *All Hands* (January 1987): 27.

Zellen, Barry Scott. *Arctic Doom, Arctic Boom: The Geopolitics of Climate Change in the Arctic.* Santa Barbara, Calif.: Praeger, 2009.

INDEX

Torrijos-Carter Treaty, 51
Toshiba–Kongsberg incident, 217
Toshiba Machine Company, 128
Tower, John, xxii, 63–64, 240
Train, Harry, 67–68, 84, 87, 99–100
Trident submarine, 36
Tromsø, Norway, 80, 82
Trost, Carlisle, 237, 250, 263
Truman, Harry S., and administration
    and atomic bomb, 13
    and beginning of Cold War, 16–17,
        19–22
    and Korean War, 23–26, 89
Truman Doctrine, 20
Tsygichko, Vitaly, 145–46
Tu-16 Badger aircraft, 85–86, 106
Tu-20 Bear D aircraft, 221–22
Tu-22 Backfire bombers, 58, 110, 121,
    133
Tu-22M Backfire bomber, 80, 267
Tu-95 Bear aircraft, xv, xvi, 85–86, 106,
    114, 135
Tuttle Jerry O., xvii, 75, 77, 78, 83, 109
Typhoon-class submarine, 147, 148

U-boat, 14
Udaloy-class destroyer, 133, 142, 143
Ulyanovsk (ship), 241
United Effort '83, 154–55
United Nations, 20, 186, 229, 239–40
United States, USS (supercarrier), 22
U.S. Naval Institute Proceedings. See
    Proceedings
"U.S. Relations with the USSR"
    (NSDD 75), 254
"United States Relations with the
    Soviet Union" (NSD 23), 254
U.S.–Soviet Agreement on Reciprocal
    Advance Notification of Major
    Strategic Exercises, 254–55

Valiant Blitz exercise, 249–50
Valley Forge, USS (carrier), 25
Velikhov, Yevgeni P., 252
"velvet revolution," 246
Vestfjord, Norway, 169–70, 170, 197,
    198
Victor I-class submarine, 124
Victor III-class nuclear attack
    submarines, 56–57, 57, 126, 153–
    54, 221–22, 298n220

Vienna Document, 265
Vietnam
    and Cambodian war, 232, 246, 269
    Cam Ranh Bay air base, 136, 229,
        247
Vietnam War, xxii–xxiii, xxvii, 32–33,
    36, 44–45, 281
Vilnius Massacre, 265–66
Vincennes, USS (Aegis cruiser), 191
Vinson. See Carl Vinson, USS
Vinson, Carl, 12, 21, 21
Visakhapatnam, India, 220
Vladivostok, USSR, 105, 106, 120–21,
    263
Voennaya Mysl (Military Thought), 258
V/STOL (vertical/short takeoff and
    landing), 122, 123, 132, 241, 243

Walker, John, 58, 86, 125–29, 216
Warner, John, 40, 40
War of 1812, 4, 5
War Plan Orange, 11
Warsaw Pact
    and balance of powers in late 1970s,
        272
    and CFE treaty, 265
    disbanding of, 266
    in early years of Cold War, 28
    and Gorbachev's renunciation of
        Brezhnev Doctrine, 235
    and NATO nuclear strategy, 29, 30
    NATO–Warsaw Pact arms limitation
        talks, 231
    and perestroika, 164, 211
    Soyuz '81, 131
    troop levels compared to NATO,
        272
    Zapad '81, 132
Wasp, USS (aircraft carrier), 30
Watkins, Jim, 100, 122, 124, 177–78
Weinberger, Caspar, xxv, 167, 177
    1982 defense budget testimony, 109
    and naval funding, 155–56
    and Arthur D. Nicholson's death,
        129
    Ocean Venture '81, xxvi
    on Reagan's national security team,
        65
    submarine intelligence briefing with
        Reagan, 100
West, Francis "Bing," 51, 52, 54, 55